People keep telling me I can be a great man.
I'd rather be a good one.

—JOHN

ALSO BY CHRISTOPHER ANDERSEN

The Good Son

JFK JR. *and the* MOTHER HE LOVED

CHRISTOPHER ANDERSEN

GALLERY BOOKS

New York   London   Toronto   Sydney   New Delhi

My John is such a happy little boy, you know.
I think sometimes I worry about him too much.

—Jackie

G Gallery Books
A Division of Simon & Schuster, Inc.
1230 Avenue of the Americas
New York, NY 10020

Photo credits:
John F. Kennedy Presidential Library and Museum: 1, 2, 3, 4, 6, 8, 44;
Bettmann/Stanley Tretick 1963/CORBIS: 5; Rex USA: 7, 9, 10, 11, 12, 14, 25,
31; Hutton-Deutsch Collection/CORBIS: 13; Bettmann/CORBIS: 15, 17, 19, 41,
27, 30; Henri Buseau/Sygma/CORBIS: 18; Associated Press: 29; Brooks Kraft/
Sygma/CORBIS: 32; Charles Kruppa/AP/CORBIS: 33; Ralf-Finn HEstoft/
CORBIS: 35; Reuters/CORBIS: 36,38; Lawrence Schwartzwald/Sygma/CORBIS:
40; Globe Photos: 16, 20, 21, 22, 23, 26, 34, 38 39, 41, 42; John Barrett/Globe
Photos: 28; Laura Cavanaugh/Globe Photos: 43.

First Gallery Books hardcover edition October 2014

GALLERY BOOKS and colophon are registered
trademarks of Simon & Schuster, Inc.

For information about special discounts for bulk purchases,
please contact Simon & Schuster Special Sales at
1-866-506-1949 or business@simonandschuster.com.

The Simon & Schuster Speakers Bureau can bring authors to your live event. For
more information or to book an event contact the Simon & Schuster Speakers
Bureau at 1-866-248-3049 or visit our website at www.simonspeakers.com.

Interior design by Renato Stanisic
Cover design by Janet Perr
Cover image © Condé Nast Archive/CORBIS

Manufactured in the United States of America

10 9 8 7 6 5 4 3 2 1

Library of Congress Cataloging-in-Publication Data

Andersen, Christopher.
   The good son : JFK Jr. and the mother he loved / Christopher Andersen.
      pages   cm
   1. Kennedy, John F. Jr., 1960–1999.   2. Children of presidents—United
States—Biography.   3. Onassis, Jacqueline Kennedy, 1929–1994.   I. Title.
   E843.K42A73   2014
   973.922092—dc23
      [B]   2014024249

ISBN 978-1-4767-7556-2
ISBN 978-1-4767-7558-6 (ebook)

For my granddaughter,
Charlotte Beatrice Brower,
aka "Charlie"

Contents

*The whole world knew his name
before he did. John seemed to belong
not only to our family, but to the
American family.*

—TED KENNEDY

"A Certain Gallantry"

He was the most brilliant star in the Kennedy firmament—the only son of two figures who captured the world's attention more than a half century ago and have yet to relinquish it. John Fitzgerald Kennedy Jr. would spend his entire life trying to come to terms with the world's obsessive interest in the people he knew simply as Mummy and Daddy—and its similarly obsessive interest in him.

For the rest of us, it was no mystery at all. As a dynamic, attractive, and impossibly glamorous couple living with their young children in the White House, Jack and Jackie Kennedy embodied all the hopes and dreams of the postwar era. When a sniper's bullet brought a bloody end to it all, Americans realized that, however shocked and saddened they may have been for the nation's loss, it paled in comparison to the burden his wife and children would bear.

In the days and weeks following Dallas, Jackie's natural dignity and quiet strength were the glue that held a stunned and grieving nation together. Yet it fell to the little boy known throughout the world as John-John, whose mother well understood the enduring power of symbolism, to provide the most memorably heart-melting moment of all. With her eye undoubtedly on John's future, Jackie bent down and instructed the three-year-old to deliver history's most famous salute as his father's horse-drawn casket passed before him—in that moment securing his place forever in the national consciousness.

At the time, young John was merely a supporting character in the larger narrative being spun by his mother. Terrified that her husband's time in the White House was too short for him to be remembered as a great president, Jackie concocted the myth of an American Camelot. Then she spent the rest of her life cultivating a personal mystique that, in the end, made her the most talked-about, written-about, speculated-about personality of her generation—arguably the most celebrated American woman of the twentieth century.

"It's hard to talk about a legacy or a mystique," John once observed. "It's my family. It's my mother. It's my sister. It's my father. We're a family like any other. We look out for one another. The fact that there have been difficulties and hardships, or obstacles, makes us closer."

Caroline's big-sisterly affection for John was certainly never in doubt. Nor was her role in the Kennedy family saga any less significant. Like her brother, high-spirited Caroline was one of the few remaining links to a more innocent and hopeful period in American history—the time before Vietnam, Watergate, AIDS, and the specter of terrorism. At dedications and graduations and weddings and funerals too numerous to mention, Caroline stood alongside her brother, sharing equally in the joys and the heartaches.

In the patriarchal world of the Kennedys, however, the heavy burden of expectation was John's to bear alone. Starting with his wildly ambitious grandfather, Joseph P. Kennedy Sr., the men of each generation were expected to carry the dynastic torch forward. When Joe Jr. was killed on a bombing run during World War II, the torch was passed to Jack, then from Jack to Bobby, from Bobby to Teddy—and on to the next generation.

For John, the pressure to follow in his father's footsteps was an inescapable part of daily life. In JFK's absence, it seemed as if the entire world had stepped up to remind John more or less continuously that he was destined for political greatness.

John came to understand why so much was expected of him, but he also often wondered what, if Dallas had never happened, his larger-than-life dad would have wanted for him. In one grainy black-and-white television interview, JFK cautiously admitted that he wanted his son to enter politics because he had found public service to be both challenging and personally fulfilling. At the same time, the young president was quick to add, "I want him to do whatever makes him happy—whatever that is."

John's mother was another matter entirely. No less a force of nature than her husband, Jackie also wanted her son to do whatever made him happy—as long as he fulfilled what she firmly believed to be his destiny. Along the way, she urged him to take risks, to forge his own path, and to cherish his legacy without letting it overwhelm him.

"I think the most interesting thing about him," John once said of his father, "is that you realize he was just a man, that he lived a life, like anybody else." John did precisely that—living his life to the fullest and on his own terms, with a kind of easy, unadorned grace born of a life spent entirely in the public eye. In the end, he eagerly embraced all that was expected of him—and, in a move that might well have altered the course of U.S. political history, prepared to challenge one of the most formidable public personages of our time.

When she died of lymphoma in May 1994, Jackie took comfort in the fact that, unlike so many other members of their famous family, her children had escaped the famous "Kennedy Curse." John believed it, too. During the five years that followed, it became clear that he, like his mother before him, shared in what Arthur Schlesinger called "a certain gallantry."

In the end, John could no more escape his fate than his parents could escape theirs. His is a bittersweet boy-to-man saga of family, fate, love, loss, and promise unfulfilled.

It is the story of *The Good Son*.

PART ONE

His Mother's Son

"Please Don't Do It"

July 16, 1999

t was nearly 8:30 on this torrid Friday evening, and the sun was already sinking into the strange, yellowish haze that consumed the horizon. If he had left two hours earlier as originally planned, John F. Kennedy Jr. would have arrived at Martha's Vineyard in time to see Gay Head's majestic gray, white, and crimson clay cliffs standing in sharp relief against the darkening sky. Gliding over the cliffs, John and his two passengers in the Piper Saratoga—his wife, Carolyn Bessette, and Carolyn's sister Lauren—would all have been treated to a gull's-eye view of Red Gate Farm, the 474-acre estate that had been his mother Jacqueline's true refuge—a Shangri-la of dunes, marshes, Scotch pines, and scrub oaks, bordered on one side by square-shaped Squibnocket Pond and on the other by 4,620 sandy white feet of private oceanfront.

Kennedy family friend George Plimpton called it "a dream place, a sunlit place. It's hard to explain the effect it all had on you—all the variations in color, water sparkling like diamonds everywhere you looked."

That had been the original plan—to leave Manhattan at 6:30 p.m. and be in the air by 7:15 so that John, who had yet to learn how to rely solely on his instruments, could fly under visual flight rules. John was accustomed to cutting things close, and given the Piper's cruising speed of 180 miles per hour, leaving at 7:15 would put them safely on the ground at Martha's Vineyard Airport well before nightfall. They would drop Lauren off with friends, and then make the quick hop over to Hyannis Port for the wedding of John's cousin Rory—all before Cape Cod, the islands, and the ocean that separated them were engulfed in darkness.

Even if they had managed to leave on time and make it the Vineyard before sunset, Carolyn was far from enthusiastic about boarding a small plane with her husband alone at the controls. She was well aware of just how much her husband enjoyed pushing the envelope—like the time just a few years earlier when a group of John's friends watched as he swam out to sea off the coast of Baja California and simply vanished. John's terrified pals began to run for help when, as one recalled, "all of a sudden he just reappeared." Then there were the kayaking trips in which John would take off alone for long stretches at a time and simply materialize at base camp, filthy, wrung out, and deliriously happy. John simply showed no sign of outgrowing his daredevil streak: Just that spring South Dakota authorities denied his request to rappel down the face of Mount Rushmore, the sort of stunt that prompted his closest friends to call him "Master of Disaster."

It was a part of John's personality that Carolyn's celebrated mother-in-law took great pride in. Jackie made a point of indulging, even encouraging her son's instinctive adventurous streak. Whether he was mountain climbing, scuba diving, playing football, skiing, or simply zipping in and out of midtown Manhattan traffic, Jackie was proud of her son's unfettered athleticism. She did not even protest when he disappeared into the wilderness for as much as a week at a time.

John's obsession with taking to the skies at the controls of his own plane was an entirely different matter.

"Please don't do it," she pleaded with John when she discovered he was pursuing his pilot's license. "There have been too many deaths in the family already." Given the Kennedys' track record when it came to flying, Jackie clearly had a point. Joe Kennedy Jr., the eldest of John's uncles, died when his plane exploded over the English Channel during

World War II. Four years later, in 1948, John's aunt, Kathleen "Kick" Kennedy, perished with her lover, Earl Fitzwilliam, when their plane crashed into France's Cévennes Mountains.

John's aunt Ethel lost both her parents in a 1955 plane crash, and her brother when his plane crashed eleven years later. In 1964, John's uncle Ted was flying to Springfield, Massachusetts, in a storm to accept the Democratic nomination for a second U.S. Senate term when his small campaign plane crashed into an apple orchard. Both his aide and pilot were killed, but Ted managed to survive—albeit with a broken back. In 1973, John's twenty-four-year-old stepbrother—Aristotle Onassis's only son, Alexander—died when his plane crashed immediately after takeoff.

Jackie confided to Maurice Tempelsman, the wealthy diamond merchant who shared the last fifteen years of her life, that there was another reason for her concern. In recent years, she was experiencing a series of premonitions regarding both her children, and the strongest and most persistent of these involved John perishing at the controls of his own plane. She had made John swear that he would not pursue his pilot's license, and on her deathbed in 1994 made Tempelsman and her brother-in-law Ted Kennedy swear that they would do whatever was necessary to keep him from becoming a licensed aviator.

John abided by his mother's wishes during her lifetime, but by late 1997 he was enrolled in a Florida flight school. Although John took Tempelsman's financial advice—Maurice had managed to parlay Jackie's $26 million settlement from the estate of her late husband Aristotle Onassis into a $200 million fortune—John turned a deaf ear to Tempelsman's pleas and warnings when it came to flying. The open sky, he tried to explain, was the only place where he felt truly liberated. "You know," explained his college pal Richard Wiese, "it was just him up there, away from everybody and it made him feel free."

Neither Tempelsman nor Uncle Teddy would fly with John alone at the controls, and while she told friends she would have loved to oblige her husband, Carolyn was equally reticent. In addition to John's well-documented penchant for risk taking, Carolyn also worried about his lack of focus (John suffered from attention deficit disorder) and his chronic absentmindedness. John routinely misplaced things—his gloves, his credit cards, his wallet. It didn't help that he kept his keys on a chain fastened to his belt loop; they still disappeared with frustrating regularity—so often that he kept a spare set of keys to their TriBeCa apartment tucked under the front stoop. This inability to concentrate for extended periods of time—something a pilot would obviously be required to do—was of particular concern to the meticulously organized Carolyn. "We spend hours every day just looking for his stuff," she complained. "It drives me so crazy."

More to the point, it had been only six weeks since John took to the skies over Red Gate Farm in a $14,300 Buckeye ultralight powered parachute—a flimsy contraption that resembled a go-cart with an engine-drive propeller at the back—and crashed, snapping his right ankle. Undaunted, and with his foot still in a cast, John flew back up to the Vineyard for the Fourth of July. This time, Carolyn agreed to go as John's passenger—but only because there was a licensed instructor sitting next to him in the cockpit. Otherwise, she would buy a seat on one of the scheduled airline flights or drive the five hours to Hyannis and then take a ferry to the island. Once while she waited to meet John at the Martha's Vineyard airport café, Carolyn told her waitress, Joan Ford, why she was reluctant to fly with John. "I don't," she said without hesitation, "trust him."

On today's trip up from New Jersey, Jay Biederman, the flight instructor who had recently helped John pass his written instrument test and was preparing him for his instrument flight test, was scheduled to go along as he had several times before. But when Biederman canceled to join his parents on a hiking trip in Switzerland, John made the fateful decision not to find a replacement.

Carolyn's thirty-four-year-old investment banker sister harbored no reservations about John's piloting skills. Lauren Bessette was a Wharton School graduate with a command of Mandarin Chinese, and a rising star at Morgan Stanley. She could be most persuasive. Over lunch at the Stanhope Hotel's Café M that Wednesday, July 14, John was overheard enlisting Lauren's help in talking his wife into going. "Oh, come on now," Lauren urged Carolyn, "we'll have fun."

Kyle Bailey was also planning to fly to Martha's Vineyard that night, but when he arrived at New Jersey's Essex County Airport he could see that "something was not quite right."

Instead of the clear five-to-ten-mile visibility being reported by the Federal Aviation Administration, an odd haze was blanketing the region. He picked out a fixed point on the horizon—a ridge he would normally be able to make out in the distance. "But I couldn't see it at all," Kyle said. "There was this really strange, thick haze. Heavy but sort of shimmering at the same time. It was already getting dark, and the wind was picking up. So I decided it wasn't worth the risk."

John made a different decision. Since the cast had been removed from his injured foot just twenty-four hours earlier, he hobbled to the plane on crutches, tossed them into the baggage compartment, then gingerly pulled himself up into the cockpit—all the while wincing in pain. Behind him, Carolyn and Lauren belted themselves into the Piper's tan leather seats. They faced forward, with two empty rear-facing seats opposite them.

Now, as he walked to his car, something made Bailey turn around. "It was so spooky," he said, "but I watched as they taxied into position and waited to be cleared for takeoff." The aircraft's registration number, N92539A, was emblazoned on its fuselage. Bailey noticed that this was different from the number on John's older, less powerful Cessna. John was actually having that number, N529JK, transferred to the new plane. N529JK was a reference to his father's May 29 birthday.

Bailey found himself standing, unable to move—"as if something was telling me it was important to keep watching." Since Lauren was seated on the opposite side of the plane, Bailey could not see her. But as the Piper idled on the runway, John and Carolyn—she seated directly behind him and facing forward—were plainly visible in profile. "It was hazy but their silhouettes were so clear. I was struck at the time by how ethereal it looked, how eerie."

There was no obligation to file an official flight plan that night, but John did inform the control tower at Essex County Airport that he intended to fly due north and then east to Martha's Vineyard. Just twelve minutes after sundown, at 8:38 p.m., the tower cleared John for takeoff. He advanced the throttle, and the Piper Saratoga rolled down Runway 22. In a matter of seconds, the plane carrying JFK Jr., his wife, Carolyn, and sister-in-law Lauren Bessette lifted off the tarmac and sailed smoothly into the twilight sky—heading due south at first, over a golf course, then banking right before making a gentle turn toward the northeast. "North of Teterboro," he told the control tower in his only radio communication that night.

"Eastward . . ."

Had he known about his new plane's many remarkable capabilities, John could simply have pushed two buttons to activate the Piper Saratoga's automatic pilot feature and it would have flown him all the way from New Jersey to Massachusetts. Once there, it would have even executed a perfect three-point landing at Martha's Vineyard Airport.

If he was even aware that he could put his plane on automatic pilot, John gave no hint of it. "The Piper was his shiny new toy, and he was thrilled with it," a friend said. "But it was an awful lot of plane to handle, and John was still learning the ropes."

As it climbed at a speed of 104 miles per hour toward its cruising altitude of 5,600 feet, the plane crossed over the Hudson and headed toward Long Island Sound. It had been in the air only a matter of minutes when an air traffic controller on Long Island spotted an unexpected blip on his radar screen. A small plane of unknown origin—since John hadn't filed a flight plan there was no way for anyone to know precisely who he was or where he was heading—seemed to be edging perilously close to an American Airlines passenger jet.

Alerted to the danger, the pilot of the airliner was taken aback by the sight of the Piper Saratoga emerging from the mist just off the tip of his right wing. Careful not to upset his 160 passengers, he made a subtle maneuver to put distance between his airliner and the smaller craft—and avert the midair collision that otherwise would have been inevitable.

Inside the Piper, everyone was blissfully unaware of how they had just cheated death—at least for the time being. To protect their ears from the earsplitting whine of the engines, John and the Bessette sisters wore headphones that made it possible for them to talk about their weekend plans and trade gossip about their wide circle of friends in New York as they leafed through fashion magazines spread out on the small foldout table between them.

John must have thought he was playing it safe at that point—never straying far from the Connecticut coastline, ticking off the names of the cities and towns as they appeared one by one just over his left shoulder: Greenwich, Bridgeport, New Haven, Old Saybrook, New London, Mystic.

He could make them out—just barely. But after forty minutes in the air, nothing was visible. The murk was now so dense that neither the comforting sight of the city lights below nor the stars above were available to help guide John on his way.

At any time, John could have pushed those two lifesaving buttons to turn on the automatic pilot. Dr. Bob Arnot, flying just twenty minutes ahead of Kennedy, considered doing just that. When he approached the Vineyard and searched for the lights of Oak Bluffs, Edgartown, and Vineyard Haven, Arnot saw nothing. "It's as if someone put you in a closet and shut the door." Arnot wondered if the island had suffered a power failure.

"There was no horizon and no light," he said. "The night could best be described as inky black."

At 9:24, John still had the option of simply pushing the two buttons that put his plane on autopilot. Now, forty-six minutes into his planned flight, John instead scanned the coastline for familiar landmarks as he flew over Westerly, Rhode Island.

Nothing.

Looking to the right, he searched for the hatchet-shaped outline of Block Island, but there was only darkness below.

Anyone flying strictly by visual flight rules and not relying solely on instruments would normally have borne left once he reached Point

Judith and clung to the coastline until he reached Buzzards Bay. Then he could make a right turn and fly straight out to Martha's Vineyard over eight miles of open water. Instead, John decided to maintain his course straight ahead to the Vineyard over thirty-five miles of ocean. This final leg of the trip would take only six minutes, but it meant that John would have no visual reference points, lights, or landmarks. Without them, local pilot Tom Freeman observed, "you are totally, completely in the dark—literally as well as figuratively—if you don't know how to rely on your instruments. It's a sickening, scary feeling."

By this point, other pilots in the region were either radioing for assistance or asking for permission to put down at alternate airports inland until the fog lifted.

John, however, pressed on.

His first instinct, understandably, was to try to drop below the cloud layer. Fifty-six minutes after takeoff, at precisely 9:34 p.m., John pushed the yoke forward and with the airspeed indicator reading 150 knots (173 miles per hour), swiftly descended at the rate of 700 feet per minute. Leveling off at 2,300 feet, he was at last below the haze and could see Gay Head Lighthouse and, not far beyond, the lights of Jackie's beloved Red Gate Farm.

But within five minutes, John was back to flying blind. Another pilot in the area that night describes the sensation as being in a room with the windows painted white. John's instructors had warned him about spatial disorientation, and how, deprived of visual cues, the human brain can quickly confuse down with up and up with down. Even the most experienced pilots, he remembered being told, developed debilitating vertigo—and that was why, under these conditions, the only way to safely arrive at his destination was to rely solely on his instruments and ignore what his body was telling him.

In the cockpit, John tried to square what his body seemed to be saying with the readings on the gauges and dials directly in front of him. The off-kilter reading on the directional gyro in the lower center of the instrument panel would have contradicted whatever it was he was feeling. A quick glance at the turn-and-bank indicator in the lower left-hand corner would have shown that the red ball was not centered and that his wings were not level—no matter what his own senses were telling him.

His head swimming, John made a sharp right turn and took the plane back up three hundred feet—a last, frantic maneuver to somehow get above the haze. By this point John's body was, in the words of veteran military pilot Edward Francis, "undoubtedly playing all sorts of tricks on him. You can be upside down and turning to the left and your body is telling you you're right side up and turning right." Add to this confusion the mounting panic of the two women behind him. "By now they would have been bounced around enough to know something was seriously wrong," Francis speculated. "They may have been screaming. They certainly would have been asking John what was happening."

Unfortunately, John had not yet gone through the phase of instrument training that might have helped him cope with pandemonium in the cockpit. In the air, instructors simulate an emergency and then try to rattle a novice any way they can—by yelling, grabbing at the controls, or even popping a paper bag—all to reinforce the pilot's ability to ignore distractions and focus on the problem at hand. "They train you," Kyle Bailey said, "to have nerves of steel."

Still, John managed to level off at 2,600 feet and steer the plane straight for Martha's Vineyard Airport, now just twenty miles ahead. He maintained this course for a full minute before he must have again begun listening to the mixed messages his senses and the instruments were sending him. At 9:40 p.m., John, clearly disoriented, turned south, away from the island. He then began to bring the plane down, descending gradually until the plane reached 2,200 feet. It was then that the Piper Saratoga suddenly surged downward at an alarming 5,000 feet per minute—ten times the normal airspeed.

Yet the situation was not hopeless—not yet. If he could just have maintained the presence of mind to level his wings *before* pulling up on the yoke, he could have regained altitude and saved the plane. To accomplish this, the notoriously absentminded John would have had to bring to bear all his powers of concentration, and he would have had to rely solely on his instruments. Instead, he made a classic—and fatal—mistake: pulling up on the yoke without bothering to level the plane. As a result, the Piper Saratoga started to turn clockwise in a corkscrew fashion, picking up speed as it headed downward in what aviators refer to as a "graveyard spiral."

Inside the cabin, John, Carolyn, and Lauren were pressed back into their leather seats as the plane spun wildly toward the ocean's surface at a rate of ninety-nine feet per second. They would no longer be able to scream; the G-forces pressing against their chests would have already forced the air out of their lungs. All they would have been able to do was listen in terror to the wail of the engine and the wind shrieking past the windows.

Listen, and wait.

Now my wife and I prepare
for a new administration,
and a new baby.
—JFK's victory speech, November 9, 1960

It was clear that John was the light of his life.
—John's uncle Jamie Auchincloss, on JFK

Sometimes I can't remember what
really happened, and what I saw
in pictures.
—John

2.

The Son He Had Longed For

November 24, 1960
Aboard the Kennedy campaign plane *Caroline*

The president-elect was in an upbeat mood, nursing a cocktail and talking about the makeup of his administration, when word came from the cockpit that his pregnant wife had collapsed at their Georgetown home. He was devastated—"stricken with remorse," his aide Kenneth O'Donnell recalled, "because he was not with his wife."

John F. Kennedy had reason to feel guilty. Although Caroline's birth in 1957 had been an easy one, Jackie had already endured a miscarriage and a stillbirth that nearly killed her. In the closing weeks of the 1960 presidential campaign, Jack had pressured Jackie to join him on the campaign trail.

She defied her doctors and reluctantly agreed, pushing herself to the edge. This final campaign surge ended with a ticker-tape parade through New York's fabled "Canyon of Heroes"—a frenzied blur of mass hysteria during which the candidate and his wife perched precariously on the back of an open car. Several times, they were both nearly yanked from the car by overzealous fans tugging at their sleeves.

After taking such risks to ensure her husband's narrow victory margin—less than one-fifth of one percent—Jackie might have expected that Jack could make more time for her and for Caroline, the daughter he called "Buttons." Instead, their redbrick townhouse on Georgetown's narrow N Street became "transition central," overrun with both hard-boiled rank-and-file members of Kennedy's Irish "Murphia" as well as the youthful and energetic Ivy Leaguers who made up JFK's personal brain trust.

The scene was no less chaotic outside, where reporters and onlookers pressed against police barricades across the street. Several times a day, Jack, still determined to accommodate the faithful whenever possible, strode across the street to shake hands and parry with the press.

Jackie, sensing that all was not right with her pregnancy, was now determined to obey her obstetrician's orders not to leave the house. Holed up upstairs, she begged Jack to spend time with her and Caroline. Instead, he began shuttling between Georgetown and La Guerida (roughly "Spoils of War" in Spanish), Joseph Kennedy's sprawling oceanfront estate in Palm Beach, Florida. There JFK and his father, tended to by a household staff of twelve, sunbathed in the nude while discussing possible cabinet appointments.

Jack did agree to fly back to Georgetown to share a quiet Thanksgiving dinner with his wife and daughter, but only as long as he could fly back to Palm Beach that same night. Understandably apprehensive now that the due date was only three weeks away, Jackie pleaded with him to stay. "Why can't you stay here until I have the baby," she asked, "and then we can go down together."

Jack refused. Caroline had been born right on schedule, and Jack had no reason to think the next baby would be any different. Besides, three weeks "might as well have been six months to him," their friend Bill Walton said. "He was not about to put everything on hold just because Jackie was a little nervous. He had a country to run."

As soon as he finished his pumpkin pie, Jack departed for Palm Beach, leaving a crestfallen Jackie behind. The president-elect's plane had only been in the air a matter of minutes when Caroline's nanny, Maud Shaw, heard Jackie's screams. Rushed by ambulance to Georgetown University Hospital, Jackie was immediately prepped for an emergency caesarean.

Once he touched down in Florida, Jack commandeered the fastest aircraft available—the DC-6 press plane that trailed the *Caroline*—and headed straight back to Washington. En route, he put on the cockpit headphones and waited for any news. It wasn't until shortly before l a.m. on November 25, 1960, that passengers and crew could breathe a sigh of relief. When Press Secretary Pierre Salinger announced over the intercom that Mrs. Kennedy had just given birth by caesarean section to a healthy six-pound, three-ounce boy, the reporters cheered and JFK, smiling broadly, took a deep bow.

While the press was spoon-fed glowing reports that mother and child were "doing well and resting comfortably," both Jackie and her baby remained in guarded condition. Once the anesthesia wore off, Jackie, still in considerable pain from her ordeal, demanded to see her son. She could see her baby, but was forbidden to hold him; the infant, suffering from what would turn out to be an undiagnosed respiratory ailment, spent the first six days of his life in an incubator. Jackie's condition, meanwhile, was also problematic. It would take months for Jackie and her baby to fully recover, but only after each suffered setbacks severe enough to take them to the brink of death.

Chastened, Jack rushed to his wife's third-floor suite at the hospital and then popped into the nursery to visit his son. "Now, that's the most beautiful boy I've seen," the president-elect gushed. "Maybe I'll name him Abraham Lincoln." To make up for the worry he had cause her, Jack visited Jackie and the baby three times a day.

For now, a carnival atmosphere prevailed at the hospital—"buoyant and joyous" were the words *Life* magazine's Gail Wescott used to describe it. "It was innocent and exhilarating. It did not seem that anything could ever go wrong." One of the stars of the show was Buttons, eager to see the baby brother born just two days before she turned three—her "birthday present," she was told by her parents, and she believed it. "Caroline thought for a long time," Nanny Shaw said, "that he belonged to her."

Determined to keep John's christening a low-key affair, Jackie convinced her husband that it should take place at the hospital and away from the press. But when the president-elect wheeled his wife and their week-old son outside her room toward the hospital chapel, a cadre of photographers were poised for action at the far end of the corridor. "Oh, God," Jackie said. "Don't stop, Jack. Just keep going." But Jack was not about to disappoint the Washington press corps—or the public that had voted him into office. He stopped pushing Jackie's wheelchair for a moment to allow a few shots to be taken of the infant, who was dressed for the occasion in his father's forty-three-year-old silk-and-lace baptismal gown.

When the closed-door christening was over thirty minutes later, a noticeably more relaxed Jackie emerged. "Look at those pretty eyes," she said as she looked down at her son. "Isn't he sweet?" Jack nodded in agreement, but his mind was clearly elsewhere.

On December 9, just hours after an exhausted Jackie was led on a punishing White House tour by outgoing first lady Mamie Eisenhower, America's new first family departed for Palm Beach aboard the *Caroline*. Settling in, JFK lit a cigar and chatted animatedly with his advisers. They had been aloft only a matter of minutes when Jackie, who for years had encouraged Jack's cigar smoking to disguise her own cigarette habit, noticed that a cloud of smoke was encircling the baby's bassinet. This time, Jackie called a halt to the conversation and directed Jack and his stogie-chomping cronies to the far end of the cabin.

Jackie spent the next two weeks in bed, trying to recover from her emergency caesarean as well as her grueling trek through the Executive Mansion with a clueless Mamie Eisenhower. Her baby, meanwhile, was losing weight, crying nonstop, and—most disturbingly—at times struggling for breath. "John's health really wasn't doing so well," she later said. "There was, thank God, this brilliant pediatrician in Palm Beach who really saved his life, as he was going downhill."

John was, in fact, suffering from an inflammation of the lung's hyaline membrane, a condition not uncommon among premature infants.

Sadly, this was the same respiratory problem that would later kill his infant brother, Patrick.

"Jackie came perilously close to dying after John's birth—and so did the baby," said JFK's physician Janet Travell, who added that the press corps was kept "entirely in the dark." Jackie's own health suffered because she was "consumed with worry" over the baby. "Jackie was very emotional about losing her son," Travell said. "It was the thing she feared more than losing her own life."

John was not even three weeks old, but he had already come close to death twice and was about to again. On the morning of December 11, 1960, would-be suicide bomber Richard Pavlick was parked outside the Kennedys' Palm Beach mansion waiting for the president-elect to head out for Sunday Mass at St. Edward's Church just a few blocks away. Pavlick planned to crash his 1950 Buick, packed with seven sticks of dynamite, into the Kennedys' car as it pulled away from the house.

Pavlick was about to floor his car when Jackie and Caroline suddenly appeared in the doorway to wave goodbye to Daddy. Behind them was the Kennedy family's private nurse, Luella Hennessey, holding Baby John in her arms. Touched by this warm family tableau, Pavlick did not go through with his gruesome plan.

It was only after he was arrested for drunk driving a few days later that Pavlick's weird assassination plot was uncovered. For his part, Pavlick was unrepentant. He told police he did not wish to harm Jackie or the Kennedy children, but that he still planned to "get" JFK. Pavlick was charged with attempted murder and later sent to prison.

Jack, who suffered from a variety of life-threatening illnesses and narrowly escaped death during World War II combat in the Pacific, barely blinked when he was told the news. His own experiences, coupled with the tragic early deaths of his brother Joe and sister Kathleen, had convinced Jack that he would die young—"and that there was nothing he or anyone else could do about it," said his longtime friend Senator George Smathers of Florida. Another Kennedy intimate, fashion designer Oleg Cassini, called this Jack's "sublime streak of elegant fatalism."

Jackie, on the other hand, was anything but stoic. She had blithely assumed that bodyguards and Secret Service agents would provide them with all the protection they needed, and was outwardly distraught when she was told how close she and her children had come to being blown to pieces. "We're nothing," she said, "but sitting ducks in a shooting gallery."

"I don't think it ever really occurred to Jackie that somebody could get past all those people who constantly surrounded Jack," said Letitia "Tish" Baldrige, Jackie's classmate from Miss Porter's School and the woman she hired to be her White House social secretary. "Jackie always worried about people violating her family's privacy. I never heard her say a peep about somebody wanting to do them harm."

There were only a few weeks left until inauguration day, and Jack had no time to think about anything beyond putting his administration together. The frenetic pace he set back in Georgetown continued beneath Florida's swaying palms.

While Jackie tried to rest upstairs, bow-tied Harvard intellectuals, polished Washington operatives, and grizzled Boston pols all vied for her husband's attention. If she wanted to make her way from her bedroom to the upstairs bathroom, a nightgown-clad Jackie risked bumping into a stranger on her way there. Making matters worse was the added presence of her noisy Kennedy in-laws, whose frat house antics had always annoyed Jack's decidedly more civilized bride. "Ethel and Bobby are here. Mayhem," she complained to Baldrige. "Complete and utter chaos."

By comparison, John, even with his health issues, was no trouble at all. Like millions of mothers in the 1960s, Jackie had no interest in breastfeeding. It was left to Luella Hennessey to heat up the baby's bottle, change his diapers, and get up several times during the course of the night to feed John and then rock him back to sleep. Shaw happily took care of Caroline, who periodically upstaged her father during press conferences by teetering around the room in her mother's stiletto heels.

Shutting herself upstairs with the drapes drawn, Jackie refused to join Jack's boisterous relatives for dinner on the main floor. "I couldn't hold food down," she recalled. "I guess I was just in physical and nervous exhaustion because the month after the baby's birth had been the opposite of recuperation."

Nevertheless, Jackie, who had her own plans for the White House, made the most of those hours alone in her bedroom. "It's the worst place in the world," she had told a friend after her long march with Mamie. "So cold and dreary. A dungeon like the Lubyanka . . . I can't bear the thought of moving in. I hate it, hate it, hate it." Unable to sleep, she pored over blueprints and photographs of the Executive Mansion, laying the groundwork for what she already envisioned as a historic restoration.

Still shaky, Jackie returned to Georgetown alone on January 14, less than a week before the inauguration. She explained to Jack that she wanted to go ahead of the rest of the family because there was no way she could unpack and introduce the children to their new home at the same time. So John and his big sister remained behind with their father, Maud Shaw, and Elsie Philips, the new nanny hired to take care of John.

At exactly noon on January 20, 1961, Jackie appeared impervious to the teeth-chattering twenty-degree cold as she watched her husband being sworn in by Chief Justice Earl Warren. Jack was the country's first Roman Catholic president, the first born in the twentieth century, and at forty-three the youngest ever elected to office—although Jackie, just thirty-one, had always viewed him as a much older and wiser man.

He proved it with his inaugural address, which called the younger generation to action with its enduring "Ask not what your country can do for you" message. But Jackie had no opportunity to congratulate him; Jack, who had always resisted public displays of affection, did not follow tradition by kissing his wife after he took the oath. And once Marian Anderson had closed the ceremonies with a stirring rendition of the national anthem, JFK bounded off the platform without his wife.

Bravely weathering the icy conditions, the new first couple kicked off the inaugural parade, riding in an open car from the Capitol to the White House. Jackie climbed onto the reviewing stand but could stay for only an hour. Bone-weary and freezing, she now dreaded the long night of inaugural balls that stretched before her. "I'm exhausted, Jack," she said, excusing herself from the parade festivities. "I'll see you at home." She would later acknowledge that it took a moment for it all to sink in. She was not heading back to their "sweet little house that leans slightly to one side" on N Street; home was now 1600 Pennsylvania Avenue.

Trying to recover her strength, Jackie went straight to the Queen's Bedroom (so named because five queens had slept there) and refused to budge—not even to greet family members at a private reception in the State Dining Room. Instead of dining that night with her husband and members of his cabinet, she had dinner on a tray in bed.

None of it worked. Jackie was unable to summon the strength to get out of bed. "I can't do it," Jackie told Dr. Travell. "I just can't move." In the weeks leading up to the election, the infamous "Dr. Feelgood," Max Jacobson, had been injecting the candidate, his wife, and several members of the Kennedy inner circle with amphetamines. Now Dr. Travell was handing Jackie a little orange pill—Dexedrine—to give her the energy boost needed to make it through the rest of the evening.

An hour later, the nation's glamorous first lady felt strong enough to accompany her dashing husband to the first three of five inaugural balls they were scheduled to attend. The reaction at each was the same: As the orchestra struck up "Hail to the Chief" and the first couple—he in white tie and tails, she in a dramatic floor-length white silk cape—made their entrance, a collective gasp went up from the throng, which then exploded in cheers and applause.

By the fourth ball, however, Jackie's Dexedrine-fueled high had worn off. "It was like Cinderella and the clock striking midnight. I just crumbled," she said. "All my strength was finally gone." She excused herself, sending her husband along to attend the final two balls solo.

"I always wish I could have participated more in those first shining hours with Jack," Jackie later said. "But at least I thought I had given him our John, the son he had longed for so much."

WITH THE INAUGURAL festivities behind them, Jackie now felt free to fly the children up from Palm Beach—something Jack had been urging her to do for weeks. To the surprise of everyone who knew him, Caroline's arrival in 1957 had transformed the notoriously libidinous JFK into a doting and devoted dad. "He wanted the children around all the time," said Jacques Lowe, Kennedy's longtime official photographer and friend. "Like a lot of fathers who are smitten with their kids, he couldn't keep his hands off them. But Jackie called the shots when it came to Caroline and John."

Jackie's excuse for keeping the children in Palm Beach was credible enough: their rooms in the family quarters of the White House were being painted, and she didn't want them exposed to the noxious fumes. Just as important, she wanted to shield them at least for a little while longer from the pomp and circumstance that from now on would be an inescapable part of their lives. "I want my children to be brought up in more personal surroundings," she told Baldrige. And, while everyone in the family had a code name—the president was "Lancer," Jackie was "Lace," Caroline "Lyric," and John "Lark"—Jackie made it abundantly clear to everyone working at the White House that she would be a hands-on mom. "I don't want them to be raised by nurses and Secret Service agents," she told Baldrige.

Flying in the face of reality—and the inescapable fact that her children would always be cared for by nannies and governesses—Jackie vowed that John and Caroline would have something approaching a normal childhood. "It isn't fair to children in the limelight to leave them in the care of others and then expect that they will turn out all right," she said. "They need their mother's affection and guidance and long periods of time alone with her. That is what gives them security in an often confusing world."

The first lady was pleased to learn that John's and Caroline's toys had been stashed away in the closet of White House Chief Usher J. B. West. "We'll bring them out as soon as the children's room are ready," she had instructed him. The toys were, in fact, the first things to arrive from the N Street house, covertly smuggled in while the Eisenhowers were still very much in residence.

Before she took on the daunting task of restoring the long-neglected public rooms of the White House to their former glory, Jackie first tackled the upstairs living quarters. "Sometimes I wondered, 'How are we going to live as a family in this enormous place?'" she later recalled. "I'm afraid it will always be a little impossible for the people who live here. It's an office building."

Jackie quickly set about to purge the place of the motel modern décor favored by her predecessors. Her own chandeliered French provincial bedroom was done up in hues of green and blue, with leopard-skin throws draped here and there for drama. The president's bedroom, connected to his wife's by a walk-in closet that contained a stereo system, was decorated in blue and white. On one wall, Jackie hung Childe Hassam's American impressionist masterpiece *Flag Day*.

The children's rooms were just across from the Yellow Oval Room. Jackie decided to make John's spacious nursery a reflection of his father's room. The walls were white, and the crown molding a vivid blue. Caroline's room, not surprisingly, was all done in shades of pink and white, with rosebud-patterned drapes that matched the linens, and a country scene by Grandma Moses hanging opposite the white-canopied bed.

The nanny slept in her own small room positioned right between John and Caroline. "Maud Shaw won't need much," Jackie wrote in a memo to J. B. West. "Just find a wicker wastebasket for her banana peels and a little table for her false teeth at night."

Those first few nights in the White House, Nanny Shaw was getting little sleep. Jackie was upset that her infant cried constantly and didn't seem to be gaining any weight. "John had been in such delicate health," Baldrige said, "that naturally any little sign of something going wrong was cause for alarm."

Shaw doubled the amount of formula the baby was getting and switched his morning meal of beef extract to lunchtime. Within six weeks, John was no longer crying incessantly, and had developed a healthy appetite for cereals, soup, strained fruit, vegetables, and meats.

By that time, Jackie's makeover of the upstairs living quarters of the White House was complete. "She wanted to cozy things up with flowers and family photographs and the paintings that she liked," Baldrige said. "She turned this drafty, cold old place into a warm environment for a young family overnight."

As an adult, John conceded that he could not actually distinguish between his firsthand recollections and what he learned from newsreels, photographs, and the endless stream of Camelot tales spun by relatives and family friends. In the end he believed that his earliest memories were of playing with his father on the floor of the president's bedroom, part of the daily routine that seldom varied during their thousand days in the White House.

By design, the president and first lady seldom saw each other in the morning. "That time," Baldrige said, "was the children's time." By the time Shaw brought them into their father's bedroom, he had already spent thirty minutes going over cables and scanning the morning newspapers while soaking in the tub.

After the kids kissed their father, he went to the dressing room to change while they sat on the floor watching cartoons. At 9 a.m. they switched to TV exercise pioneer Jack LaLanne, and the president clapped along as Caroline followed LaLanne's signature regime of jumping jacks and stretches. At first, Shaw sat in a corner chair tending to Baby John while father and daughter enjoyed this time together.

Later, when John was a toddler, Jack spent less time clapping and more time actually rolling around on the floor with both children. "He was absolutely crazy about Caroline. He adored her," their old friend Chuck Spalding said. "But there was a special connection with John. Even before John was able to walk, Jack threw him in the air, tossed him around, tickled him—things he did with Caroline, but to a greater extent with John."

That he could do any of these things at all was remarkable in itself.

In addition to his often incapacitating allergies and a medical history that included scarlet fever, anemia, an underactive thyroid, colitis, and a cholesterol level of 350, JFK had long been secretly battling Addison's disease, a degeneration of the adrenal glands that—like AIDS—destroys the immune system. He also endured crippling back pain—pain so severe that he spent most of his time hobbling around on crutches.

As a result, the president risked a visit to the emergency room every time he roughhoused with his kids. "You'd see that look on his face that told you the pain was terrible," Jacques Lowe said, "but he never complained. To see the sheer joy on his face when he was playing with John—obviously to him it was all worth it."

Once the president was dressed, John was handed off to Maud Shaw and Caroline walked hand in hand with her father to the Oval Office. When he was old enough, John joined them. "It was very touching to see the president walking down the corridor holding hands with the children," JFK's longtime secretary Evelyn Lincoln said. "He was always talking to them, asking them questions. He never talked baby talk to them. Both the president and Mrs. Kennedy always spoke to Caroline and John as if they were little adults."

Not that it was always easy to comprehend what John was trying to say. At her father's behest, Caroline sometimes acted as interpreter, often appending commentary of her own. When John toddled into the Oval Office in the middle of a meeting between JFK and his uncle Bobby, the attorney general, everything stopped while the most powerful man in the world strained to understand his son's gibberish. "He's saying he wants a cookie," Caroline explained authoritatively. "But he shouldn't have one because he's been a very naughty boy."

Unlike other children who saw little of their parents during working hours, John and his sister encountered theirs several times throughout the day. Caroline spent the rest of the morning at the school Jackie set up on the third floor for the president's children and the sixteen or so offspring of several White House staffers and a few close friends. During the school's morning recess, JFK stepped out into the garden and clapped his hands to summon Caroline and her classmates. The first ones to make it to the president were rewarded with a piece of candy—something that did not go over well with Caroline's teachers.

JFK summoned John in much the same way—calling the boy's name repeatedly ("John. John!") while he clapped his hands. It usually took a few tries before the easily distracted toddler actually showed up, prompting staffers to start calling the president's son "John-John." It was a nickname neither parent embraced. "Jackie hated the whole 'John-John' thing and would cast a withering glance in the direction of anyone who used it," Baldrige said. "To her and to the president, he was always just John."

At noon, Jackie joined John and Caroline as they ate lunch in the "High Chair Room," the small dining area for the children she had set up off the kitchen. Then Caroline returned to class and John, under the watchful eyes of two Secret Service agents and nannies Shaw and Phillips, headed for the play area his mother had designed for the children just outside the president's office window. The space included a tree house with a slide, a leather swing, a barrel tunnel, and a small trampoline.

Adding to the general mayhem was the first family's growing menagerie. The Kennedys arrived at the White House with just one dog, their Welsh terrier Charlie. But soon Pushinka, a gift from Soviet premier Nikita Khrushchev, would arrive. "We trained that dog to slide down the slide we had in the back of the White House," John later said. Pushing Pushinka down the slide, he added wistfully, "is probably my first memory."

Charlie and Pushinka were joined by Wolf, an aptly named Irish wolfhound that had been given to the family by a Dublin priest. Joe Kennedy then gave Jackie a German shepherd, Clipper. The most celebrated Kennedy pet, Caroline's pony Macaroni, had a stable all his own. Few people were aware of the existence of John's pony Leprechaun. The boy did not share his father's allergic reaction to dogs and cats, but horses were another matter.

Jackie simply turned a blind eye to the boy's discomfort. An accomplished equestrienne, the first lady was thrilled that Caroline had turned out to be "an absolute natural" on horseback. She saw no reason why her son couldn't be as well. "The poor kid's eyes would water and he'd be sneezing away," Chuck Spalding said, "but Jackie just figured he'd get over it."

John's earliest childhood memories also included Caroline's cat Tom Kitten, who eventually had to be given away because of their father's allergies; a beer-drinking rabbit named Zsa Zsa (after the actress Zsa Zsa Gabor, a friend of Jack); and a rotating cast of lambs, ducks, and guinea pigs. Aside from the dogs, the Kennedy children spent the most time playing with the few animals allowed to be kept in cages in Caroline's room: Bluebell and Marybell the hamsters, and Caroline's favorite pet, a canary she insisted on naming Robin.

Whenever she could spare even a minutes away from her first lady duties, Jackie would run down to the play area and push John on the swing or guide him down the slide. She also managed to squeeze in a little relaxation time for herself, watching the children play as she bounced on the trampoline.

"Everyone thought Jackie was this very aristocratic personality," Baldrige said, "and she certainly could be absolutely regal when she wanted to be. She also took the *job* of being a mother very seriously— actually more seriously than most women of her generation, I think." Around the children, however, she was "a very different, more light-hearted person. There was this marvelous little girl inside of her that came out when she was around Caroline and John."

Jackie may have been a more earnest mother than most because of her own unhappy childhood. Growing up in Manhattan and in the moneyed Long Island enclave of East Hampton in the 1930s, Jackie and her little sister, Lee, were caught in the crossfire between their domineering mother, Janet, and their swashbuckling playboy father, "Black Jack" Bouvier. The marriage ended in divorce, and soon after the Bouvier girls went to live with Janet and their new stepfather, the wealthy Hugh D. Auchincloss II. Jackie called him "Uncle Hughdie."

With their mother's remarriage, Jackie and Lee suddenly found themselves adjusting to life with a new set of stepsiblings. One of them was Gore Vidal, Hugh Auchincloss's stepson by a former marriage. According to Vidal, Janet had rushed Auchincloss into marriage "because she had to. She was a financially desperate social climber with two small daughters to raise."

Jackie's privileged upbringing continued without interruption at Merrywood, the Auchinclosses' palatial forty-six-acre estate outside Washington, and at Hammersmith Farm, the family's lavish, twenty-eight-room "summer cottage" in Newport, Rhode Island. Jackie grew particularly fond of her stepbrother Hugh "Yusha" Auchincloss, and the two children her mother had with Hugh Auchincloss—her stepsiblings Janet and Jamie.

At fifteen, Jackie was shipped off to Miss Porter's School in Farmington, Connecticut, one of the finest finishing schools in New England. Yet even then she was never allowed to forget that she was only a poor step-relation of the rich and influential Auchincloss clan. "Jackie and I were in the same boat," Gore Vidal explained. "We were brought up in style, allowed to live in their very comfortable, rather Jamesian world. But the money was *theirs*. We—Jackie, Lee, and I—were penniless, and were made painfully aware of the fact."

Even as first lady, Jackie was plagued by feelings of insecurity and inadequacy—feelings that, her Bouvier cousin John Davis once suggested, "stemmed from her parents' terribly bitter, unhappy marriage. And then to never quite know where she stood with her stepfather . . . it left her feeling abandoned emotionally at a very young age."

Of course nothing compared to the pressures brought to bear on the wife of the American president. Public expectations were high, and Jackie admitted she was "panic-stricken" at the thought of disappointing her husband. Behind the scenes, John's parents were also dealing with their own medical issues—and the mounting tensions in their relationship caused by his flagrant infidelity.

Still, there was a general consensus among their friends and those working in the White House that Jackie went to great lengths to shield John and Caroline from the strains in their parents' marriage. In the end, Jack and Jackie "enjoyed each other," insisted Jackie's stepbrother Yusha. "That's what John grew up with. He was born into a house filled with love and fun and laughter, just like millions of other children."

Well, obviously not exactly like millions of other children. The public could not get enough of the adorable tots who inhabited the Executive Mansion, and no one understood the political value of that better than the president. He made sure national publications like *Newsweek, Life, Look,* and *Time* were filled with heart-melting photos of John playing with his toy helicopter; Caroline astride Macaroni; Jackie helping her son into his pajamas; the two Kennedy children merrily dancing in the Oval Office while Daddy looked on; and John and Caroline cavorting with their cousins at the Kennedy family compound in Hyannis Port.

To satisfy her husband's need to placate the Washington press corps, Jackie grudgingly signed off on a handful of these carefully circumscribed photo shoots. But for the most part, she made it her mission to block access to the children. "She didn't want them exploited in that way," Pierre Salinger said, "and the president did. That always left me holding the bag, because as soon as Jackie's back was turned, he told me to invite the photographers in." It was understood that, once the photos ran, Salinger would take the rap. "It was a part of my job," he said, "that I could easily have done without."

"Jackie Kennedy was the most warm and delightful woman you could ever imagine," said legendary *Life* photojournalist Alfred Eisenstaedt, echoing the sentiments of his colleagues. "But if you even pointed a camera at John or Caroline without her permission, it was over. You could not cross her when it came to the children. If you did you were done, out."

Jack still had ample opportunity to work his magic, particularly since Jackie spent long stretches of time at Glen Ora, the family's retreat in the heart of Virginia's horse country. What photographers often found themselves treated to was a glimpse of the growing bond between the young president and his little boy.

JFK delighted in tickling his son, leaning down at staff meetings so that the boy could babble in his ear, or tossing him into the air—regardless of the often painful consequences. John famously hid under his father's desk while the president teased, "Is there a rabbit in there?" But the game father and son played most frequently was "Going Through the Tunnel," which simply involved scampering between the president's legs and back again. At some point, JFK would gently spank John's behind or playfully grab the boy as he tried to make it through.

All the while, the president took obvious delight in simply touching the boy—a connection that Jackie and others called "sensual" in nature. "He would nuzzle John the way a bear nuzzles its cub," Baldrige observed, "pausing for a moment to inhale his smell and feel his skin. It was really very moving, because President Kennedy was very reserved otherwise. You never saw him hugging or kissing anyone in public, not even his wife." The children gave JFK a "chance to behave just like any other loving, affectionate American dad," Baldrige added. "It began with Caroline, but it was really John who opened up the president's heart."

Stanley Tretick, the *Look* magazine photographer who took some of the most memorable White House shots of JFK and his children, remembered that JFK's "interest in the boy was incredible . . . And you know, it was a genuine thing between the two of them. The boy also sensed his father. I think it would have really grown . . ."

No one was more delighted than Jackie, who often watched silently on the sidelines as her husband tumbled around on the floor with their son. "You could tell how thrilled she was," said Baldrige, who on more than one occasion caught Jackie spying on the two Kennedy men. "Jackie got such a kick out of watching them enjoy each other. The weight of the world was on this man's shoulders. He was trying to keep us from getting into a nuclear war with the Russians, among other things. But for a few moments he could roll around with John and forget all that. Jackie was proud she could provide him with a happy family life. She felt it was the most important part of her job as his wife."

From the very beginning, there was also the palpable sense that John, not his big sister Caroline, would someday be the Kennedy standard-bearer. "No question about it," said writer George Plimpton, an old friend of Jackie. "Everyone loved Caroline and we all knew she was exceptional, but great things were expected of John. I think Jackie in particular believed the world of politics was a man's world."

Given the fact that JFK was the first president to be born in the twentieth century, expectations regarding John's future—not Caroline's—made sense in the context of the times. "The Kennedys were already a dynasty, so the sky was the limit for John," veteran Washington journalist Helen Thomas said. "Back then, every *boy* was told he could grow up to be president. Well, John-John was no ordinary American boy."

"People forget that Jackie detested politics," Gore Vidal observed, "but she loved being in close proximity to power. Daughters were raised for the express purpose of marrying rich and powerful men, which is what Jackie did—spectacularly. Sons carried the torch."

For the time being, aviation—not politics—was foremost on the mind of young John Kennedy Jr. At thirteen months, he took his first public steps at the Palm Beach airport, seeing his father off to Washington. Less than a month later John was scampering up and down the center aisle of Air Force One, playing peekaboo with members of the White House press corps.

Soon newsreels and photos captured John jumping up and down with anticipation as his father's helicopter set down on the South Lawn of the White House. "Nothing got him more excited than that helicopter," Salinger said. "President Kennedy would get off and lean down to scoop John-John up, and the boy would run right past him with his toy helicopter in his hand. As much as he missed his father, John-John *really* wanted a ride in that chopper."

When a real helicopter wasn't around, John simply became one, spinning around in circles with his arms outstretched until he collapsed on the ground. "The president thought this was hysterical," Chuck Spalding said. "He even came up with a new nickname name for John. He started calling him 'Helicopter Head.'"

"He was absolutely determined to spoil John from the beginning," George Smathers said. "He could not deny that boy anything. If the

President was talking to a cabinet member or some head of state, it didn't matter—he'd stop everything if John came skipping into the Oval Office."

If JFK had one concern about his son, it was that John was being seduced by the trappings of war—the marching bands, the wreath layings at the Tomb of the Unknown Soldier, not to mention the twenty-one-gun salutes and flyovers that often greeted visiting dignitaries. John was "right there," the president said, whenever "guns, swords, or anyone wearing a uniform" were involved.

White House photographer Cecil Stoughton had a simple enough solution: stop letting the boy watch the parades and ceremonies that seemed to take place there several times a week. That wasn't going to be easy. Jackie, whose father had served as an Army major during World War I, had always been fascinated with the military. "A man in uniform always seemed to get to her," said Baldrige. "She had immense respect for soldiers and was terribly kind to the Marine guards and the military aides at the White House. They loved her."

It was the first lady who actively encouraged John's interest in military pageantry, making sure he had an unobstructed view whenever a marching band or honor guard was on the premises. "John loved it because she loved it," Baldrige said. "And don't all little boys love that sort of thing anyway?"

By October 1962, when U.S. intelligence discovered the presence of offensive Soviet nuclear missiles in Cuba, Jack was, according to Oleg Cassini, "in many ways a changed man. Caroline and John had really opened him up emotionally. He was worried about all children, and what might happen if he made the wrong decision. Can you imagine carrying that kind of burden?"

Over those perilous thirteen days in October, JFK was consumed with the task of pulling the world back from the brink of nuclear war. For a full week, top State Department and Pentagon officials secretly met around the clock with the president to hammer out a response to the Soviets' blatantly provocative act. Even White House staff members were kept in the dark. So as not to arouse suspicion, key advisers were smuggled in through service entrances and slept behind closed doors on couches and cots.

Somehow, JFK still managed to eke out some time to spend with Caroline and John, who had taken ill and was now in bed with a 104-degree temperature. Jackie reassured her husband that Dr. Travell had already seen the boy, and that it was a run-of-the-mill case of the flu.

"Jackie didn't want anything adding to his burden," Salinger said. "She loved the fact that he was a devoted father, but she was also a very smart woman who respected the fact that he was doing the world's toughest job. She was a real team player in that sense—and never more so than during the Cuban Missile Crisis."

For her part, Jackie had refused to be sent off to a bomb shelter with the wives of other top administration officials, vowing instead to perish along with her husband on the lawn of the White House if that's what it came to. In the meantime, she arranged a number of small dinner parties at the White House to lighten her husband's mood.

"Jack was reflective, even melancholy," recalled Cassini, one of those invited by Jackie to cheer up her husband. "He felt a nuclear war with the Soviets was inevitable, whether now or later." The first couple took several quiet strolls on the White House grounds during this period, and at one point JFK confessed his fears to Jackie. "We've already had a chance," he said. "But what about all the children?"

Hours later, JFK addressed the nation. He had ordered a naval blockade of Cuba, and now it was up to the notoriously belligerent, saber-rattling Soviet premier, Nikita Khrushchev, to make the next move. After thirteen tension-filled days, Soviet ships carrying missiles bound for Cuba turned back on October 24, 1962. "We're eyeball-to-eyeball," said Secretary of State Dean Rusk, uttering the most memorable phrase to come out of the Cuban Missile Crisis, "and I think the other guy just blinked."

That same day, John's fever broke. Within twenty-four hours, he was peering from behind pillars, scampering down hallways, and twirling like a helicopter. "Overnight, things were back to normal," Baldrige said. "It's hard to describe the sense of relief everyone felt. I mean, just hours before people were heading for the fallout shelters and saying goodbye to loved ones. We really thought it could be the end—Armageddon. Then suddenly, everything was going to be OK. We were getting a new chance at life. The president had saved the day."

Now that John was feeling better, Jackie started making plans for the children to go trick-or-treating—the first time John would be permitted to accompany his sister on her appointed rounds. On Halloween night, Arthur Schlesinger opened the door of his Georgetown house to find several goblins hopping up and down. "After a moment a masked mother in the background called out that it was time to go to their next house." The voice was unmistakably Jackie's. They had already stopped at the homes of former New York governor Averell Harriman and noted columnist Joseph Alsop. Former secretary of state Dean Acheson was next.

"The children must never feel vulnerable or frightened," Jackie later told another friend, Kitty Carlisle Hart. "It's a mother's job to make them feel secure, no matter what's going on in the larger world." With things now somewhat back to normal, the first family celebrated Thanksgiving with the rest of the raucous Kennedy clan at Hyannis Port. As usual, John careened wildly about the living room, at one point bumping into the wheelchair of Grandpa Joe Kennedy, who by this time had suffered a debilitating stroke. The elder Kennedy took it all in stride, never happier than when he was surrounded by his tribe of children and grandchildren.

Only days later, Jackie oversaw a joint party celebrating her children's birthdays—Caroline's fifth and John's second. Creamed chicken, cake, and ice cream were served, and then Jackie helped them blow out the candles on each of their birthday cakes.

The Marine Band provided the entertainment, and at one point John grabbed a pair of maracas and joined in. Once they finished opening their presents, Caroline and John led their guests to the White House movie theater for an afternoon of cartoons. "Too bad Daddy isn't here," Caroline said of the kids-only affair. "Cartoons and cowboy movies are his favorites."

With JFK's popularity still soaring in the wake of the Cuban Missile Crisis, a sense of euphoria permeated the air that Christmas of 1962. At the Kennedy mansion in Palm Beach, Jack and Jackie fully embraced the holiday spirit by surrounding themselves with family and friends.

Certainly no one was the wiser on January 8, 1963, when the most famous painting in the world, Leonardo da Vinci's *Mona Lisa*, was unveiled at Washington's National Gallery of Art. Almost solely because of his deep personal affection for Jackie, French minister of culture André Malraux agreed to have the masterpiece taken down from its wall in the Louvre and lent personally to the president of the United States. Wearing a bejeweled, strapless mauve gown to the opening, Jackie caused a bigger sensation than the painting itself.

A week later, Jackie announced to Tish Baldrige that she was "taking the veil"—cutting back drastically on her official schedule and, for the foreseeable future at least, devoting herself to her family. She did not tell them the real reason for her decision, but they guessed it just the same. Jackie was pregnant.

As much as JFK adored Caroline, John had awakened something in the president that surprised Jackie. Jack now seemed more committed to his family—and to his marriage—than he had ever been. "What he wants more than anything else in the world," Jackie told her friend Roswell Gilpatric, "is another wonderful little boy."

This time, Jack and Jackie were not about to take any unnecessary risks. With a miscarriage, a stillbirth, and two difficult pregnancies behind her, Jackie decided to take the advice of her obstetrician, Dr. John Walsh, and stick close to home.

Jack did his part, as well. To spare his wife any unnecessary emotional distress that might trigger problems with her pregnancy, the president systematically put an end to his extramarital affairs—several of which he had been carrying on for years right under his wife's nose. One of those women, White House intern Mimi Beardsley, realized that the president was "winding things down" by January 1963. Jack told Mary Meyer, the sister-in-law of his longtime journalist pal Ben

Bradlee, that their clandestine affair was over during a dinner dance at the White House on March 8.

Jackie confided to United Nations ambassador Adlai Stevenson, the two-time Democratic presidential nominee, that she appreciated what her husband was doing. "The new baby was going to be a turning point for them," Smathers said. "She was absolutely convinced of that." Although there was no way of determining the child's sex—this was decades before the use of ultrasound for that purpose—Jackie was also convinced she was carrying another son. "She called the unborn baby 'he' all the time," Salinger said. "With a wink, of course, but she believed it."

The son they already had was proving himself to be quite the handful. Celebrating the Easter holiday in Palm Beach, Jackie and Maud Shaw exhausted themselves trying to corral John as he scampered across the neighbor's lawn in search of colored eggs. He later threw a full-fledged tantrum at a White House reception for Luxembourg's Grand Duchess Charlotte, and nearly clobbered Yugoslavian president Marshal Tito when he accidentally dropped his toy gun from the Truman Balcony while Tito and JFK stood below.

That summer, Jackie and the children settled into the Kennedys' rented beach house on Squaw Island, just a stone's throw from the Hyannis Port compound, and she devoted herself to nothing more strenuous than reading, painting, and napping. "She wanted that baby more than anything," Jack later told George Smathers. "*We* wanted him . . ."

On the morning of August 7, 1963—halfway through her seventh month—Jackie took Caroline to her riding lesson at a local stable when she suddenly began to experience labor pains. Within twenty minutes a helicopter was carrying her to the hospital at nearby Otis Air Force Base. "Please hurry!" she begged Dr. Walsh. "This baby mustn't be born dead."

At 12:52, Jackie gave birth by caesarean section to the boy she had prayed for. Weighing just four pounds, ten ounces, the baby was immediately placed in an incubator. In 1963, few babies of this size survived. To further complicate matters, he suffered from the same lung disorder—hyaline membrane disease—that afflicted their stillborn daughter Arabella and had nearly killed John.

The base chaplain was summoned immediately to baptize the boy Patrick Bouvier Kennedy, after Jack's paternal grandfather and Black Jack Bouvier. Patrick was forty minutes old when his father arrived from Washington. Although the press was being told only that Jackie and the baby were in "good condition," the decision was quickly made to transport Patrick by ambulance to Children's Hospital in Boston.

Jack spent some time with his wife, whose postoperative condition was serious enough to require multiple blood transfusions, then joined John and Caroline at Squaw Island to reassure them that everything was going to be fine.

But it wasn't. Soon the nation was holding its collective breath, and praying for the child's recovery. By the next day, Patrick's condition had deteriorated to the point where he was moved to a hyperbaric chamber in the adjacent Harvard School of Public Health. Using a suite at Boston's Ritz-Carlton hotel as his base, JFK visited his son four times, then helicoptered to Otis Air Force Base to check in on Jackie.

While reporters swarmed outside, the president decided to spend the night at the Boston hospital where Patrick was undergoing treatment. Jack was holding his son when the baby died at 4:04 a.m. on Friday, August 9. "He put up quite a fight," the president told his closest aide, Dave Powers. "He was a beautiful baby."

The president rushed to his wife's side. Once at Otis Air Force Hospital, he strode purposely past rows of red-eyed medical personnel toward the first lady's room. "Oh, Jack, oh, Jack," Jackie sobbed as they broke down in each other's arms. "There's only one thing I could not bear now—if I ever lost you."

Jack made John the mischievous,
independent boy he is.
Bobby is keeping that alive.
—JACKIE

John, from the earliest age,
was a natural politician,
a diplomat, a person who lit up a room.
—JAMIE AUCHINCLOSS

3.

"John, You Can Salute Daddy Now"

November 22, 1963
Washington, D.C.

Someone would have to tell them. But not Jackie. She could not bear the thought of facing John and Caroline and trying to explain that they would never see their father again. It had been only hours since she held her husband's brains in her hand. Now she had so much to deal with—the funeral, leaving the White House, finding a way to go on without him—and it seemed only fair that someone else should shoulder this particular burden. It had to be someone who wouldn't collapse from the strain of performing it, as Jackie feared she would.

"I think Miss Shaw should do exactly what she feels she should do," Jackie told her mother, Janet Auchincloss. "Miss Shaw will have to judge how much the children have seen or heard, or whether they are wondering. She will just have to use her own judgment."

From the moment she heard that shots had rung out in Dallas, Maud Shaw feared that Jackie would ask her to break the news to the children. Less than four months earlier, the no-nonsense, resolutely dependable Shaw had broken the news of Patrick's death to John and Caroline.

But this! She was close—perhaps too close—to the children. It would break Miss Shaw's heart to tell them that their father had been killed by an assassin's bullet, every bit as much as it would break their mother's heart.

Family and friends had been gathering at the White House, and Shaw approached them all—as well as members of the Secret Service "Kiddie Detail"—pleading for someone else, anyone else, to volunteer. "I haven't the heart to tell them," she said. "Why can't someone else do this? I can't . . . I can't . . ."

Ben Bradlee had almost taken care of the job for her. Before leaving the White House to join Jackie at Bethesda Navy Hospital in Maryland, where the president's autopsy was being conducted, Jack's journalist friend declared "I'm going to tell them myself" before his wife, Tony, pulled him back. Instead, he wound up doing his best to distract the children.

"Tell me a story!" John demanded. "Tell me a story!" Bradlee did—again and again, until it was obvious he'd have to come up with something else. "Chase me around the house!" Bradlee commanded, and John happily obliged, squealing with delight as he chased Bradlee down the hall into the West Sitting Room, through the family dining room, and into the Yellow Oval Room.

Miss Shaw only felt worse as she watched John play, oblivious to the monumental events swirling around him. High-ranking government officials were arriving throughout the night, some by helicopter. Every time a chopper touched down on the lawn, John stopped whatever he was doing and screamed, "Daddy's home! Daddy's home!"

Shaw put John to bed without saying anything. He was too young to understand, she reasoned, and there was certainly no harm in waiting until morning. The nanny decided Caroline required an entirely different approach. "It's better for children Caroline's age to get a sadness and a shock before they go to sleep at night," Shaw later explained to Jackie. "That way it won't hit them hard when they wake up in the morning."

Shaw waited until Caroline had changed into her pink pajamas and brushed her teeth before tucking her in. The nanny sat on the edge of the bed, and Caroline snuggled with her favorite pink teddy bear. As

Shaw took Caroline's hand in hers, the little girl could see her eyes welling up with tears.

"What's wrong, Miss Shaw?" she asked. "Why are you crying?"

"I can't help crying, Caroline, because I have some very sad news to tell you," Shaw said. "Your father has been shot. They took him to a hospital, but they couldn't make him better. He's gone to look after Patrick. Patrick was so lonely in heaven. He didn't know anyone there. Now he has the best friend anyone could have. And your father will be so very glad to see Patrick."

Caroline instantly burst into tears. "But what will Daddy do in heaven?" she wanted to know.

"I am sure God is giving him enough things to do, because he was always such a busy man," Shaw tried to explain. "God has made your daddy a guardian angel for you and for Mommy and for John."

Shaw remained with Caroline for more than an hour, stroking her hair gently as the little girl buried her head in her pillow and sobbed herself to sleep. There would be no sleep for the nanny; her heartbreaking assignment was only half done.

At 8:30 the following morning, Nanny Shaw went into John's room and gently woke him. "John, your father has gone to heaven to take care of Patrick," she said.

"Did Daddy take his big plane with him?" the boy asked.

"Yes," she answered.

"I wonder," John said, "when he's coming back."

Father John C. Cavanaugh, a former president of the University of Notre Dame, arrived at the White House that morning to say Mass in the East Room for a small gathering of family and friends. Miss Shaw, in the meantime, dressed the children and brought them to their mother's bedroom. Until this moment, Jackie had not been able to face them since returning from Dallas. Without shedding a tear, she embraced them both, silently took their hands, and led them downstairs.

John and Caroline were too young to attend the Mass, but they were allowed to peer through the door from the adjacent Green Room. Afterward, while the adults milled about the East Room where JFK lay in state, Jamie and Janet Auchincloss (Jackie's half siblings), hatched a plan to—if only for a moment—take the children's mind off their father's brutal murder. With the German shepherd and Grandma Janet's French poodle in tow, they asked a member of the Kiddie Detail to drive them the thirty miles to Manassas Battlefield.

Caroline and her little brother took turns walking the dogs—John shrieking with joy as he tried to hold on to the leash, his sister hot on his heels. "We let them walk the dogs for a while," Jamie said, "and then took the leashes off so they could run." Within minutes, they were spotted by a National Park Service ranger. "Hey! No dogs allowed," he shouted angrily. Walking closer, the burly ranger suddenly realized he was yelling at the children of the slain president—and, suddenly overcome with emotion, began to sob.

"I felt sorry for the ranger," Auchincloss said. "It was a reminder that this wasn't just a tragedy that was happening to us. Everyone in the world was dealing with the same feelings of shock and grief." As for Caroline and John: "Everyone really looked at my niece and nephew the way they looked at their own children," he added. "They felt they knew John and Caroline. I think for all Americans it really felt like a death in the family."

After the Mass, J. B. West accompanied Jackie over to the Oval Office for one last look before her husband's things were packed up. With "eyes like saucers," as West put it, she memorized everything in the room—right down to the embossed white-and-gold leatherette frame that held photos of herself and the children. Jack had placed the triptych on his desk at the height of the Cuban Missile Crisis to remind him of what was at stake.

"My children," Jackie said, "they're good children, aren't they, Mr. West?"

"They're not spoiled?"

"No, indeed."

That night, Jackie opened notes the new president had written to each of the children just hours after their father was killed. "It will be many years before you understand fully what a great man your father was," Lyndon Johnson wrote to John. "His loss is a deep personal trag-edy for all of us, but I wanted you to know particularly that I share your grief—you can always be proud of him."

In his handwritten note to Caroline, LBJ wrote, "Your father's death has been a great tragedy for the nation, as well as for you, and I wanted you to know how much my thoughts are of you at this time. He was a wise and devoted man. You can always be proud of what he did for his country."

Jackie read the notes aloud to John and Caroline, then asked Maud Shaw to bring pencils and paper for the children.

"You must write a letter to Daddy now," she told Caroline, "and tell him how much you love him."

Caroline covered the page with large block print. "DEAR DADDY," her letter read, "WE ARE ALL GOING TO MISS YOU. DADDY, I LOVE YOU VERY MUCH, CAROLINE." Jackie then told her son to add something of his own, and John, who was not yet three, scribbled a large X on the page.

Jackie stayed up until dawn writing her own rambling, five-page letter to Jack. It was drenched in tears by the time she was finished.

Jackie was physically and emotionally drained. Fearing that she would crumble under the strain of what lay ahead, she turned once again to Dr. Max Jacobson. She was changing into her black mourning dress when "Dr. Feelgood" was ushered into the White House, as usual, through a side entrance. Once upstairs, he greeted Jackie warmly and was soon digging through his battered black medical bag for vials and syringes.

The president and the first lady had long relied on Jacobson's injections—amphetamines (mostly Dexedrine) mixed with steroids—for the energy boost they needed to make it through their frantically busy day. Dr. Max's potent "cocktails" were perfectly legal at the time. Although Dr. Travell and the rest of the White House medical team urged caution, the official position of the Food and Drug Administra-tion at the time was that amphetamines and steroids were neither harm-ful nor habit-forming.

No one disputed that, without a little pharmaceutical assistance from Dr. Max, Jackie would have fallen apart. Over the next few days, Jacobson remained in the shadows but always close at hand. "I was there when she needed me," he later said. "And she needed me quite a lot."

Soon the president's body would be moved to the Capitol Rotunda, where more than a quarter million mourners would stand in line for hours to pay their last respects. Jackie and Jack's brother Bobby, described by Bradlee as "catatonic" with grief, walked down to the East Room to see JFK one last time. The lid was gently opened, and Jackie placed the two letters—the children's and the one Jackie had written— inside, along with a pair of gold cufflinks and a favorite piece of scrimshaw, a whale's tooth carved with the presidential seal. Bobby put in a clip of his own hair, a silver rosary, and the gold PT-109 clip Jack had given him.

Jackie had offered words of comfort to Jack's devoted personal secretary, Evelyn Lincoln, and now dropped into Pierre Salinger's office looking, in Salinger's words, "almost ghostly." As she began to speak, JFK's longtime press secretary and friend struggled to contain his own emotions. "Pierre," she said, "I have nothing else to do in life but help my children deal with this terrible problem, the effect of their father's assassination, to bring them up well, and see that they become decent, caring, and intelligent people. I have to make sure they survive."

As Jackie spoke, in Dallas a nightclub owner named Jack Ruby lunged from the shadows and shot accused assassin Lee Harvey Oswald—another shocking scene broadcast live into millions of homes across the nation. Although conspiracy theorists would speculate for decades on Ruby's true motive, he claimed he shot Oswald to both spare Jackie the ordeal of a trial and avenge her children.

———

ELEVEN MINUTES AFTER Oswald was pronounced dead, Jackie and her children were in the Capital Rotunda, leading a nation in mourning. Unlike their Kennedy cousins who were dressed in black, Caroline and John wore powder blue jackets and red shoes. Now more than ever,

Jackie had told Maud Shaw, she wanted her children to look like children, not like miniature adults.

Cabinet members, senators, bemedaled members of the Joint Chiefs of Staff, and Supreme Court justices alike fought back tears as the president's young widow took their daughter by the hand and led her to the coffin. But first Jackie leaned down and whispered, "We're going to say goodbye to Daddy now, and we're going to kiss him goodbye and tell Daddy how much we love him and how much we'll always miss him." Then they walked up to the bier, knelt, took the flag that covered the coffin in their gloved hands, and pressed it tenderly to their lips.

More than anyone, Jackie understood how important such moments were in shaping history. Her triumphant tours of Europe and the Indian subcontinent, her painstaking restoration of the White House and its unveiling before what was then the largest television audience in history, the glittering state dinners and gala evenings for the arts that had transformed the White House into an American Versailles, her own unique sense of style—all were reflections of Jackie's love of symbolism and spectacle.

To ensure that Jack would have a funeral befitting his place in history, Jackie focused on even the most minute detail—from the black bunting in the East Room ("Find out how Lincoln was buried," she had told Bobby Kennedy) to the design of the Mass cards to the number of horses that would pull the caisson carrying her husband's casket. "I think it was also her coping mechanism," Salinger said. "As long as she put one foot in front of the other, going through the motions of lying in state and the funeral, she didn't have to dwell on the horror of what happened in Dallas. That came later."

She had planned for John to join her and Caroline in the Capitol Rotunda, but things didn't quite work out that way. John had managed to follow his father's casket up the Capitol's thirty-five steps alongside Caroline and his mother, but once at the top, he began to squirm. Maud Shaw instantly whisked the boy off to an office down the hall. He was instantly drawn to a bulletin board covered with dozens of tiny American flags.

"Would you like one?" asked a congressional aide.

"Yes, please," John responded, "and one for my sister, please." The man plucked two flags off the bulletin board and bent down to hand them to the toddler. John turned to leave, but then realized he had forgotten something. "Oh," he said, "and may I have one for my daddy?" Startled, the aide handed him a third flag, and John scampered off to proudly present it to his mother.

The night before Jack's state funeral, the president's widow dined in the West Sitting Room with Bobby and Ethel Kennedy, as well as her sister Lee and Lee's husband, Prince Stanislaw ("Stas") Radziwill. Down the corridor, Jackie's shell-shocked Kennedy in-laws, Eunice and Sargent Shriver and Pat and Peter Lawford, ate with Dave Powers, Defense Secretary Robert McNamara, and a few others in the family dining room.

A surprising last-minute addition that night was the notorious Greek shipping tycoon Aristotle Onassis, whose dubious business dealings had made him the target of several criminal investigations. Following Patrick's death, Lee had been searching for ways to lift her sister's spirits, and Onassis had generously invited them both on an Aegean cruise aboard his magnificent 325-foot yacht, *Christina*. The legendary opera diva Maria Callas had been Onassis's mistress for years, and now Lee was rumored to be intent on replacing her. But when the cruise was over, it was Jackie who accepted a ruby-and-diamond necklace from her host, leaving Lee to grouse about her gift from Onassis—three "dinky little bracelets Caroline wouldn't even wear to her own birthday party."

That trip had generated such negative press that Jackie pledged to make it up to Jack. Her first step toward making amends: Jackie agreed to accompany her husband during his reelection campaign, starting with Dallas. Bobby and the rest of the Kennedy camp regarded the man they simply called "The Greek" as little more than a corrupt, uncouth social climber. But that didn't stop Jackie from summoning Onassis to her side.

Party-loving Onassis was well aware that Irish wakes could be raucous affairs, but the lighthearted mood that prevailed that night in the White House surprised even him. As soon as Ari arrived, Jack's close friend Lem Billings recalled, "we all piled into a sports car and raced to Arlington to the spot where Jack was going to be buried. Later we all laughed and sang and carried on with great hilarity back to the White House."

Incredibly, while the rest of the world was still in a state of shock, Dave Powers was cracking Jackie and the others up with stories of the early days campaigning in Boston. "You'd never know there was a funeral," said family friend Milt Ebbins, who dined in the White House on November 23, 24, and 25. "Jokes were being told at the table. Ethel was very funny. I tried to tell Pat [Lawford] about seeing Bobby crying in the East Room and she curtly cut me off—'We don't want to hear about that.'"

As the evening wore on, the crowd became increasingly soused. As Jackie watched, someone snatched the blond wig off Ethel's head and tossed it around the room. Soon the junior senator from Massachusetts, Ted Kennedy, was leading the group in boozy renditions of "When Irish Eyes Are Smiling" and "That Old Gang of Mine."

"People were shrieking with laughter, crying with laughter," JFK's brother-in-law Peter Lawford said. "Everybody was up, drinking and smiling and trying to make the best of it. Not being Irish, I tried to get in the swing of it, but I was thoroughly destroyed."

Later over coffee and brandy, Bobby began ribbing Onassis about his questionable business dealings. At one point RFK pointed out that Onassis had made his first million dollars in Argentina. The attorney general then dashed out the door and returned minutes later with a document stipulating that Onassis would give half his estimated $500 million fortune (then second only to the fortunes of Howard Hughes and oilman J. Paul Getty) to the poor people of Latin America. Happy to play along, Onassis signed the bogus contract and toasted the deal with champagne.

There were times that evening, Ben Bradlee remembered, that Jackie seemed "completely detached, as if she were someone else watching the ceremony of that other person's grief. Sometimes she was silent, obviously torn. Often she would turn to a friend and reminisce, and everyone would join in with their remembrance of things forever past."

Jack's close friend Chuck Spalding, who slept over at the White

House that night, was at first taken aback by the Kennedy clan's hijinks—although he knew Jack would have approved. "It's a very Irish thing," Spalding explained. "They make bad jokes and drink too much just to keep from going crazy. It's how they cope." Jackie, however, "was a completely different type. It didn't come naturally to her, but she understood the whole Irish thing and tried to be a part of it."

————

WHAT IMPACT ALL this manic behavior had on her children remained to be seen. John and Caroline ate that night, as usual, in their little High Chair Room off the kitchen. Maud Shaw bathed and dressed them in their pajamas and then, as she always did when the Kennedys had company in the family quarters, brought them in to say good night to the grown-ups. The merriment "obviously confused Caroline," Shaw conceded, although John was "probably too young to really understand."

Once she realized John and Caroline were standing in the room in their pajamas, Jackie pulled them toward her, kissed them, and then sent them off to bed. "Everyone saw the children," Spalding said, "but they just kept whooping it up. Nobody seemed to care, which struck me as very sad."

It was only as she began walking the children to their rooms that it occurred to Maud Shaw that Monday, November 25, was more than the day of JFK's funeral. It was John's third birthday. As in previous years, it was understood that the children would have a joint party halfway between John's birthday and Caroline's—this year she was turning six—on November 27. But what, the nanny pondered, was the right thing to do on John's actual birthday, the day his father was to be laid to rest before a television audience of millions?

Over breakfast that morning, Miss Shaw and Caroline sang "Happy Birthday" to John over breakfast. Then he unwrapped two gifts—yet another toy helicopter from Caroline and a book about planes from his nanny.

Barely an hour after he opened his presents, John was sitting alongside his sister in a limousine bound for St. Matthew's Cathedral. They were to wait for their mother to join them there. In the meantime, to the eerie, unforgettable cadence of muffled drums, Jackie—flanked by Bobby, Teddy and the rest of the Kennedy family—walked behind the horse-drawn caisson bearing the president's body from the White House to St. Matthew's. The same caisson that had carried Franklin Roosevelt's coffin was pulled by three pairs of perfectly matched gray horses, and following close behind was the traditional "riderless horse" named, coincidentally, "Black Jack."

The cortege that followed on foot behind Jackie and the family included 220 representatives from 102 nations, including such historic figures as Ethiopian Emperor Haile Selassie, Great Britain's Prince Philip, French President Charles De Gaulle, Israel's Foreign Minister Golda Meir, and German Chancellor Ludwig Erhard.

Inside the cathedral, Jackie sat between her children as Boston's raspy-voiced Richard Cardinal Cushing began reciting the Latin Mass. Midway through, the cardinal switched to English: "May the angels, dear Jack, lead you into paradise . . ."

No longer able to maintain the façade, Jackie broke down. "You'll be all right, Mommy," Caroline whispered as she reached up with a handkerchief to wipe away her mother's tears. "Don't cry, I'll take care of you."

Later, Jackie would praise her daughter for holding her hand "like a soldier. She's my helper. She's mine now." But she doubted she would have the same influence over her son—certainly not in the patriarchal world of the Kennedys. "John," she predicted, "is going to belong to the men now."

As he squirmed in this seat at the cathedral, it seemed clear that, regardless of whom he "belonged" to, JFK's inexhaustibly frisky son was going to be a handful. Jackie asked Bob Foster, a member of the Secret Service Kiddie Detail, to take her son to a small room at the rear of the cathedral. Among the many officers standing near the door to the room was an Army colonel with a chest full of medals. He knelt down and, by way of entertaining the bored little boy, patiently explained what each medallion, cross, star, battle ribbon, and leaf cluster meant.

After a few minutes, Agent Foster whispered that it was time to go back inside the church. John turned to salute the colonel, but with his left hand. "Oh, no, John," the colonel said, "that's not the right way to salute. You salute with your right hand." After a few practice tries, the officer was satisfied John had gotten the hang of it.

Only a few weeks earlier, John had marched noisily into his catechism class with his make-believe rifle—a stick—over his shoulder. "He thinks he's a soldier," Caroline sighed to their teacher, Sister Joanne Frey, "and he doesn't even know how to salute."

Now he was about to prove his sister wrong. As everyone gathered outside the cathedral to watch the flag-draped coffin leave for the final journey to Arlington National Cemetery, John took his place at his mother's side. Jackie's tearstained face, only partially concealed behind a fluttering veil of black lace, leaned down to her son and said quietly, "John, you can salute Daddy now and say goodbye to him."

John snapped to attention, lifted up his right hand, and snapped off the salute that came to symbolize a nation's grief. It may have been the moment that secured John's place in the hearts of his countrymen, but once again he would find it difficult to separate his own memories from what he had seen and read over the years. "I've seen that photograph so many times, and I'd like to say I remember that moment," he mused thirty years later. "But I don't."

Just forty-five minutes after lighting the Eternal Flame atop her husband's grave at Arlington, Jackie shook hands with more than two hundred dignitaries as she stood in a White House receiving line. Maud Shaw spirited John upstairs for his afternoon nap. No one was quite sure what to do with Caroline, who long ago had outgrown the need for a nap. Just to take her mind off things, one of the Secret Service agents assigned to protect Lyric offered to take her for a ride.

After driving around aimlessly for half an hour, they finally wound up at Georgetown Visitation Academy, where Sister Joanne Frey was preparing to teach another catechism class. Suddenly Caroline appeared in the doorway looking, the nun said, "so lost and alone."

"Oh, I'm glad you're here," Frey said brightly. "I have so many things to do to get the class ready—you can help me!"

That afternoon, there was a small birthday party for John in the family dining room. Jackie had decided that, while they would still have a joint celebration for the children later in the week, her son deserved to be happy on his special day. "John knows today is his birthday," she said, "and I did not want to disappoint him." Besides, she added, "we need a party on this day more than any other, don't you think?"

After blowing out the three candles on his cake with a little help from Caroline, John wasted no time tearing through the wrapping paper on his gifts. Not everyone was in a festive mood. Emotions, said Jamie Auchincloss, were in fact "strained to the very limit." When Dave Powers burst into "Heart of My Heart," a favorite tune of Jack's, Uncle Bobby again began weeping and darted from the room.

There was one more sorrowful duty for JFK's young widow to perform. She had wanted her stillborn daughter Arabella and son Patrick reburied next to their father. In a top-secret mission directed by Bobby, the children's bodies were disinterred and flown to Arlington aboard the *Caroline*. Late that night, Jamie Auchincloss joined Bobby, Teddy, and Jackie at JFK's grave site for a brief, clandestine burial—the second in only a matter of hours. "It was incredibly touching, but Jackie had that look of resolve," said Auchincloss, who remembered that the ceremony took place in almost total darkness, with JFK's "eerie, flickering" Eternal Flame as the sole source of light. "Jackie wanted to bring them all together again, and she did."

Jackie and the children flew to Hyannis Port to spend Thanksgiving with the rest of the Kennedy clan. While John and Caroline played with their unruly cousins, their mother spent an hour consoling her wheelchair-bound father-in-law behind closed doors. The mere presence of Jack's wife and children unleashed a torrent of emotion among the staff. "Tears everywhere," said Secret Service agent Ham Brown. "Secretaries, nurses, Secret Service. We were all a mess."

Mirroring the scenes played out in millions of homes that Thanksgiving, John and Caroline sat at the children's table while Bobby's un-disciplined tribe made rude faces and threw food at each other. "Even at the age of three, John was a complete gentleman compared to that bunch," Jackie's friend George Plimpton said. "He and Caroline were spirited, but they weren't spoiled brats. They knew how to behave because their mother drilled it into them."

Just one week after the assassination, Jackie sat down with veteran *Life* magazine journalist Theodore White, a longtime friend of Jack's. Worried that somehow JFK would be forgotten, she set out to create a new American myth that would guarantee her husband's place in history.

With John and Caroline tucked in bed upstairs, Jackie, wearing black slacks and a beige pullover sweater, curled up on the sofa with a cigarette and began to talk. Pudgy, bespectacled White then began to scribble frantically while Jackie described Jack's murder in riveting, often grisly detail—the puzzled expression on JFK's face when the first bullet tore through his windpipe, how the final bullet seemed to tear off a piece of her husband's skull in slow motion, how his brain matter sprayed over her, how she cradled his head as they raced to Parkland Memorial Hospital.

More important, over the next three and a half hours Jackie carefully sowed the seeds of a new American myth that would guarantee her husband's place in history. To help him cope with his back pain, she told White, Jackie often played what she claimed was Jack's favorite record—the cast album from the Lerner and Lowe musical *Camelot*. It was the title song, which wistfully recalled the mythical realm's "one brief shining moment," that Jackie felt best summed up her husband's legacy.

"There will be great presidents again," she told White, speaking, he said, as if she were in a trance. "But there'll never be another Camelot again." As White used a phone in the kitchen to dictate his story to *Life*'s editors in New York, Jackie hovered over him, insisting he resist any efforts by his bosses to downplay the Camelot analogy.

"She had always been described as a fairy-tale princess," White later said, "and now she wanted Jack to take his place in history as a modern King Arthur." She had "obviously thought long and hard about how she wanted her handsome, heroic young husband remembered," White said. But did she consider the burden this placed on her children? "By extension," White mused, "John was cast as a prince of the realm, and heir apparent to the throne."

Their last night in the White House as a family, Jackie threw the promised joint birthday party for John and Caroline. There was another cake—a big one this time—and more presents, which the children took turns opening. Caroline's favorite gift was a large pink teddy bear to add to her growing collection of stuffed animals. This time John had two favorites: a model of Air Force One, and a one-of-a-kind authentic Marine uniform custom-made by military tailors for the only son of the late commander in chief.

Although at parties she had lampooned her husband's vice president and his wife, Lady Bird, as "Colonel Cornpone and his little pork chop," Jackie now publicly praised Lyndon Johnson for his kindnesses to her. Nevertheless, LBJ was eager to move into his home. Jackie stayed in the White House eleven days after her husband's murder, compared to the one day Eleanor Roosevelt took to pack up and leave after FDR suddenly died.

No matter. Now that fate had chosen him to head the Democratic ticket in the coming election, LBJ wanted Jackie in his corner. With a little nudging, he reasoned, she might even be willing to campaign for him. The day before Jackie and her children left the White House, LBJ, aware of Jackie's Bouvier heritage and her fondness for all things French, took Pierre Salinger aside. "I want to do something nice for Jackie," Johnson told Salinger. "I'll name her ambassador to France." Salinger passed along the offer to Jackie, who promptly rejected it.

LBJ knew that Jackie, who had charmed the residents of New York's Spanish Harlem as well as thousands of Cuban exiles in Florida, spoke fluent Spanish as well as flawless French. She had also been a huge hit when, as first lady, she visited Mexico City. "Ambassador to Mexico, then?" Lyndon asked her. But Jackie turned that offer down, as well.

True to his reputation for getting his way as the longtime leader of the Democrats in the U.S. Senate, Johnson persevered. JFK and Jackie were also extremely popular in the United Kingdom, despite the fact that Joe Kennedy had been a disaster during this tenure as the ambassador to the Court of St. James's in the years leading up to World War II.

One of Jackie's closest friends, in fact, was David Ormsby-Gore, who was serving as Britain's ambassador to the United States at the time. "The British Invasion was just starting," Oleg Cassini said. "They were about to change everything in music, fashion, the arts. They were the future. At least from that standpoint, Jackie and the British would not have been a bad fit."

Just weeks before the Beatles made their U.S. debut, Johnson asked Jackie to be his ambassador to Great Britain. Again the answer was no. Exasperated, LBJ put all his cards on the table. "President Johnson said I could have anything I wanted," Jackie told her longtime friend Charlie Bartlett. "But I'm just not interested."

What Jackie wanted was a familiar environment for her children, and that precluded a foreign posting. "I'm *never* going to live in Europe. I'm not going to 'travel extensively abroad,'" she protested, pooh-poohing the rumors that she intended to move to France. "That's a desecration. I'm going to live in the places I lived with Jack. In Georgetown, and with the Kennedys at the Cape. They're my family. I'm going to bring up my children. I want John to grow up to be a good boy."

However, Jackie was in no position to simply pick up and move into a new home. John Kenneth Galbraith, the Harvard economist then serving as the U.S. ambassador to India, convinced another old Washington hand to offer his Georgetown residence as a temporary home for the displaced first lady. While Jackie hunted for a new place to live, she would move into Undersecretary of State Averell Harriman's palatial redbrick mansion on N Street, just three blocks down from the modest house where she and JFK had lived before his election as president. By contrast, the Harriman house featured seven bedrooms, a dining room that comfortably sat eighteen, its own swimming pool, and one of the finest private collections of Impressionist paintings in the world.

THE DAY BEFORE the big move, John spotted a cardboard box marked "John's Toys—N Street" and began to cry, convinced that his toys were leaving without him. After assuring John that he and his toys would soon be reunited, Maud Shaw suggested he put on his new Marine uniform and then pick out a few select items they could hand-carry to their new house. John sat on the floor and dipped into the packing carton to retrieve some toy swords, a cowboy gun, and a helicopter.

On December 6, the White House staff lined up to say goodbye to Jackie and the children. "It was very sad, of course," J. B. West said. "Everyone was very, very emotional, but Mrs. Kennedy couldn't have been more gracious." Secret Service agent Bob Foster decided to distract John by taking his hand and leading the boy on a quick stroll around the grounds.

It wasn't long before John declared he was thirsty, and as Foster lifted him up to drink from a water fountain, a White House photographer suddenly appeared. John stopped and glared at the man. "What are you taking my picture for?" the boy asked. "My daddy's dead." The photographer and Foster both broke down in tears.

An hour later, a White House limousine pulled up in front of the Harriman house. Caroline stepped out, then her mother and brother. John carried a small box containing his father's posthumously bestowed Presidential Medal of Freedom in one hand and waved a small American flag in the other. Uncle Bobby and Aunt Ethel were close behind, chased by photographers.

That afternoon, John and Caroline managed to duck out for some play time at a local park. While they bobbed up and down on teeter-totters, two Secret Service agents stood guard. The law in 1963 stipulated that Jackie and her children were entitled to government protection for only two more years. That period was later extended to cover the children of ex-presidents until age sixteen, and a presidential widow until remarriage or death.

Unfortunately, it quickly became evident that the Secret Service was virtually powerless to shield JFK's young family from the prying eyes of an insatiable public. Gawkers pressed up against police barricades on both sides of the street just outside the Harriman house, and traffic was at a standstill as drivers and their passengers craned their necks to catch a glimpse of the world's most famous family.

Uncle Bobby and Dave Powers came to visit every day, much of that time spent playing games with John and Caroline, trying to fill the void left by their father. Uncles Teddy Kennedy and Jamie Auchincloss, the Radziwills, Jackie's half sister Janet, and old friends like Oleg Cassini, Chuck Spalding, and his wife, Betty, and Galbraith—all made the effort to come at least once or twice a week. Stuck behind locked doors, her drapes drawn, Jackie complained to everyone who dropped in that she felt like "a carnival freak."

It didn't help that, almost as soon as they set foot in the Harriman house, John and Caroline both came down with the chicken pox. Caroline followed orders and stayed in bed. But John? Once outside the door to his room, Maud Shaw knew "full well what he was going to do. I would hear his little feet padding across the bedroom carpet, the door would open ever so slowly, then his head popped 'round the door, his face bright with mischief."

Not even John's antics could brighten Jackie's mood, or keep her from replaying what happened that day in Dallas over and over again in her mind. "She was just flattened, lost," Chuck Spalding said." You'd try to change the subject but she kept coming back to Jack." During one weekend at Wexford, the country home she and Jack had built in Atoka, Virginia, Jackie tearfully confessed to Betty Spalding that she had no idea how she was going to manage raising Caroline and John alone, or even where she was going to live. "No one knows what it's like," Jackie said, staring blankly. "No one knows what it's like."

When Robert McNamara took Jackie out for lunch at a small Washington restaurant, the rude stares and loud mutterings from the other diners became so unbearable that they picked up and left halfway through their meal. "There was no possibility of her forgetting who she was or the terrible thing that happened," McNamara said. "Not even for a moment."

Before he returned to his practice in New York the first week in December, Max Jacobson made sure to leave behind an array of potent sedatives and sleeping pills for Jackie to take. Nothing seemed to work. A few days before Christmas, she summoned Jacobson to Georgetown. "My life is over, Max," she said as she rolled up her sleeve for another of Jacobson's injections. "Just empty, meaningless."

Jacobson spent nearly an hour trying to convince Jackie that she had much to live for, and that she had an "obligation" to her children. "I tried my best to impress upon her that life would go on, eventually, and the sooner she realized it, the better it would be."

From her "lifeless stare," Jacobson concluded that his words had had little impact. Once back in Manhattan, Dr. Max prepared one of his "C.A.R.E. packages" to send to Jackie. Each package contained ten disposable syringes and a vial of Dr. Max's powerful amphetamine-steroid "cocktail." Before leaving her that day in Georgetown, Jacobson carefully taught Jackie how to administer the injections herself.

Shortly before Christmas, Jackie paid $175,000 for a three-story, fourteen-room, beige brick colonial townhouse at 3017 N Street, not far from the Harrimans'. Unfortunately, it was only after they moved in that Jackie realized she had made a serious miscalculation. In contrast to the Harriman house, all the rooms at 3017 N Street faced the front—including the living room, study, dining room, and even several bedrooms—and were completely exposed to anyone who happened to be passing by.

One morning, a fusillade of flashbulbs went off when John pulled back the curtains to peek out the living room window at the noisy mob in the street. "What," he asked Maud Shaw, "are all these silly people taking my picture for?"

"Outside the crowd of spectators grew and grew," said decorator Billy Baldwin, whom Jackie had hired to design the interior of her new home. "There was bumper-to-bumper traffic."

"I can't even change my clothes in private because they look in my bedroom window," Jackie complained. If she felt like a "carnival freak" at the Harriman house, observed Jacques Lowe, JFK's widow now likened herself to a "caged animal."

One afternoon during a violent winter storm, Baldwin and Jackie were unpacking boxes at the new house when she suddenly got up and wandered over to window. For a few moments, she gazed at the gawkers huddled outside in the subfreezing temperatures, then returned to Baldwin—this time with tears streaming down her face. "I'm afraid I'm going to embarrass you," she said as she collapsed on the sofa, burying her face in her hands as she wept.

Once she composed herself, Jackie told Baldwin that her biggest concern was for her children's emotional well-being. Hysterical women were breaking through police lines to hug and kiss Caroline and John. "The world is pouring terrible adoration at their feet," she said, "and I fear for them."

More than anything, Jackie wanted John and Caroline to experience the carefree joys of something akin to a normal childhood. To make their move to a new house less jarring, she showed Baldwin photographs of the children's bedrooms at the White House and asked him to furnish their new rooms identically. "She wanted their lives to be disrupted as little as possible," he said. "She was trying for some semblance of constancy, of continuity. Sadly, this was impossible."

At least the familiar presence of Nanny Shaw, the family's longtime maid Providencia "Provi" Paredes, Jackie's personal secretary Mary Gallagher, and a few others was clearly making the transition easier for John and his sister. But one grown-up face was missing, and it belonged to Daddy's loyal secretary. Evelyn Lincoln and John had developed a strong bond, based in part on the fact that she often doled out candy to him whenever he dropped by the Oval Office to visit his father. Transferred to a small office in the Executive Office Building, Evelyn Lincoln now faced the monumental task of organizing her late boss's belongings and papers.

John asked if he could call Mrs. Lincoln to let her know they would soon be paying her a visit. Nanny Shaw held the phone up to John's ear.

"Hello, Mrs. Lincoln," John said. "This is John."

"Why, John," she answered, "what a wonderful surprise."

"I'm going to visit you with Mrs. Shaw soon."

"That would be lovely, John," Lincoln said. "I'm looking forward to seeing you."

"Me, too."

Lincoln waited for John to go on, but there was only silence on the line. The boy, she concluded, "was obviously thinking."

"Mrs. Lincoln?" he asked tentatively.

"Yes, John?" This time, there was an even longer pause.

"Is Daddy there?"

It was going to be a melancholy Christmas. No phone calls to the North Pole—Daddy was no longer there to tell the White House switchboard operators to imitate Mrs. Claus. Nor was Daddy there to hang up the stockings on the mantel, as he did every year. But Caroline had been allowed to continue classes at the little White House school Jackie had established until the end of the year, and that meant that she could still play an angel in the annual children's Christmas pageant. The Kennedys, the Auchinclosses, and family friends clapped and cheered and sang carols, but John and Caroline knew holidays would never be the same. "No one could forget," Sister Joanne Frey said, "that someone was missing."

Jackie and the children joined the rest of the Kennedys in Palm Beach for Christmas, and while they were decorating the tree Caroline blurted out a question about Daddy. "Will Patrick be looking after him in heaven?" she wanted to know.

Before anyone could speak, John, who had been trying to guess the contents of wrapped packages beneath the tree, piped up, "Is there fish chowder in heaven?" Everyone laughed, including Jackie. JFK, as his family and friends knew so well, was a certified fish chowder fanatic.

Such lighthearted moments were few and far between.

Even for the sake of her children, Jackie found it impossible to pull out of her deep depression. "I'm a living wound," she said. "My life is over. I'm dried up—I have nothing more to give and some days I can't even get out of bed. I cry all day and all night until I'm so exhausted I can't function. Then I drink."

There were touching reminders that Jackie wasn't the only one in the immediate family who was grieving. During one family dinner, Caroline pulled one end of a wishbone as Jackie's teenage half sister, Janet Auchincloss, held the other. "Can I wish for anything I want?" she asked.

"Anything," Aunt Janet promised.

"I want," Caroline said without hesitating, "to see my daddy."

Her own pain notwithstanding, Caroline took it upon herself to comfort her mother. "After my daddy died, my mommy is always crying," she told Sister Joanne in the middle of a catechism class. Caroline described how she would crawl into bed with her mother and "tell her everything is all right and tell her to stop crying. But she doesn't. My mommy is always crying. My mommy is always crying . . ."

Perhaps only one other adult could fully fathom the depth of Jackie's grief. "Bobby was very tough—in many ways tougher than JFK," Pierre Salinger said. "But he worshiped his brother, just idolized him. Everything he did he did for the president, and in a terrible instant it was all gone." Chuck Spalding agreed that RFK was now "one of the walking wounded. As sad as Jackie looked, Bobby looked even worse."

David Halberstam, who wrote extensively about the Kennedy White House in his landmark book *The Best and the Brightest* and whose own brother was a murder victim, understood how both Bobby and Jackie must have felt. "You ask yourself over and over again if there was something you could have done or said that might have changed things," Halberstam said. "The feelings of rage, despair, and even guilt—guilt over being here when your brother isn't anymore—you know, 'Why him and not me?' It all just eats away at you."

Like his sister-in-law, Bobby found it all but impossible to sleep. He would get out of bed at Hickory Hill, his historic Virginia estate in McLean, Virginia, and drive aimlessly around Washington and its suburbs. "If you've ever lost a loved one under circumstances like that," Halberstam observed, "you know that it is just too painful to keep reliving the moment. You want to put the horror behind you as quickly as you can and move on with your life. But it's not that easy if no one around you understands what you're feeling."

Jackie understood. During his nocturnal wanderings, Bobby sometimes turned up at her house in Georgetown. There they talked until dawn, taking comfort in their shared grief. "I think he is the most compassionate person I know," Jackie said, acknowledging that, away from family and friends, Bobby was "too shy and too proud" to let that side of his character show.

Indeed, compassion was not one of RFK's better-known attributes; a ruthless competitor in politics and in life, he took pride in his reputation as the president's enforcer. Within and without his own party, Bobby was feared more than respected.

At the same time, Bobby's bona fides as a family man were impeccable. All of which made him the perfect surrogate father to his brother's children—a role he undertook with enthusiasm. "Let's face it," Chuck Spalding said, "Bobby was in every way the logical choice to be a surrogate father to those kids." For both John and Caroline, it "must have been very comfortable having him around, reminding them of their father," Spalding continued. "The way he sounded, the body language, the hair, those teeth!"

Over the next six months, Jackie took her children to Hickory Hill almost daily to play with Bobby and Ethel's brood of eight.

"They think of Hickory Hill as their own home," Jackie said. If there were any Father's Day activities at school, Bobby showed up for Caroline. She, in turn, showed her report cards to RFK. Her artwork during this period was invariably marked "To Uncle Bobby," and brought to him for his approval.

RFK was equally hands-on in his treatment of his nephew, picking John up early each morning and driving him to his Justice Department office, where he played with his cousins Michael and Kerry. To re-create the child-friendly atmosphere that had prevailed in the Oval Office, Bobby periodically stopped conferences and staff meetings so he could play leapfrog or hide-and-seek—or simply toss a squealing John in the air.

When Uncle Bobby wasn't around, John had no qualms about approaching others to perform this important service. On one of several trips to New York that February, John was playing with the children of Deputy Peace Corps Director Bill Haddad when he suddenly asked his host, "Are you a daddy?" When Haddad said yes, John brightened. "Then, will you throw me up in the air?" he asked. Haddad, trying hard to contain his emotions, obliged.

Jackie welcomed the influence of such positive male figures in her little boy's life—to a point. Not surprisingly, John became attached to several of the men whose job it was to protect him. Foremost among these was Agent Foster, who tried in vain to keep John from calling him "Daddy." Understandably concerned that her son had perhaps grown too close to Foster, Jackie made the painful decision to request that he be reassigned. "Jackie was consumed with the fear that the world was going to forget Jack," Teddy White said. "She certainly didn't want their son to forget him." To show their gratitude, Jackie and the children gave Foster their Welsh terrier Charlie.

What Jackie did want was for the Secret Service to serve as a bulwark against intrusions on her family's privacy. One morning she dropped into a newsstand in Hyannis Port with John, attracting what one Secret Service agent described in his official report as a small crowd of "harmless onlookers"—mostly "elderly ladies with cameras" trying to snap a few photos. "Mrs. Kennedy turned a cold shoulder and refused to permit any photographs," the agent recalled. Later, she scolded him for not taking action. "Do something," she said, "when there are people around like that!"

In truth, there was really only one person Jackie trusted to protect her family—the same man her husband had leaned on heavily both in the Senate and throughout his presidency. It was a decision that, in a sense, had been made long before Jack's death. Jackie and JFK had stipulated in their wills that if anything ever happened to both of them, John and Caroline would be raised by Bobby and Ethel. "Now I want them [Caroline and John] to be part of that family," Jackie said. "Bobby wants to look after his brother's children. There's John, with his brother's name. He's going to make sure John turns out as he should."

If you bungle raising your children,
I don't think whatever else you do
well matters very much.
—JACKIE

Not being a Kennedy, my mother could
recognize the perils and the positive aspects.
—JOHN

Jackie worried more about John than she did
about Caroline, who matured quickly and
was very influenced by her father.
Jackie paid special attention to John.
—YUSHA AUCHINCLOSS, JACKIE'S STEPBROTHER

4.

"A Kennedy Never Gives Up"

It was not long before Jackie, convinced that only Bobby could replace Jack in her children's lives, asked RFK to legally adopt them—a move that would have given Jackie and Bobby equal status as guardians. Ethel, who had never been particularly fond of her idolized sister-in-law, vetoed the plan.

Adoption notwithstanding, John was soon learning what it meant to be a Kennedy—the hard way. At Hickory Hill, RFK spent the better part of one afternoon trying to teach his nephew how to kick a football. John's approach was to kick at the ball, watch it roll a few feet in front of him, and then fall on the ground.

"Get up, try again," Bobby told the boy. John did, kicking at the ball until it rolled away from him—and then collapsing.

This went on three, four more times before John finally fell to the ground—and stayed there.

"Come on," an exasperated Uncle Bobby said. "A Kennedy never gives up."

Refusing to budge, John looked up and said, "Hmmph, here's one that does."

That St. Patrick's Day afternoon, Sister Joanne Frey, the children's catechism teacher, was driving by Washington's Rock Creek Park when she spotted a familiar figure. "It was Mrs. Kennedy," recalled Sister

Joanne, who rolled down the car window and called out to her. "I was wearing my habit," the nun said, "so she recognized me immediately and came over to the car. I looked around for a Secret Service agent, but didn't see anybody. She seemed to be just wandering through the park alone, lost in her thoughts."

As Jackie came closer, it appeared she was wearing "a sort of babushka over her head," Sister Joanne said, "and no makeup—her eyes were red, her face was swollen, it was obvious she had been crying." At home that night, the nun opened her afternoon paper to see a photo of Jackie on the front page, placing a shamrock on the president's grave earlier that day. "She was wearing a mink coat and looked beautiful in the photograph. Then it hit me: This is the face the public sees. I just saw the *real* Mrs. Kennedy—alone, sad, completely devastated."

There were more onerous tasks ahead. Not one to leave such important matters to others, Jackie had quietly approached John Stevens Stone Masons in Newport, Rhode Island, and asked them to pick out six black slate slabs—one of which she would personally select to be the permanent marker for her husband's grave at Arlington. The slabs, each weighing hundreds of pounds, were transported to Hammersmith Farm and arranged in a semicircle in the Auchinclosses' formal garden.

Jamie Auchincloss was there when Jackie arrived at Hammersmith Farm in late March to make the final selection. Jackie's half brother felt there was "a sad symmetry to Jackie choosing the president's grave marker at Hammersmith. It was where she and Jack were married, where Jackie had come of age." Although Jamie remembered his sister going about "the whole process in a very businesslike way"—walking from stone to stone, methodically running her hand over each as she looked for flaws and imperfections—everybody watching "was fighting back tears, including the stonemasons."

At the end of the month, Jackie took John and Caroline along on a ski holiday in Stowe, Vermont. There they were joined on the slopes by their uncles Bobby and Teddy and their families. This time the press was in hot pursuit. At one point, John watched as his big sister was knocked to the ground by photographers trying to get a picture of their grieving mom. "How," Jackie later asked her friend Arthur Schlesinger incredulously, "do you explain *that* to a child?"

From Stowe, Jackie and Bobby left—sans children and sans Ethel—to spend a week with Chuck Spalding and Lee and Stas Radziwill at heiress Bunny Mellon's hilltop villa in Antigua. For several days, they water-skied, sailed, and explored some of the remote, uninhabited islands in the area. At night, they drank and joked and played Jack's favorite songs as loudly as they could—all, Spalding said, in an effort to "drown out the bad memories any way they could."

To the other members of their party, it was clear that Jackie and Bobby were becoming something more than just in-laws. They paired off from the others, holding hands as they huddled together in corners, lost in conversation and whispered confidences. Spalding described them as "definitely a unit—a twosome. She relied on him for everything, and he adored her. There was definitely an intimacy there."

In Jackie's case, there was the added desire to provide Jack's children—particularly John—with a father figure who mirrored all the qualities of her late husband. Clearly, no one came closer to accomplishing that than Bobby. "Jackie wanted Bobby to continue indefinitely as Jack's substitute in the children's lives," Spalding said. "She felt particularly strongly that John needed a strong male figure—preferably a Kennedy—to shape Jack's only son."

Jackie was not the only Bouvier falling for Jack's younger brother. Lee threw two parties for RFK in London early in 1964, sparking rumors that theirs might be more than just the standard in-law relationship. "Lee wanted to sleep with Bobby," said her close friend Truman Capote, "and Bobby, like all those Kennedy men, was not one to pass up the opportunity."

Not that Jackie was operating under the illusion that she somehow had exclusive claim on Bobby's affections. Still emotionally unmoored some five months after Dallas, Jackie reverted to her old habit of seeking out solace and reassurance from attractive, invariably married, men.

One night during this period, Jackie showed up at Billy Martin's, a popular Georgetown restaurant, with Robert McNamara. She often told Jack she thought his secretary of defense was the most attractive man in the cabinet. According to one patron, Jackie, clearly intoxicated by the end of the evening, was "hugging and kissing" McNamara. When she got up to go to the ladies' room, she was, said another witness, "weaving and terribly unsteady on her feet. Everyone probably assumed she had good reason to drink." Out of sympathy for JFK's widow, the incident was never reported in the press.

Just a few weeks later, Jackie lunched at Washington's Jockey Club with Lee, Hollywood business manager George Englund, and Englund's client Marlon Brando. Beguiled by the smoldering, brutishly handsome Brando, Jackie listened intently as he shared behind-the-scenes details of filming *Mutiny on the Bounty* in the South Pacific. She was equally intrigued by the fact that Brando, a passionate civil rights activist who had been one of Jack's most ardent Hollywood supporters, was now protesting on behalf of Native Americans and India's oppressed class of "untouchables." When the lunch was over, Jackie had to wade through a sea of reporters and photographers—yet another reminder that she would have no peace as long as she lived in Washington.

"Like half the other women on the planet at the time," Chuck Spalding said, "Jackie found Marlon Brando completely irresistible." She later rhapsodized to her friend Franklin Roosevelt Jr. that the "Stella!"-bellowing star of *A Streetcar Named Desire* was no real-life Stanley Kowalski. He was, she reported, well read, articulate, serious, and of course "*extremely* attractive."

After the mob scene at the Jockey Club, Lee was more concerned than ever that the circus atmosphere surrounding Jackie's life in Washington was beginning to take its toll. The crowd outside 3017 N Street now seemed larger than ever, and grew more unruly with each passing day. "I worry so much about John," she told her friend Roswell Gilpatric, who had served as Jack's deputy defense secretary. "The crazy women focus on him even more than they do Caroline, and I think it's really starting to frighten him."

Lee urged her sister to move to Manhattan and leave Washington behind—boorish gawkers, pushy photographers, painful memories and all. It would be a homecoming of sorts—the Kennedys and Bouviers had roots in New York, and Jackie and Jack had spent some of their happiest times there. Besides, Jackie knew from personal experience that the studied nonchalance of New Yorkers made them far less likely to accost a celebrity; as counterintuitive as it seemed, she and the children would be permitted to live their lives there in comparative peace.

To make the transition for her sister even easier, Lee persuaded her husband to purchase an eleven-room apartment for the Radziwills at 969 Fifth Avenue—just a few blocks from Peter and Pat Kennedy Lawford, Steven and Jean Kennedy, and an assortment of Bouvier and Auchincloss relatives.

In the short run, Jackie seized every opportunity to get out of Washington. Not wanting to abandon the family's tradition of spending Easter with the rest of the Kennedy clan, she and the children flew to Palm Beach. This time Jackie hosted an Easter egg hunt for forty local children that included special prizes supplied by FAO Schwarz, the famous Fifth Avenue toy store.

Things seemed to be going smoothly until John and a four-year-old named Richard began fighting over what was then one of the hottest toys for boys—a GI Joe action figure. Jackie jumped into the middle of the fray and managed to pull the battling tots apart, but not before a wrought-iron end table was overturned. Mortified, Jackie handed the GI Joe in question to the other little boy and eventually fetched another one for her son—but not before carrying John inside, bending him over her knee, and spanking him. The sound of the little boy's wailing brought an abrupt end to the merriment outside. "My mother was very strict with me," John later said. "Caroline could do just about anything, but if I stepped out of line, I got a swat."

In truth, Jackie knew that John would inevitably be more closely linked with JFK in the public mind. "Jackie hated bratty behavior, really hated it—and in the Kennedy family you didn't have to look far to see kids who were just spoiled rotten," her friend Cleveland Amory said. Jackie spent more time disciplining her son for the simple reason that, Amory observed, "Caroline was always so well behaved, so eager to please. John, in a word, wasn't. As a small child, John was what you would call a handful."

It was a side of the boy the public did not often see. At public ceremonies honoring his father, John could be counted on to follow his mother's stage direction with meticulous precision—just as he had done when he saluted Daddy's passing coffin. On May 29, 1964—what would have been President Kennedy's forty-seventh birthday—Jackie and the children attended what turned out to be a tear-filled Mass at St. Matthew's Cathedral, the site of JFK's funeral just six months earlier.

From there, the family drove to Arlington, where they knelt and prayed at Jack's grave while a mob of more than one thousand onlookers held back by police barricades snapped photos and shouted their names. While Caroline placed flowers on her father's final resting place, John was assigned the task of leaving behind something special—a tie clasp in the shape of PT-109, the legendary patrol boat Jack had skippered in the Solomon Islands during World War II. Carefully following his mother's instructions, John removed the clasp from the lapel of his white linen coat, leaned over, and placed the pin on the boughs that covered Daddy's grave.

This visit to Arlington was the beginning of what would become an annual ritual—for the nation as well as Jack's widow and children. "She would take the children to the grave on the anniversary of the president's birthday," Tish Baldrige said. "His birthday, not his death. She believed in celebrating life, not death."

From Washington, John flew with his mother and sister to Hyannis Port. While they played outside with their boisterous Kennedy cousins, Jackie, still worried that Jack's time in the White House was too short for him to be remembered, made a televised pitch on behalf of the John F. Kennedy Library. "His office will be there," she said, describing the Oval Office replica she had envisioned as the library's centerpiece. "You can hear every speech he made, you can see all the manuscripts of his speeches and how he changed them."

Once the cameras were gone, Jackie went upstairs to her room and looked out the window at John and Caroline cavorting on the lawn with a dozen other tousle-haired Kennedy children. Just nine months earlier, Jackie had watched as John, Caroline, and nine of their cousins greeted JFK as he climbed out of his presidential helicopter and got behind the wheel of a golf cart. Squealing with delight, the children piled onto the cart, then held on for dear life as the president took off at breakneck speed across this same stretch of emerald-green lawn.

The memories that came flooding back weren't all happy ones. It had also been only nine months since Jackie was rushed from Hyannis Port to Otis Air Force Base Hospital, where her son Patrick was delivered five and a half weeks prematurely by caesarean section. "I never thought that any pain could cut more deeply than what I felt then for little Patrick," she told Pierre Salinger. "But I was wrong."

Heeding her sister's advice, Jackie went apartment hunting in New York in June 1964. To throw off the press, her best friend and assistant, Nancy Tuckerman, played the role of prospective buyer while Jackie went along disguised as the Tuckerman family's nanny. Jackie made several apartment-hunting trips to Manhattan before paying $200,000 for a five-bedroom, five-bath, fifteenth-floor apartment at 1040 Fifth Avenue. The co-op was owned by Mrs. Lowell Weicker, whose husband would later serve as Connecticut's Republican senator and as the state's governor. It was steps from one of Jackie's favorite haunts—the Metropolitan Museum of Art—and boasted sweeping views of Central Park and the reservoir.

By way of making a complete break from her life in Washington, Jackie sold the weekend house in Wexford for $130,000 and replaced it with a rental not far from Bobby's summer home in Glen Cove, Long Island. Angered by LBJ's decision not to pick him as his 1964 presidential running mate (Johnson chose Minnesota senator Hubert H. Humphrey instead), Bobby now planned to become a permanent resident of New York and run for the U.S. Senate.

While John and Caroline remained in the care of Maud Shaw back in Georgetown, Jackie would spend the next few months and more than $125,000 renovating her new apartment. Headquarters for this operation was the Carlyle, the same hotel where Jack had maintained a sprawling suite for years. He considered the Carlyle to be his home away from the White House, and took full advantage of the hotel's labyrinth of underground tunnels that allowed him to walk undetected to those Upper East Side town houses occupied by some of New York's most beautiful socialites.

John was with his sister and mother in Georgetown when tragedy struck the family again. On June 19, 1964, Bobby called Jackie to tell her that his brother Teddy had insisted on flying through a storm to Springfield, Massachusetts, to accept his party's nomination for a second term in the U.S. Senate. Ted's small plane crashed, killing the pilot and Ted's aide and breaking the senator's back. "Somebody up there," Bobby joked when he and Jackie visited Ted at the hospital, "doesn't like us."

Just days after Uncle Teddy's plane crash, John and Caroline joined Uncle Bobby as he posed for the cover of *Life*. On the eve of launching his own career in politics, Bobby was more than willing to use his fallen brother's children to advance his own interests. Part paterfamilias, part pied piper, RFK was photographed with six of his extended brood climbing all over him. In sharp contrast to the other children, all of whom were captured in a moment of gleeful hysteria, freckle-faced Caroline sat in her uncle's lap looking pensive, perhaps a little sad. In the foreground, eager-to-please John obliged the photographer with a broad, gap-toothed grin worthy of Norman Rockwell.

Operating out of her suite at the Carlyle that summer in Washington, Jackie oversaw the small army of workmen who were transforming the somewhat shabby apartment at 1040 Fifth into a showplace. No longer surrounded by the painful memories of her days as first lady, she was beginning to feel like a human being again. "New York gave her the one thing she so desperately needed," said Nancy Dickerson, the pioneering TV journalist who was also a friend of JFK's. "It gave her room to breathe."

It was more than that. "I think she saw her return to the city," Nancy Tuckerman said of her friend, "as coming home. And more than anything she hoped—perhaps even expected—that in a city of such size and diversity, she'd be able to find the anonymity she longed for. But this was unrealistic, and intellectually she probably knew it."

Thrilled at the prospect of being able to live life on her terms, Jackie now felt free to spend time with a number of handsome escorts, including McNamara and Ros Gilpatric. She even invited the lethally seductive Brando, who was so promiscuous he later confessed to keeping two abortionists on retainer, to her Carlyle suite.

The couple met on several occasions before the inevitable happened: After one too many drinks, Jackie and Brando fell into bed together. Brando wrote about his brief, steamy affair with Jackie in an original draft of his 1994 memoirs, but his Random House editor, Joe Fox, convinced him to take it out. Fox, as it happened, was a friend of Jackie's. The affair ended quickly, which was the norm for Brando. "I have always been lucky with women," he said, "though I hardly ever spent more than a couple of minutes with any of them."

(Told of Jackie's fling with Brando after his mother's death, John seemed intrigued by what he viewed as simply more evidence of her adventurous spirit—and by the fact that Brando had known his father well enough to needle the president about his weight. When JFK chided the then-svelte Brando for being "too fat" for his next part, Marlon shot back: "Have you looked in a mirror lately? Your jowls won't even fit in the frame of the television screen!" John, who as an adult completely accepted that his father was a compulsive womanizer, also appeared fascinated by the fact that both JFK and Brando—not to mention Uncle Bobby—had had torrid affairs with Marilyn Monroe.)

Although they were still months from actually moving into their new apartment, Jackie was eager for John and Caroline to start their new lives in New York. On September 15, 1964, Caroline joined her cousins Sydney and Victoria Lawford at the Convent of the Sacred Heart, just a few blocks up from 1040 Fifth. This was the exclusive Catholic girls' school that their grandmother Rose had attended more than a half century earlier.

Since John would not be enrolling at New York's prestigious

St. David's School until February 1965, Jackie made sure his Secret Service detail kept him well occupied with trips to the Central Park Zoo, marathon sessions on the swings at the park's Eighty-fifth Street playground, and plenty of tricycle time. Whenever she could, Jackie broke away from meetings with decorators to spend time with the kids; at one point the former first lady was photographed rowing John and Caroline around the Central Park lake dressed in a double-breasted white wool Chanel suit and pearls.

Such interludes were fewer and farther between as Jackie was enlisted in Bobby's campaign to unseat New York's incumbent Republican senator Kenneth Keating. That August, she had appeared at the Democratic National Convention in Atlantic City and all but eclipsed the party's nominee for president, Lyndon Johnson.

When the convention was over, LBJ used Air Force One to literally block Jackie's plane from departing for Newport—refusing to move until she came out onto the tarmac and posed with him for a picture. Johnson knew that she was now focused on getting Bobby elected to the Senate, but wouldn't she make this one gesture that would mean so much to the Democrats in this election year?

"She said, gently but firmly, no," Jamie Auchincloss recalled. "My sister could not be budged once her mind was made up, and the one thing she hated above all else was being exploited—even by the president." Especially not this president, whose crass behavior—among other things, LBJ liked to confer with aides, both male and female, while sitting on the toilet—often made her cringe.

Jackie was "appalled by Johnson's earthiness," observed historian William Manchester. What LBJ had to say about her good friend Adlai Stevenson ("You know, he squats to piss") simply "horrified" Jackie. She confided to Manchester that the remark left her "stunned" and speechless.

Getting Bobby elected to the Senate was an obvious next step toward putting the Kennedys back in the White House in 1968, and Jackie was willing to do all she could to help make that happen. When she wasn't getting her new home ready or squeezing in a few moments with the children, Jackie was courting influential New York opinion makers on Bobby's behalf.

"He must win," she told Dorothy Schiff, powerful publisher of the *New York Post*, over tea in her Carlyle suite. "People say he's ruthless and cold . . . but, being younger than his two brothers and so much smaller . . . he hasn't got the graciousness they had. He is really very shy, but he has the kindest heart in the world." Not surprisingly, RFK would win the *Post*'s coveted endorsement—in large part, Schiff later conceded, because of Jackie's impassioned plea on his behalf.

Bobby wasn't above using John, either. When JFK's only son showed up at the World's Fair in Flushing Meadow, Queens, that September, he created a minor sensation—largely because the Kennedy campaign had tipped off the press in advance. Perched on the back of one of his four Secret Service agents, John cheerfully answered questions lobbed to him by reporters.

"Where's Caroline?" one asked.

"She's in school," answered John, "but I'm too young."

At Walt Disney's futuristic Magic Skyway exhibit, John was presented a toy car. "Hi, everybody!" he shouted to the assembled crowd as he grabbed the toy and plopped down on the ground. "I'm going to play car!"

The *Tyrannosaurus rex* exhibit at Sinclair Oil's Dinoland, however, turned out to have a sobering effect on Jackie's boy. "The lights and the dinosaurs," an uncharacteristically somber John told the pack of reporters, made him feel "a little bit scared."

"Jackie and John had enormous, really universal appeal," David Halberstam said. "Dallas was still so fresh, so raw. Just looking at Jack Kennedy's young family—especially John-John—it was hard not to feel a tug of emotion." They "made it impossible to forget that Bobby was carrying the torch for Camelot and the New Frontier, not LBJ."

That November, Bobby clobbered his opponent at the polls, racking up a 700,000-vote margin of victory. Ironically, Jackie's was not among them. She refused to cast her vote for anyone in the 1964 election—not for Bobby, and certainly not for LBJ. "This is very emotional, but I'd never voted until I was married to Jack," she later explained. The 1964 vote "would have been his—he would have been alive for that vote. And I thought, I'm not going to vote for anyone because this vote would have been his."

Jackie understood full well how Lyndon would react. "I know," she conceded, "that LBJ was hurt." But not Bobby, who publicly acknowledged that he, too, refused to cast a vote for the Texan who had replaced his brother in the White House.

It would be another two weeks before Jackie finally checked out of the Carlyle and took up residence in her new home. The apartment at 1040 Fifth was the axis on which John's world would spin for the next thirty years, and would, for the most part, remain frozen in time.

"It was Jackie's haven, her refuge," Tish Baldrige said. "And a magical place for any child to call home." Anyone stepping into this magical place for the first time was instantly drawn to the apartment's paramount feature: its jaw-dropping panoramic view of Central Park in the foreground, with the Hudson River and New Jersey stretching to the horizon. Just across the street and to the left was the limestone-sheathed, neoclassical Metropolitan Museum of Art. Later, John would be able to look down on a reminder of his father: the glass-enclosed Temple of Dendur, which Jackie picked out when Egyptian president Gamal Abdel Nasser offered to honor JFK by giving the United States one of his country's ancient ruins.

Jackie, who had a talent for illustration that dated back to her days at Miss Porter's School, spent hours at the window trying to capture the view on canvas. Occasionally, she invited John and Caroline to set up their own child-size easels and join her.

They also enjoyed peeping at neighbors and the pedestrians below through a high-powered telescope set up on a tripod. Her friend and frequent escort Charles Addams, the celebrated cartoonist, explained that Jackie liked "prying into *other people's* lives for a change." Like any other boy his age, John was keen on looking but had a difficult time at first mastering the lens. Once he did, "there was no stopping him."

While Mommy focused on people, John tended to zero in on ships ply-
ing the Hudson, or the dogs, horses, and pigeons that also populated the
park—not to mention the moon and the stars. "John shared his mother's
love of adventure and her tremendous curiosity," Plimpton said. "The
whole business of peering through a telescope as if you were a captain
on the high seas or an astronomer—it was just incredibly exciting."

To ease the children's transition into their new life, Jackie flooded
the apartment with furniture, decorative objects, and mementos that
had been part of the family's time in the White House. As John and his
sister stepped directly out of the elevator and into the apartment's long,
mirrored entrance hall, they instantly recognized the marble torso of a
Roman god displayed on a table between two yellow porcelain vases.
"Look, look, it's Daddy's man," John shouted. The torso had been part
of JFK's antiquities collection. Several other pieces from the collection,
including the two-thousand-year-old bust of a young boy and a small
rendering of Hercules circa 500 B.C., sat atop an elaborately detailed
nineteenth-century French chest.

Exploring their new home for the first time, Caroline and John
clicked off each familiar item they spied—starting with John Singer
Sargent's *Venetian Girl* displayed on an easel in the living room. Nearby
was *Study of a Snow Owl* by Peter Paillon, and Sargent's striking *Head
of an Arab*. The dining room scarcely resembled a dining room at all.
With its crimson damask wallpaper, bookcases, comfy overstuffed
couches, marble fireplace, and black baby-grand piano, it contrasted
sharply with the stark formality of the other rooms. On one wall was
a world map covered with colored pins, each denoting a spot JFK had
visited as president. From now on, John would take first-time visitors
straight to the map and proclaim, "See those pins? My daddy went to
all those places!"

As in nearly every other house in America with small children, John's
finger paintings and Caroline's watercolors were proudly displayed
along with family photos on a bulletin board in the kitchen. Down
the hall, in the direction of John's room, were several framed four-
by-six-foot collages made up of family snapshots. John's friend Robert

Littell described each as a "joyful pastiche—pictures of poignant moments and happy days." By design, none of the photos in the collages, which she would replicate and hang in the family's other homes, predated November 22, 1963.

In fact, images of Jack were made conspicuous by their absence. In the entire apartment there was only one silver-framed head shot of JFK to be found, and it sat with other family photos on the dresser in her chartreuse-and-white corner bedroom. "She was trying to move on," Billy Baldwin said, "and she didn't want Caroline and especially John to have their whole lives dominated by the ghost of their father."

The welcoming, almost-but-not-quite casual environment Jackie tried to create for guests belied her attention to detail and an obsessive need for order. The closets in her bedroom were nothing short of immaculate, the contents arranged according to Jackie's exacting standards. Hundreds of pairs of shoes were organized by color and style. Evening dresses were lined up by length, day suits and evening suits were separated, and all clothes were arranged according to the spectrum, starting with primary colors and then shades of color. Hanging in their own section were forty pairs of identical white slacks.

Housewarming gifts from political leaders, celebrities, and social movers-and-shakers were soon landing on her doorstep—a Louis XV bed from Bunny Mellon, the forty-nine collected works of Winston Churchill from his son Randolph. President Johnson dropped in to pay his respects, as did ballet great Rudolf Nureyev, Ethiopian Emperor Haile Selassie, her old friend Leonard Bernstein, and King Hassan of Morocco.

For Jackie, most days were spent in an unmarked office at 200 Park Avenue, one of several Manhattan buildings owned by her father-in-law, Joe Kennedy, and for years the headquarters of his financial empire. There, with the help of Tuckerman and Pamela Turnure, the Jackie Kennedy look-alike who was both Jack's lover and the first lady's press secretary, she went about the business of sorting through letters of condolence that were still pouring in from all over the world.

Yet for the first time in months, Jackie was no longer crying herself to sleep. She could get through an entire day without mentioning Jack's name, now concentrating on beginning the next chapter of her life as the world's most famous single mother.

An early challenge was to convince the other mothers not to shy away from asking Caroline and John to parties and playdates. When Caroline asked why all the other girls in her class at Sacred Heart were being asked to birthday parties and she wasn't, Jackie picked up the phone and called one of the other mothers directly. "Of course we'd love to invite Caroline," the woman sputtered, "but we all felt it might be presumptuous to ask."

"Oh," Jackie replied, "but she's just a little girl. Please invite Caroline to everything. She's dying to come!" Caroline quickly became the most sought-after children's birthday party guest in New York.

Unfortunately, John was missing out on all the fun—and let everybody know it. "How come Caroline gets to go birthday parties and I don't?" he demanded whenever she headed out the door wearing a party dress and clutching an elaborately wrapped gift. "I want to go, too!"

A solution came in the improbable form of Morocco's King Hassan II and his son, Crown Prince Mohammed. During their White House years, the Kennedys had grown especially fond of the dashing monarch and his young family. Now Jackie seized the opportunity to throw a birthday party at her apartment for the crown prince, who was turning four.

No one was more excited than John, who joined his sister at the table alongside the crown prince. "Oh, John just loved it," Jackie later said. "He was so tired of hearing Caroline chatter on about all the wonderful parties she'd been to."

Not so thrilled was the birthday boy himself. When seventeen-year-old Jamie Auchincloss arrived to lend his sister a hand, the crown prince "was sitting at the table and looking terrified." Four bodyguards were lurking in the background, and hovering over the festivities was a royal nanny who, Jamie recalled, "looked even more intimidating than the bodyguards."

Everyone jumped when Jackie suddenly burst out of the kitchen carrying a huge birthday cake and singing a comically off-key rendition of "Happy Birthday" at the top of her lungs. When Jackie embellished the lyrics—"Happy Birthday, Dear Mohammed, Crown Prince, Li-on of Juu-dah"—everyone laughed. Everyone but the birthday boy and his entourage.

Matters only got worse when the little prince tried and failed to blow out his candles. The nanny and the bodyguards quickly joined in, huffing and puffing furiously, only to see the flames flicker back to life.

JFK's mischief-loving widow had put trick candles in the cake, convinced that it would liven up the festivities. What she hadn't considered was the fact that Prince Mohammed was considered infallible in his part of the world. Unaccustomed to things not going his way, the little boy burst into tears—and his nanny angrily confronted Jackie.

"Look what you have done!" she shouted in Jackie's face. "How terrible! I suppose you think you are funny?"

It was something the nanny "shouldn't have done," Jamie recalled. "Jackie was not accustomed to being talked to that way—especially by a servant." Jamie held his breath as his sister fixed the woman with a withering stare.

"It's too bad if he didn't understand the joke," Jackie said. "But this is my house and in it I will do as I damn well please."

Perhaps with the exception of her Moroccan guests, everyone in the room "felt like applauding," Jamie said. "I was very proud of her." So was John, who laughed so long and hard at the prince trying to blow out his candles that he fell off his chair.

John's zany antics were more than a match for his mother's, and during those first few weeks at 1040 Fifth she could count on him to keep her spirits high while Caroline was at school. John still spent most of his day with Nanny Shaw or roughhousing with Secret Service agents, who—whether Jackie approved or not—still helped fill the void left by his father. But when they were together—hanging out at the circus or digging into butterscotch sundaes at their favorite spot, Serendipity off Third Avenue—it had to have been clear to John that his mother was happier than she had been in months.

"The spark had returned to her eyes," said her friend Kitty Carlisle Hart, who not long before sat in stunned silence as Jackie obses-
sively recounted every moment of Jack's murder in horrific detail. Only
a year earlier, Hart had lost her husband, the legendary playwright
Moss Hart, and the two women bonded over concerns that their children might be emotionally scarred by the loss of their father at such a
young age. Now Kitty Hart, who had previously doubted that Jackie
was capable of letting go of the past, was struck by her friend's upbeat
demeanor. "She was finally giving herself permission to rejoin the land
of the living." Pierre Salinger agreed. "The black cloud had lifted, so
they could start to get on with their lives."

But the black cloud soon returned, and John and Caroline were
the first to notice. Mommy had stopped smiling and laughing, and her
eyes were once again red from weeping. Caroline quickly figured out
the reason: Everywhere there were black-bordered photographs of her
father—on the sides of buses, in store windows, on newsstands, and on
television. Mommy was crying herself to sleep again.

The approaching first anniversary of JFK's assassination hit his
widow hard. "She knew it was coming, of course, and assumed she
could just soldier through it," said Baldrige. "She hadn't counted on
not being able to look anywhere without seeing his picture, or seeing
the assassination recounted again and again on television. The nation
was living it all over again, and that meant she had to as well. It was
agony for her."

Jackie had planned to cancel her newspaper delivery for the week
leading up to the first anniversary of Dallas, but forgot. So when she
looked at the front page of the *New York Times* as she did every morning, there was another painful reminder—a banner headline trumpet-
ing the release of the Warren Report.

She went about her business, but soon realized there was no escaping the painful reminders of what had happened just twelve months
earlier in Dallas. As Jackie walked down Fifth Avenue toward Kenneth's Salon, every single store window she passed displayed a picture
of her martyred husband. Once she got to the salon and closed the door

behind her, she walked up to the receptionist's desk and broke down. "For the next several minutes, she just stood there, weeping," another customer said. "It broke your heart to see it."

Settling into a salon chair, Jackie managed to regain her composure and instinctively reached for a magazine. Jack stared back at her from the black-bordered cover of *Life*'s special memorial issue. "I can't stand it," she told her hairdresser, Rosemary Sorrentino. "Why do they remember the assassination? Why can't they celebrate his birthday?"

On November 22, 1964, Jackie took John and Caroline to the Seventy-ninth Street playground in Central Park. While the usual contingent of Secret Service agents looked after them, Jackie wandered down one of the park's winding paths until she found a secluded bench. She spent the next several hours sitting in that same spot, she later said, "crying my eyes out."

The first-anniversary hysteria proved so devastating for Jackie, in fact, that she admitted to Ros Gilpatric that she had considered suicide. "I have enough pills to do it," Jackie told him.

Gilpatric did not take the threat seriously. She would never take her own life, he said, "because of the children." But he was still worried about her mental state. "Everyone who loved her," he said, "was very much concerned."

"People tell me that time will heal," she told Dorothy Schiff. "How *much* time?" Schiff was shocked by the change in her friend. "She is odd and different," Schiff said of Jackie, "very much less the queen than she was."

That fall, several of Jackie's friends were taking turns inviting her to small dinner parties at their Park Avenue penthouses and Upper East Side brownstones. These were "always groups of four or six—never more than that," said George Plimpton, one of her frequent escorts. But in late November, all that changed. "Nancy Tuckerman would call and say Jackie was in her room, too ill to keep our dinner date," said Gilpatric. "All of the terrible memories had flooded back." To the dismay of her friends, Jackie "was back at square one—shattered, inconsolable."

Three days after the world marked the anniversary of his father's murder, John blew out the four candles on his birthday cake. "See, Mommy," he said, making a sly allusion to Prince Mohammed's futile attempt to extinguish the fake candles on his cake. "*I* can do it!"

John ripped into his presents—puzzles, books, a toy truck, and a model plane, of course—with the kind of unfettered abandon that reminded Jackie of his father. Then the birthday boy and his twenty-five guests, mostly cousins and a smattering of friends, joined in a spirited game of musical chairs, followed by pin-the-tail-on-the-donkey.

As she watched her son and his sister laughing with their little friends, Jackie turned to one of the other mothers. "My John is such a happy little boy, you know," she said. "I think sometimes I worry about him too much. But every mother worries about her children, of course."

Inviting children—even total strangers—over to the apartment was part of Jackie's overall strategy to keep John and Caroline grounded. "Quite often we invited children we met in the park home to the Fifth Avenue apartment for dinner," Maud Shaw recalled. "Mrs. Kennedy was very good about that. I always used to ask her beforehand, of course, but her reply was always the same. 'Certainly they can come,' she would say. 'I leave it to you. I like the children to have new friends. It's good for them.'"

Still, John's mood was inevitably tethered to that of his mother, and her mental state remained precarious. It was clear to both children that Mummy, as they now called her, was happiest when she was in the company of one person—Uncle Bobby.

Even Ros Gilpatric, who competed with RFK for Jackie's affections, conceded that after Dallas Jackie clung to her brother-in-law for emotional support—and vice versa. "Bobby," Gilpatric said, "was the only one who could pull her out of her depression."

By the time Jackie and the children joined the Radziwills for Christmas in Palm Beach, Jackie and Bobby were lovers. Rightly believing that the press would never dare to report the story—the fallen president's family was still sacrosanct—Bobby and Jackie did little to conceal their feelings for each other. They still openly held hands, embraced, even kissed.

"Jackie and Bobby were definitely having an affair," Nancy Dickerson said. "You must remember this was years before anyone wrote about Jack's infidelities. When the stories about JFK and Marilyn Monroe started to surface, they were dismissed as preposterous. After Dallas, no one would have believed St. Jackie and St. Bobby were sleeping together, no matter how obvious it was. It would have been considered sacrilege."

Gore Vidal also believed that Jackie was now in love with Bobby. "There was always something oddly intense in her voice," he said, "when she mentioned him to me." Clare Boothe Luce, one of Joe's closest friends, was also convinced. "Well, of course *everybody* knew Jackie and Bobby were 'involved.' . . . At least everyone who knew them knew what was going on."

A favorite trysting place was the bar of the Sherry-Netherland Hotel on Fifth Avenue, where Kennedy brother-in-law Peter Lawford shared an apartment with flamboyant Greek-born journalist Taki Theodoracopulos, better known simply as "Taki." As it happened, Taki was having an affair with Jackie's sister, Lee. "Lawford was telling me at the time," Theodoracopulos said, "that Jackie was sleeping with Bobby." Lawford also told his wife that Bobby was filling in for Jack "in all departments."

Indeed, for the next three years Bobby and Jackie would be spotted cozying up in the early-morning hours at various out-of-the-way New York nightspots. On Long Island, where Jackie leased a country house near Bobby's, locals spoke of seeing them nearly every weekend, cuddling in the rear booth of a quiet restaurant or walking arm in arm along the beach. According to Bruce Balding, who owned the stable where Jackie boarded her horses, "many people often saw Jackie and Bobby off by themselves, heads together, or looking fondly at each other in various hotels in the area, so they got the idea."

Ethel, who like other Kennedy wives was accustomed to such behavior, receded into the background. She even remained behind at Hyannis Port and Hickory Hill, caring for the children, while her husband and

Jackie vacationed together, openly sharing a bedroom at the Montego Bay, Jamaica, villa owned by a mutual friend.

Not only was the attorney general's office rife with speculation about RFK and Jackie—she frequently called, asking for him—but even the Kennedy faithful confessed to the distinct probability that Bobby and his brother's widow had become romantically entangled. JFK's close friend Paul "Red" Fay remembered that after Dallas she "went into hibernation and Bobby was over there practically every day with her. She's a fascinating woman. If she'd throw her charm at you, why, you'd be emotionally swayed." By the same token, Fay noted that RFK was a "controlling individual, and I think that probably if Bobby felt something, why, she was going to go along."

———

WITH RFK ENSCONCED as New York's junior senator, John saw more of his uncle than ever before. Caroline certainly was aware that Uncle Bobby and their mother enjoyed a warm and tender relationship—a relationship that was looking more and more like the one their parents enjoyed. "Caroline was very, very intuitive for a seven-year-old," Plimpton said. "She got the signals Bobby and Jackie were sending to each other, and I'm sure she encouraged John in thinking that her mother and Bobby were in love."

By the holidays, the beguiling, assertive Jackie of old was back. The day after Christmas she packed the kids up and joined Bobby and his Hickory Hill gang for a ski holiday, this time in Aspen, Colorado. There was no escaping the press, which breathlessly chronicled every moment—from furious snowball fights between John and his Kennedy cousins to Jackie's frustration as she tried to fasten her son's ski boots.

There were two more ski trips in early 1965—one to the Catskills and the other aboard a Pepsi corporate jet to Keene, New Hampshire. In Keene, photographers again had a field day snapping JFK's son as he tried unsuccessfully to make it down the bunny slope without taking a tumble.

On one ski trip, Jackie and her friend Joan Braden were watching John and Caroline zip down a hill on a sled when, out of the blue, Jackie turned to Braden and said, "You know, there'll never be another Jack." There were "escorts, companions, and another husband," Braden mused later, "but there was never another Jack for her."

Nor was Jackie really ready to see another man take the oath of office on the Capitol steps—not when she believed it was her husband who should have been standing there. She was still in a state of shock and had not even changed out of her blood-spattered Chanel suit when she agreed to stand by Lyndon Johnson while he was sworn in the first time aboard Air Force One. Now, viewing Johnson as little more than a placeholder for Bobby, she refused to be moved by LBJ's phone calls beseeching her to attend his inauguration in January 1965.

Jackie chose instead to fill up her calendar with nights at the theater, parties, and trips. Leaving John and Caroline in the care of Maud Shaw, she took in a Greenwich Village production of *Tartuffe* and, wrapped in sable, turned heads at a Metropolitan Opera gala performance of *Tosca*. Afterward, Aristotle Onassis's future bride went backstage to meet the Greek tycoon's longtime mistress, the fabulously temperamental Maria Callas.

Her deceptively carefree existence notwithstanding, Jackie spent every spare moment with Bobby. The fact remained that neither JFK's wife nor his brother had fully come to terms with what the family obtusely referred to as "the events in Dallas."

"Jackie and Bobby were joined at the hip," Salinger said, "and to have him be such a large part of their lives was obviously a huge comfort to John and Caroline—John in particular, because he needed a strong male figure around." Bobby made no attempt to conceal his devotion to his brother's widow, and Jackie fully reciprocated. In early 1965, her old friend Frank Conniff asked Jackie to describe her feelings for Bobby. "I would," she said in deadly earnest, "jump out of the window for him."

John, well, he's something else.

—JACKIE

John was never a brat, but he was all boy.

—GEORGE PLIMPTON, FAMILY FRIEND

5.

"I Want to Help Him Go Back
and Find His Father"

———

She was absolutely devoted to her children," George Plimpton said of Jackie. "And even with all that had happened, she made sure they had a happy life." It wasn't easy. An important first step was making sure that the very agency assigned to protect her children didn't unintentionally make them fearful and dependent. Secret Service agents guarding the family would simply have to curb their enthusiasm.

Jackie was very precise about what she expected of the family's security detail, and complained bitterly when she believed they were going too far. "Mrs. Kennedy feels very strongly," wrote the head of the Kiddie Detail in a confidential Secret Service memo to the agency chief, "that though there are two children to protect, it is 'bad' to see two agents 'hovering around.'" For example, Jackie demanded that, whenever she was behind the wheel, the follow-up car not be seen by the children. "The agent must drift into the background quickly when arriving at a specific location," the memo continued, "and remain aloof and invisible until moment of departure."

Beyond mastering the art of hiding in plain sight, Secret Service agents were ordered point-blank not to spoil John and Caroline. "It's bad for the children to see grown men waiting on them," Jackie said. "I want you to tell Caroline to pick up her clothes, shoes, toys, and so on. The same goes for John."

"Mrs. Kennedy is adamant in her contention that agents must not perform special favors for John Jr. and Caroline or wait on them as servants," the confidential Secret Service memo continued. "Agents are not to carry clothes, beach articles, sand buckets, baby carriages, strollers, handbags, suitcases, etc., for Caroline and John Jr. and the children must carry their own clothing items, toys etc. . . ."

At the beach in particular, Jackie stressed that the Secret Service should back off. "Drowning is *my* responsibility," Jackie insisted, driving home her point that the agency "is not responsible for any accident sustained by the children in the usual and normal play sessions." These were to be, the memo added, "the sole responsibility of Mrs. Kennedy."

Secret Service agents did tag along when Jackie escorted John to his first day at St. David's School, at 12 East Eighty-ninth Street. Once Jackie left, one agent remained on Eighty-ninth Street while another waited in a hallway outside the classroom. There was little the agents could do to safeguard John, but it soon became clear that JFK's son could stand up for himself—and then some. His first morning at St. David's, John got into a tiff with another boy who tauntingly called him John-John. The other boy wound up with a bloody nose.

There would be other fights with other students, which one faculty member chalked up to John's "naturally high spirits." It also had something to do with the fact that, for all his mother's efforts to keep him grounded, John was used to getting his way. "He had a will of steel," the teacher said, "no doubt about it. It wasn't that he was arrogant or bratty, just determined to exhaust the opposition until they finally gave in."

It was equally true that nearly all of John's classmates seemed genuinely fond of him. "John makes friends with everybody," Jackie observed. "Immediately." It helped that his own cousin, William Kennedy Smith, also attended St. David's. The bond John and Willie Smith formed would be one of the strongest and most important in John's life, lasting well into adulthood.

———

IN THE SPRING of 1965, Jackie seized on another opportunity to spurn LBJ. This time the White House Rose Garden was being dedicated in her honor, and the president once again bombarded her with pleading phone calls. Jackie refused, but she did agree to send her mother in her place. Johnson did not give up easily. For the next four years, Jackie received an official invitation to every state dinner and countless other White House affairs. She did not deign to respond to a single one.

She did, however, slip into a flowing Yves St. Laurent gown and dance the night away at a party thrown by Lee simply to "brighten Jackie's day." Jackie's date for the night was Averell Harriman, and sprinkled among the hundred guests that night were the celebrated likes of Maurice Chevalier, Leonard Bernstein, Sammy Davis Jr., Leopold Stokowski, and Mike Nichols. One commanded more of Jackie's attention than the others: RFK, who was there sans Ethel. Bobby, said Bernstein, "hovered around Jackie like he owned her." Another guest spotted the couple huddled in a corner and sidled over to eavesdrop. "They were talking about a fistfight John had just been in at his school," she said. "Jackie sounded a little concerned, but all Bobby cared about was that John won the fight."

John was urged to be on his very best behavior when he made his first trip abroad, accompanying his mother and Caroline to England in May 1965. At Runnymede, in the meadow beside the Thames where the Magna Carta was signed in 1215, Queen Elizabeth dedicated Great Britain's memorial to JFK in a moving ceremony that ended with Jackie brushing away tears.

When it was time for the children to meet the queen, Maud Shaw held her breath; she had spent hours couching them on royal etiquette. During the lengthy ceremony, Caroline had tried to stifle a yawn but failed. However, when the time came to meet the queen, Uncles Teddy and Bobby looked on proudly as she pulled off the perfect curtsy.

Then it was John's turn to take center stage. When the queen walked up to Jack's son and smiled broadly, the little boy bowed deeply at the waist and said in a clear voice, "Pleased to meet you, Your Majesty." Nanny Shaw was relieved; all morning John had been insisting England's reigning monarch was not "Your Majesty" at all, but "*My Majesty*."

The ceremony at Runnymede was followed by tea with the queen at Windsor Castle. At one point, Jackie took aside Lord Harlech (David Ormsby-Gore, British ambassador to the United States during the Kennedy years) to thank him for the kindness he and his wife Sissie had shown her in the dark days immediately following the assassination. Maud Shaw, meanwhile, kept a wary eye on her charges. In the end, she was just happy that John managed to get through the afternoon "without spilling tea on Her Majesty or otherwise causing an international incident."

Straight from Windsor Castle, Jackie and the children moved into Aunt Lee's house in Regent's Park and started acting like any other tourists. They watched the changing of the guard at Buckingham Palace, took turns holding an executioner's ax at the Tower of London, and had their pictures taken mugging alongside Whitehall's stone-faced cavalry guards. Still obsessed with all things military, John snapped off one of his now-famous salutes to practically anything in uniform.

While Caroline and their mother took in the crown jewels, John prevailed on his Secret Service detail to help crawl inside the grimy barrel of an ancient cannon. For John, none of it compared to sharing a boat ride on Regent's Park Lake with his Radziwill cousins Tony and Tina.

Even more than their American counterparts, British reporters pursued JFK's children with dogged determination. Wily photographers surprised John and Caroline as they tried to escape out a rear door of the Radziwill house with Maud Shaw, and were on hand when John tripped and skinned his knee while running down a path in Regent's Park. When John burst into tears, Shaw tried to comfort him. Caroline was less charitable. To the delight of the press, she called her brother a "crybaby." John balled up his fist and was just about to take a swing at his sister when the nanny swept him off his feet.

Before leaving England, Jackie took John and Caroline to pose for the celebrated illustrator, designer, photographer, and artist Cecil Beaton. But obviously it was Jackie who made the greatest impression on Beaton, who scribbled in his diaries that she was "an over-life-size caricature of herself. Huge baseball players' shoulders and haunches, big boyish hands and feet . . ." Still, like everyone who ever met her, the chronically acerbic Beaton could not deny that Jackie's "very dark, beautiful, receptive" eyes were "mesmerizing."

At home and abroad, Maud Shaw was always a vigilant, caring presence in the children's lives. She made sure they were fed, dressed, and bathed, supervised their play, packed their bags, held their hands as they crossed the street, mediated their frequent disputes, read bedtime stories to them, tucked them in, and woke them in the morning. For seven years, she was as much a mother to John and Caroline as Jackie had ever been, and both the late president and his wife viewed Nanny Shaw as an indispensable part of their tight-knit family.

Yet no one, it turned out, was truly indispensable. Just as she had worried that John was growing too close to certain members of his Secret Service detail, Jackie now felt that the children had grown too emotionally dependent on Maud Shaw. Jackie told the children that Mrs. Shaw would not be returning to the United States with the family because she wanted to spend time in Sheerness, England, visiting her own relatives.

In truth, the children's beloved nanny had been sacked. Even before they left for England, Jackie had presented Miss Shaw with a leather-bound photo album commemorating her years with the family and suggested that once the trip was over she remain behind. "I loved Caroline and John very dearly, and I loved them for a very, very long time," said Mrs. Shaw, who told Evelyn Lincoln that her abrupt dismissal "came as a bit of a shock. When I came home [to her family home in England], I wept a great deal . . ."

Over lunch in London with Evangeline Bruce, the wife of U.S. ambassador to Great Britain David E. K. Bruce, Jackie explained that Miss Shaw was "good with young children" but that John and Caroline had "outgrown" her. "I want someone," Jackie said, "more attuned to their present needs."

There was another, more compelling reason, which Jackie chose not to share with her luncheon companion. In violation of the confidentiality agreement all of Jackie's employees were required to sign, Shaw had secretly signed book deals with publishers in both the United States and Britain to write a tell-all about her years of service as nanny to both Caroline and John. (Although she threatened to sue, Jackie decided not to go through with it when Shaw agreed to give her final approval of the manuscript. The book, *White House Nannie*, was released the following year and became an instant bestseller.)

In the coming months and years, Jackie made sure that John maintained a long-distance relationship with the woman who had been a mother figure to him. At first, Jackie wrote notes to Miss Shaw as if John were the author, painstakingly printing each word in her version of a child's awkward scrawl. Later, Jackie made certain that John jotted off a note to his former nanny at least once a month, updating her on what was going on in his life.

For the time being, however, the children were told only that Nanny Shaw was postponing her return to the States, and that she would be back in New York to care for them in a matter of weeks. Jackie shrewdly made sure that other familiar faces—her maid, Provi Paredes, as well as members of the Kiddie Detail, the cook, and the family's longtime driver, to name a few—filled at least some of the void left by Shaw's absence. "Caroline cried a little when she heard Mrs. Shaw wasn't coming back," said Plimpton, who had developed a special fondness for Caroline. "John was too young for any of it to mean much to him. He just kept dashing about and getting into tons of mischief—a typical four-year-old boy."

Jackie also did whatever she could to take up any slack in the aftermath of Shaw's firing. She left no doubt as to what role she intended to play in her own children's lives. "They are the center of my universe," Jackie said, "and I hope I am the center of theirs. I intend to always be there for them."

As soon as they returned to New York, Jackie resumed her morning routine of walking Caroline the six blocks up Fifth Avenue to Sacred Heart, then returning to the apartment to meet up with John and walk him four blocks to St. David's on East Eighty-ninth Street. When she could, Jackie also made the effort to meet John at his school and walk him home. "Caroline is an old hand at school," Jackie explained to her friend Charles Addams. "But it's all terribly new for John. I think he feels reassured when he sees me there waiting for him."

Evenings, however, were reserved for Mommy. That spring, Jackie became a glittering fixture on Manhattan's social scene. No longer sobbing night after night in her room, JFK's widow now seemed to be everywhere—at concerts, plays, fashion shows, museum openings, and benefits. Night after night, John and Caroline peeked in to see what Mommy was wearing before she headed off into the night. When Addams, one of her frequent escorts during this period, told Jackie she looked like a queen in her white evening gown and diamonds, Caroline and John laughed. "I've seen a queen," said Caroline, recalling their recent encounter with Queen Elizabeth, "and my mommy looks better. *Lots.*"

Jackie's frenetic social schedule now meant that she was in the papers more than at any time since she left the White House, and the public's thirst for gossip about her and the children remained unslakable. John was once again the target of photographers who lurked in the shadows outside his apartment building, hoping to snap a shot of the little boy as he and his mother departed for school.

Jackie's first instinct was to come down hard on her staff, threatening to fire anyone who divulged even the most innocuous-seeming detail of her life to the outside world. "That went double for the kids," said Addams, who noted that Jackie became "blind with rage" anytime there was a story about John or Caroline in the press.

When the family cook let slip to a reporter she knew that Jackie had lost twenty-five pounds, she was fired the next day. Jackie learned that the cook's successor planned to write a cookbook, and she met the same fate. Caroline's piano teacher made a passing comment to someone who turned out to be a reporter that she was working for the Kennedys, and was gone in a matter of hours.

This purging of anyone suspected of disloyalty did not stop there. Limousine drivers—all instructed not to speak to either John or Caroline—were replaced on a weekly basis so that none of them would become too familiar with the family's coming and goings. For entirely different reasons, Jackie was also replacing Secret Service agents more frequently; she still harbored the fear that John in particular would become too attached to them as father figures—a role that Jackie strongly felt only Uncle Bobby was qualified to fill.

"I've never known anyone who cut people off with such ease," Jamie Auchincloss said of his sister. "The phrase 'out of sight, out of mind' was invented for Jackie." Jackie's abiding distrust of those who worked for her had the unintended result of chipping away at her children's sense of security. "The way her mother dispensed with people," he went on, the children "must have found it all bewildering—and more than a little scary."

Yet Jackie's growing paranoia hadn't extinguished her sense of fun and whimsy—particularly when it came to the children. That summer, she enlisted George Plimpton to help her put together a special "treasure hunt" for John and Caroline at Hammersmith Farm. Once the children found the wooden treasure chest Jackie had filled with fake doubloons and trinkets, a Coast Guard longboat carrying angry, eye-patch-wearing "pirates"—Plimpton and a few locals—showed up to reclaim it. Taken by surprise, the other forty children who had been invited to the party—including several Kennedy cousins—ran screaming for their nannies. John, however, advanced toward the scary-looking buccaneers. "John was so *not* afraid," Plimpton recalled, "that he asked for the rubber sword I had tucked in my belt and began waving it above his head."

Jackie, watching the whole chaotic scene unfold, was "apoplectic" with laughter. "Jackie had such a great sense of mischief," Plimpton said, "and I think she thought it was absolutely hilarious that John, the youngest child there, was completely unfazed while the older children were absolutely terrified."

At one point, however, John did become upset—when, after capturing one of the pirates, the older children made the man walk the plank. When he realized the buccaneer was John Walsh, one of the substitute dads in his life, John burst into tears. "You can't die!" he sobbed. "You can't die!"

Just a few weeks after the infamous treasure hunt, John and Caroline joined the rest of the Kennedy clan at a party in Boston marking Richard Cardinal Cushing's seventieth birthday. A family friend and confidant to the family for years, Cardinal Cushing had officiated at every significant event in the lives of the Kennedys—including Jack and Jackie's marriage, the burial of Patrick, the christening of both John and Caroline, and of course, Jack's state funeral. As a young man, JFK admitted to being intimidated by the prelate's gruff demeanor and reverberating growl—but not John. "You," the boy proclaimed to the cardinal, "sound like a *bear*."

Caroline and John joined their Kennedy cousins again that Halloween, when everybody went trick-or-treating in Hyannis Port. This time, Caroline was dressed as a Dutch girl in wooden shoes and pigtails. Jackie shredded John's pants, found an old pair of men's shoes with holes in the bottom, and smudged some fireplace ash on the boy's cheeks so he could go door-to-door pretending to be a dirty-faced hobo.

Behind the scenes, John's mother was battling what she viewed as attempts by others to cash in on her private anguish. In addition to Maud Shaw, Jackie came down hard on Paul "Red" Fay when she learned he had written an account of his twenty-five-year friendship with Jack, titled *The Pleasure of His Company*. She demanded—and got—final approval.

Jackie directed the full force of her wrath at professional journalists like Jim Bishop, author of the hugely successful *The Day Lincoln Was Shot*. Jackie tried to get Random House to pull the plug on Bishop's

JFK book, *The Day Kennedy Was Shot,* and when that failed she approached historian William Manchester to write the full, authorized account of the assassination. In the end, Bishop's book would become a major critical and commercial success, and Jackie would become embroiled in a protracted war with Manchester over the content of his magnum opus, *Death of a President.*

For now, Jackie coped with stress the best she knew how—by jumping astride a horse and tearing through the countryside. She traded in her weekend rental on Long Island for a farmhouse in Bernardsville, New Jersey, and joined the exclusive Essex Hunt Club. Already an accomplished rider, Caroline was soon sailing over fences and water hazards along with her equestrienne mom. Jackie strapped a helmet on John as well, and put him through his paces with Leprechaun, the pony given to the Kennedys after JFK's triumphant visit to Ireland in the summer of 1963. Despite Jackie's best efforts and John's own fearless nature, his allergy to horses remained a serious impediment to John's chances of ever becoming a first-class horseman.

The children were scarcely wanting for excitement. That winter and into the spring of 1965, there were trips to Antigua—where John splashed around in the crystalline waters of the Caribbean while his sister learned to snorkel—as well as skiing holidays in Sun Valley, Stowe, and Gstaad. On the way back from Switzerland, Jackie and the children stopped in Rome for a private audience with Pope Paul VI, then jetted off to the Argentine pampas so John could meet some real caballeros working on the ranch of longtime Kennedy family acquaintance Miguel Carcona.

John and Caroline stayed behind that May 1966 when their mother traveled to Spain to catch Seville's famous *feria.* Still, they had no trouble charting her progress; newspapers and magazines were flooded with photographs of the "Radiant Conquistador"—looking regal in a high comb and white lace mantilla as she rode through Seville in an open carriage, sidestepping through the city streets on a white stallion, gazing down from her seat at the bullfights as three famous matadors dedicated their first kill to her while Princess Grace of Monaco sulked nearby.

Back home at 1040 Fifth, Provi showed John the latest copy of *Life* with Mommy on the cover. The photo of Jackie astride a stallion, in full Andalusian riding regalia—broad-brimmed hat, ruffled shirt, scarlet jacket, and chaps—made it clear to her countrymen that JFK's young widow had moved on with her life. While Caroline wondered aloud who owned the horse her mother was riding on, John was struck by how much she looked like the cowboys he had seen in South America. "Wow!" he told one member of the Secret Service Kiddie Detail. "Mommy looks just like a groucho!"

As soon as she got back to the United States, Jackie—named the world's most admired woman for the sixth year in a row—wasted no time making good on promises she had made to the children. On Memorial Day weekend 1966 she teamed up with Caroline to compete in a horse show in New Vernon, New Jersey, and wound up with a trophy for second place.

The next day in Hyannis Port, on what would have been Jack's forty-ninth birthday, Jackie fulfilled a promise to John that the president had made shortly before his death. She gave John a reconditioned Piper Cub observation plane. "Jack always said he was going to give John a real plane when he grew up," Jackie told JFK's friend Chuck Spalding. "Well, it's a little early, but now he has it—a real airplane." The World War II–vintage aircraft had no propeller and no engine, but that did not prevent John from climbing into the cockpit and taking off on a thrilling, make-believe aerial dogfight in the skies over Cape Cod.

Less than a month after returning from Spain, Jackie took off again—this time bringing along John and Caroline for a vacation in Hawaii with ex-Kennedy brother-in-law Peter Lawford and his children. The trip merely exacerbated tensions between Jackie and the other Kennedy women, who now referred to her contemptuously as "the Widder."

Choosing to remain behind at the Lawfords' Santa Monica, California, beach house, Pat Kennedy Lawford only learned that Jackie was going on the Hawaiian trip with her ex-husband when she read about it in the newspapers. Pat, who had officially divorced Peter just three months earlier, wasted no time ringing up his manager, Milt Ebbins.

According to Ebbins, the former Mrs. Peter Lawford was "so angry that she just kind of growled. She was *livid*."

Then Pat called Peter directly. "I won't put up with this!" she shrieked into the phone, pointing out to her ex-husband that their honeymoon had taken place in Hawaii. "How dare you go away with this woman!"

For the next seven weeks, Jackie and the children stayed in an oceanfront house near the base of Diamond Head, which they rented for three thousand dollars a month. Peter and the Lawford cousins were encamped down the beach at the Kahala Hilton.

It turned out that Pat Kennedy Lawford's suspicions—fanned by Eunice and Ethel, who now left the room anytime Jackie walked in—were warranted. Jackie and Peter had more in common than the fact that they both spoke impeccable French. Like Jackie, Lawford was an aristocrat, and often felt overwhelmed by the noisy, boisterous Kennedy clan. They also had their individual crosses to bear when it came to their Kennedy marriages. Jackie suffered though Jack's countless infidelities, while Peter confided to a friend that Pat crossed herself whenever they were about to make love.

Lawford had also suffered other indignities because of his status as "Brother-in-Lawford" to the Kennedys. After JFK decided to stay at Bing Crosby's estate instead of Frank Sinatra's when he visited Palm Springs, California, Ol' Blue Eyes blamed the perceived snub on Lawford. Shunned from that point on by one of the most powerful and feared men in the entertainment industry, Lawford would never quite regain his footing in Hollywood.

Now Jackie and the debonair British actor walked hand in hand on the beach, laughed over daiquiris at the Hilton piano bar, and exchanged knowing glances when they weren't in a quiet corner murmuring to each other in French. Things had gotten familiar enough for

Peter to start lighting two cigarettes in his mouth and then handing one to Jackie à la Paul Henreid and Bette Davis in the film *Now, Voyager.*

Lawford would later admit that he and Jackie had had a brief fling during the Hawaiian trip.

Oblivious to the intrigue that invariably swirled around his bewitchingly glamorous mother, John was having the time of his life—thanks in large part to three local boys he and Caroline met at the beach. The Miske brothers—eleven-year-old Tommy, thirteen-year-old Michael, and fourteen-year-old Gary—were dubious at first. But soon John was dashing into the surf at Wailea Beach ("John had no fear of the ocean," Gary Miske said), sliding down mud-covered hills in Nuuanu, and clambering over boulders at Sacred Falls. "You would think that we would get annoyed with a little five-year-old tagging along," said Tommy, who remembered that he and his brothers cracked up every time John pretended to be a sea captain squinting through a pretend spyglass. "But we found him to be a fun and adventuresome little kid."

John's fearless streak almost proved to be his undoing. Toward the end of their Hawaiian sojourn, one of Jackie's post-Dallas escorts, noted San Francisco architect John Warnecke, invited the children along on an overnight camping trip to the big island of Hawaii. The highlight of the evening was to be a luau, and John couldn't resist peering down into the smoldering pit where traditional dishes like Kalua pig and lomi lomi salmon were slowly cooking on hot embers.

Suddenly, Caroline let out a scream as John tumbled into the pit. The Miske brothers came running, and Secret Service agent Jack Walsh sprang into action. By the time Walsh managed to yank John to safety, Jackie's little boy had suffered severe burns to his hands, arms, and buttocks. He was rushed to the local hospital, given a battery of tests, then treated, bandaged, and released after a few hours.

To everyone's surprise, the normally vocal John remained calm and quiet throughout the whole ordeal. "That brave little kid," Tommy Miske said, "never once complained." At least John returned to New York with an unconventional souvenir—a white glove doctors in Hawaii gave him to protect the second-degree burns on his right hand—and a dramatic tale to share with his friends at St. David's.

That July, John was dolled up in a ruffled shirt, periwinkle blue shorts, and blue velvet sash for his role as a pageboy at the Newport wedding of his aunt Janet, Jackie's half sister. While he fidgeted and glowered through most of the ceremony (at one point John had to be restrained by Secret Service agents when another boy made fun of his getup), Caroline solemnly fulfilled her duties as a flower girl.

Incredibly, it had been only thirteen years since thousands of people clogged the streets of Newport to catch a glimpse of Senator Jack Kennedy and his stunning young bride as they emerged from St. Mary's Church. The crowds and the photographers had descended on Newport again, but this time to see the thirty-seven-year-old widow of the martyred president. The bride, elbowed aside by reporters and onlookers in their zeal to catch a glimpse of Jackie, turned to Lee Radziwill and wept.

After the service, Jackie and the children managed to wade through the sea of humanity to a waiting limousine—only to have paparazzi cram so tightly against the car doors that at first they couldn't be opened. Once inside the vehicle, a terrified Caroline started crying. John, however, pressed his face against the window and glowered at the photographers.

Later during the reception at Hammersmith Farm, John was able to let off steam with his equally scrappy cousins, darting in between tables and nearly knocking over an ice sculpture. His plan to surprise Jackie by letting two of Hugh Auchincloss's prize ponies into the crowded reception tent was foiled at the last minute by the father of the bride.

This playful streak notwithstanding, John was already impressing everyone with his even-tempered demeanor. "There was no one sweeter than John," St. David's assistant headmaster, Peter Clifton, remarked years later. "He had no guile in him. He's still like that. I have to give Jackie a lot of credit for that."

Even when John took a swing at another boy, it was invariably because he was being teased. "Some of the other children were jealous of all the attention that John got," the mother of another student said. "It wasn't John's fault, of course. He never struck any of the other parents as anything but a very polite, well-behaved little boy. He was not spoiled—not at all. I couldn't say that about some of the others."

Jackie was, said St. David's headmaster David Hume, "a sensible, affectionate mom who had a straight relationship with her son." Some people, he continued, "coo over their children." Jackie didn't coo. "When they reach out a hand, you should hold it. When they want to let go, you should let go. Jackie understood that."

Jackie also understood that, no matter how wonderful she was as a parent, there was little she could do to protect either of her children from those who were mentally unhinged. "I'm nerve-racked about the safety of the children," she told one of John's teachers. "There are so many nutcases about."

Jackie and Caroline were leaving St. Thomas More Church on East Eighty-ninth Street one Sunday when a woman ran up to Caroline and grabbed her by the arm. "Your mother is a wicked woman who has killed three people!" she shrieked as Jackie stood there, horrified. "And your father is still alive!"

With the help of the Secret Service, Jackie succeeded in pulling the deranged woman off, and she was taken to Bellevue Hospital for observation. "It was terrible, prying her loose," Jackie recalled years later. "I still haven't gotten over that strange woman."

Jackie always tried to walk her son home from school each day, and she was more determined than ever that November 22, 1966—the third anniversary of her husband's assassination—not be any different. As they left the school, however, Jackie realized that several students were trailing them. They were less than halfway down the block when one of the children yelled, "Your father's dead! Your father's dead!" The others quickly joined in the chant.

The cruel words were all too familiar to John's mother. "You know how children are," said Jackie. "They've even said it to me when I've run into them at school, as if . . . Well, this day John listened to them saying it over and over, and he didn't say a word."

What John did do was take his mother's hand and squeeze it firmly—without ever pausing to look back at their tormentors. Jackie later said it was "as if he was trying to reassure me that things were all right. And so we walked home together, with the children following us."

———

JOHN WAS ONLY six years old and already exhibiting a keen awareness of other people's feelings—especially his mother's. "He surprises me in so many ways," Jackie said. "He seems so much more than one would expect of a child of six. Sometimes it almost seems as if he is trying to protect me instead of just the other way around."

To be sure, Jackie was finding it impossible to shield her children from the front-page headlines being generated by her ongoing feud with William Manchester over his book *The Death of a President*. She claimed to have spoken to Manchester "in the evening and alone, and it's rather hard to stop when the floodgates open." What she feared most was exposing her children to the gory details of their father's death.

"We didn't talk about it, of course," Jackie said. "But children pick things up . . . There was no way to keep them from passing newsstands going to and from school. It was natural for them to look at the magazines and the headlines. Or be told something in school or on the street. It isn't always easy for the children."

"Jackie worried endlessly about Caroline and John," Plimpton said. "But I think she focused even more attention on John because she worried that Jack's memory would be overshadowed by her fame. Caroline was older, and she would never forget her father—Jackie was confident of that. She wasn't so sure about John."

"He'll never remember his father. He was too young," Jackie admitted saying to herself. "But now," she decided in early 1967, "I think he will." True to her nature, Jackie was not about to leave anything to chance. "I want to help him go back and find his father," she stated flatly. " It can be done . . ."

From this point on, Jackie made sure that John was constantly exposed to the people who knew John best—from longtime pals like Red

Fay, Chuck Spalding, Oleg Cassini, Bill Walton, and his ubiquitous sidekick Dave Powers to such New Frontier stalwarts as Pierre Salinger, Theodore Sorensen, and Arthur Schlesinger Jr. These were the folks "who knew Jack well and the things Jack liked to do." As long as they were around, she reasoned, "each day John will be getting to know his father."

Powers did more than just regale John with tales of his father's wartime heroism and political good deeds. Although Jack cared little about professional athletics—an uncommon trait in a politician—Powers was an avid sports fan. "There will always be a Dave Powers to talk sports with him," Jackie said, admitting that she drew a blank when John brought up the names of sports figures like Cassius Clay and Bubba Smith. "John," she sighed, "seems to know an awful lot about sports . . ."

Jackie claimed her main contribution was to fill her son in on "the little things, like 'Oh, don't worry about your spelling. Your father couldn't spell very well, either.' That pleases him, you can bet." She also walked John across the street from their first Fifth Avenue apartment to the Metropolitan Museum of Art, which housed one of the world's greatest collections of medieval armor. While the little boy gazed up in wonder at helmeted knights on horseback and the banners and flags unfurled on the Gothic stone walls, Jackie regaled him with tales of King Arthur's Round Table—and made sure he understood these were the same Camelot stories that his father loved when *he* was a boy.

No one did more to keep JFK's memory alive than John's uncles. At Hyannis Port, Bobby playfully tossed John in the surf and roughhoused with him on the lawn of the Kennedy compound while Teddy took his nephew out in Nantucket Sound aboard Jack's twenty-six-foot sailboat *Victura*. There were other, "even smaller things" that Jackie felt brought John "closer to Jack. The school insists that children even as young as John must wear neckties. That was all right with him. It gave him a chance to wear one of his father's PT-boat tie pins."

That summer of 1967, John and Caroline went along with Jackie on their first trip to Ireland. Despite attempts to hold the press at bay—they spent much of their time behind closed gates at Woodstown House, a sixty-room Georgian manor house rented for them by their wealthy New Jersey friends Murray and Peggy McDonnell—busloads of reporters following them everywhere.

One morning John was sprinting through a field when he abruptly stopped and turned back to his mother. "There's electricity in the grass," he yelled. "I got a shock! Electricity!" It didn't take long for Jackie to figure out that this was the first time John, who was used to running across the meticulously trimmed lawns at Hyannis Port, Palm Beach, and Hammersmith Farm, had ever encountered nettles.

During an afternoon jaunt to Woodstown Beach, Caroline frolicked with a group of local children in the chilly waters of Waterford Harbor and a grim-faced John built sand castles—all while dozens of photographers encircled them, snapping away. Clearly unhappy with all the attention, John broke away and, with his Secret Service detail shadowing him, headed straight for a nearby candy store.

"What do you want, dear?" the lady behind the counter asked while reporters streamed inside and began taking notes.

"Everything," John replied.

The salesclerk smiled. "Now," she said, "you know you can't have everything."

"I can, too!" John shouted back before his chagrined mom appeared to take him away.

Spending time in the ancestral home of Duganstown, John impressed his distant Kennedy cousins by singing "When Irish Eyes Are Smiling" straight through—all thanks to Uncle Teddy, who taught John all the words to the song and then rehearsed with him until he mastered it.

Their Irish escapade nearly turned to tragedy when Jackie sneaked off to a local beach and, caught in the undertow, came perilously close to being swept out to sea. "The tide was rushing in with such force," she later recalled, "that if I did not make the end spit of land opposite, I would be swept into a bay twelve miles long."

Jackie searched the coastline, but "there was no one in sight to yell to. I was becoming exhausted, swallowing water and slipping past the spit of land," she said. It was then that she "felt a great porpoise at my side." The porpoise was Jack Walsh, the same Secret Service agent who had rescued John in Hawaii. Jackie hadn't realized that Walsh, fearing for her safety but honoring her desire for privacy, had secretly followed her that night. "He set his shoulder against mine and together we made it to the spit. Then I sat on the beach coughing up seawater for half an hour while he found a poor itinerant and borrowed a blanket for me." With no idea where the sea had deposited them, Jackie and Walsh walked more than a mile before finally coming to a dirt road.

It had been the narrowest of escapes, and Jackie knew it. Although she would describe the incident in chilling detail years later, Jackie asked that the children not be told what happened. "They have suffered so much already," she explained. "Can you imagine how upsetting it would be for them to think they almost lost their mother, too?" In the meantime, she recommended that Walsh be cited for valor, and that he head up her detail in New York.

That fall, John settled back into his school routine, taking his place among the other first-graders at St. David's. Jackie was proud of both of her children's academic accomplishments—Caroline was more deserving, perhaps—but she fretted that they might become "just two kids living on Fifth Avenue and going to nice schools."

Uncle Bobby, for one, was not about to let that happen. He told them "about the rats and about terrible living conditions that exist right here in the midst of a rich city," Jackie said, and when he described "broken windows letting in the cold," John "was so touched by that that he said he'd go to work and use the money he made to put windows in those houses."

Both Kennedy children were also shocked to learn that countless thousands of children their age never had or likely would receive Christmas presents. That Christmas of 1967, John and Caroline gathered up most of their toys and asked Jackie to give them "to the poor children in Harlem."

The irrepressibly adventurous Jackie was also intent on exploring the world beyond the doorman-guarded doors of 1040 Fifth Avenue.

Before she struck out on solo excursions to Southeast Asia and Mexico, Jackie made sure the children's new nanny had matters well in hand. Dark-haired, slender Marta Sgubin was a devout Roman Catholic who spoke French, Italian, Spanish, and German as well as English. Although decidedly more reserved than Maud Shaw, Sgubin made sure they did their homework on time, and that John, in particular, behaved. She also ate dinner with the children, played games with them, tucked them into bed, and then woke them up at seven the next morning. Sgubin took turns with Jackie walking the children to school. It soon became obvious, said Plimpton, "that they both adored her."

Secure in the knowledge that John and Caroline would be safe in the new governess's capable hands, Jackie jetted off to Cambodia, ostensibly to tour the fabled ruins of Angkor Wat. In truth, Jackie was being sent on a delicate diplomatic mission to charm Cambodia's ruler, Prince Norodom Sihanouk, who in 1965 had severed relations with the United States over its growing involvement in Vietnam.

From the very beginning, Jackie's trip to Southeast Asia had all the hallmarks of a state visit. Once again following their mother's progress in the papers, John and Caroline were shown pictures of Jackie being greeted in Phnom Penh by two hundred schoolgirls in bright green *sampots*, the traditional Cambodian dress, and walking barefoot among the ancient ruins of Angkor Wat. John was particularly impressed by photos of Jackie feeding bananas to Prince Sihanouk's sacred white elephants, peels and all.

John and Caroline also came across newspaper and magazine stories linking their mother to a man—in this case, Lord Harlech. In the dark days following Dallas, Jackie leaned heavily on the former David Ormsby-Gore and his wife, Sissie, for emotional support. When Sissie was killed in a car crash in Wales just two weeks before Jackie's planned trip to Ireland, Jackie rushed to comfort her grieving friend. (Ironically, Lord Harlech himself would be killed in an automobile accident in 1985.)

Rampant speculation about a blossoming romance between Jackie, then thirty-seven, and the forty-nine-year-old British peer eventually compelled Lord Harlech to issue a formal statement. Of rumors that there was anything other than friendship between them, he could only say, "I deny it flatly."

Jackie's trip to the ancient Mayan ruins on Mexico's Yucatán Peninsula in March 1968 also proved grist for the gossip mill, only this time speculation centered on another old friend serving as her escort—Ros Gilpatric. In truth, Gilpatric, still married to the third of his five wives, was besotted with Jackie. "At that point, we were very much in love, yes," said Gilpatric, who planned to get a divorce and ask Jackie to marry him. "The trip to Mexico was very romantic, and Jackie surprised me by being so free and open about us."

He also found something else surprising—the number of times Jackie brought up the name of yet another man. "Even at the most romantic moments," Gilpatric said, "she kept mentioning Aristotle Onassis's name—what did I think of him? Was he as rich as they said he was? Was he, as some people said, a 'pirate'? She also said she felt he was very protective toward her, and that he cared about the children and their welfare. She was weighing the pros and cons, and it became very clear very fast that Onassis was the man who most intrigued her. Not me, not even Bobby."

———

NEITHER JOHN NOR Caroline was old enough to fathom what all the commotion was about. They had both met Lord Harlech and Gilpatric several times, and were not at all surprised to see newspaper photos of the two gray-haired gentlemen escorting their mother on her foreign trips. But the man who pursued Jackie more relentlessly than anyone else during this period was never even mentioned in the papers as a potential love interest for the former first lady.

John and Caroline were certainly unaware of how serious things had become between their mother and Onassis. By taking an apartment in Jackie's Upper East Side neighborhood and then showering her with flowers, gifts, and heartfelt love notes, the cigar-chomping Greek had managed to charm his way into Jackie's bed. Short (five feet four to

Jackie's five feet nine), squat, swarthy, and far from handsome, Onassis had something more than looks to recommend him. He boasted his own fleet of supertankers, his own airline (Olympic Airways), one of the world's most lavishly appointed yachts, mansions in Paris and Athens, and his own private island, Skorpios.

A relentless social climber, he used every conceivable ruse to insinuate himself into international society. Conversant in Spanish, French, German, and English as well as his native Greek, he spoke knowledgeably about every subject from British history and opera to ballet, art, and polo.

RFK viewed Onassis as "a complete rogue on the grand scale," and with good reason. It was only by ruthlessly pursuing a series of blatantly crooked business deals that Onassis was able to parlay an initial stake of only sixty dollars into a half-billion-dollar empire. In the process, he also seduced some of the twentieth century's most intriguing women—including Argentina's Evita Perón and Joe Kennedy's longtime mistress, silent screen legend Gloria Swanson of *Sunset Boulevard* fame.

To shore up an alliance with fellow shipping magnate Stavros Livanos, forty-six-year-old Onassis then married Livanos's daughter Athina ("Tina"), who was just seventeen at the time. That marriage, which produced two children, Alexander and Christina, imploded in 1959, when Tina decided to take a midnight stroll on the deck of the *Christina* and caught her husband and prima donna *assoluta* Maria Callas making love in the yacht's mirrored bar.

The ruthless tycoon and the outrageously temperamental opera star were perfectly suited for each other. Through a combination of grit, ambition, talent, and no small amount of ruthlessness, both had managed to claw their way to the peak of their chosen fields. Callas would have become Mrs. Onassis as early as 1960 had it not been for the opposition of the Onassis children. According to Ari's aide Johnny Meyer, Alexandra and Christina "hated" Callas. They called her, simply and contemptuously, "the Singer."

Now that Ari ("Aristo" to his closest friends) was making his intentions clear to Jackie, she was torn between the prospect of marrying the wealthy and powerful foreigner and her emotionally satisfying but ultimately dead-end extramarital relationship with Bobby. "She was always thinking of what was best for the children," Tish Baldrige said, "and as far as she was concerned, Bobby was always best."

That changed when Bobby decided to challenge Lyndon Johnson for his party's nomination in 1968. Jackie and Ros Gilpatric were exploring the ruins at Chichen Itza in Mexico when the news reached them that Bobby was running for president. Not long after, LBJ shocked the nation by announcing that he would not seek reelection for a second full term.

As far as Jackie was concerned, with Johnson out of the way Bobby had a clear path to the White House. "Do you know what will happen to Bobby?" she later asked Arthur Schlesinger. "The same thing that happened to Jack. There is so much hatred in this country, and more people hate Bobby than hated Jack . . . I've told Bobby this, but he isn't fatalistic, like me."

Bobby shrugged off Jackie's prophecies of doom. What troubled him now was the fact that she was seriously mulling over the idea of marrying Onassis. The mere thought of JFK's sainted widow carrying on with a shadowy foreigner would inevitably leave a sour taste in voters' mouths. But *marriage*? "For God's sake, Jackie," Bobby pleaded, "this could cost me five states."

For his part, Onassis was thrilled that Bobby had decided to run. He knew that his chief rival for Jackie's affections would now be too preoccupied with his presidential campaign to cater to Jackie's needs or, equally important, to fulfill his duties as a surrogate dad to John and Caroline. "Now," Ari told Johnny Meyer, "the kid has other fish to fry."

"The Greek" was angling for the biggest prize of all. According to one of Ari's friends, the *New York Post* columnist Doris Lilly, "everything was a contest . . . who had the most money, the biggest yacht, the grandest houses. It was no different with women, and Ari was accustomed to winning."

Onassis, whose shady business dealings made him the target of numerous Justice Department investigations over the years, had other reasons for wooing Jackie so aggressively. "Onassis knows that Jackie is an icon," Meyer said, "and he feels that if he marries her the U.S. government will get off his back." Onassis also told Meyer that by marrying Jackie he could remove all obstacles that stood in the way of the giant "super port" he had long envisioned for his tankers at Durham Point, New Hampshire.

JFK's children were also an important part of the equation. "Onassis knew that the world was in love with Caroline and John," Lilly said, "and he figured no one would want to upset them by going after their stepfather, no matter who he was." John was especially important to Onassis because "he embodied the future of the Kennedy dynasty. Ari couldn't resist the idea of shaping a future president, of having that kind of power and influence stretching into the next century."

Bobby was so appalled at the thought of Onassis becoming his brother-in-law that he dispatched Ethel and Teddy's wife, Joan, to New York to try to bring Jackie back to her senses. But it was only after Cardinal Cushing intervened that Jackie agreed to postpone her decision until after the election—ostensibly for Bobby's sake. Cushing pointed out that, over and above Onassis's checkered past, the Vatican might not look kindly on President Kennedy's widow marrying a divorced man.

Second-grader John was sitting in his class at St. David's on April 4, 1968, when an older student came into room and whispered the news in his teacher's ear: Martin Luther King had been gunned down outside his Memphis motel room. JFK had introduced his children to the Nobel Peace Prize winner in the Oval Office, and Jackie again found herself in the position of having to explain to John and Caroline why anyone would want to kill a great man like Dr. King.

In truth, Jackie loathed the civil rights leader. Bobby and Jack both learned from FBI tapes of King's private conversations that he had planned and conducted an "orgy" that took place in his hotel room after delivering his famous "I Have a Dream" speech in August 1963.

"Oh, but, Jack," she said at the time, "that's so terrible. I mean, that man is, you know, such a phony, then."

Although JFK cautioned her not to be "too judgmental" about King's sexual escapades—a stance that hardly seemed surprising, given Kennedy's own track record in this area—Jackie's doubts about King were confirmed by tapes Bobby played for her following the assassination. In them, King ridiculed Cardinal Cushing's behavior at the funeral, claiming the elderly cleric was drunk. In her own taped conversations with Arthur Schlesinger, she also pointed out that King could be heard on the FBI tapes laughing about "how they almost dropped the coffin. Well, I mean," Jackie continued to fume, "Martin Luther King is really a tricky person . . . I just can't see a picture of Martin Luther King without thinking, 'That man's terrible!' "

Her opinion of King was not about to change overnight. But now that King had joined her husband in America's pantheon of martyred leaders, Jackie did feel a kinship of sorts with his widow. Reluctant to overshadow Coretta Scott King, Jackie initially planned to meet with her at some unspecified place after the funeral, and in private. When Bobby called Mrs. King the next day to offer his condolences, however, she asked if he might arrange for Jackie to accompany him to the funeral in Atlanta. Appreciating the symbolic value of having Jackie photographed alongside King's grieving widow, RFK was all too happy to oblige.

The Roman Catholic Church, Jackie later told key RFK adviser Frank Mankiewicz, "is at its best only at the time of death. The rest of the time it's often rather silly little men running around in their black suits. I'll tell you who else understand death are the black churches." At King's funeral, she said, "I was looking at those faces, and I realized that they know death. They see it all the time and they're ready for it . . . We know death . . . As a matter of fact," she confided in this unguarded moment, "if it weren't for the children, we'd welcome it."

Always conscious of posterity, Jackie decided that now was the time to preserve her children on canvas. She commissioned New York artist

Aaron Shikler to paint portraits of ten-year-old Caroline and seven-year-old John at the New York apartment. "They look just right to me now," she told Shikler. "I would like to remember them at this age, as they are, just now."

"John was all boy—restless, impatient, all elbows and knees," the artist recalled. Despite the fact that he had his pet guinea pig to keep him company, he was "monumentally bored with the whole business. The sooner he could get out of the room," Shikler added, "the better. He hates to pose." The dreamlike portraits—of Jackie lounging on a sofa with both children and of John immersed in a book—so impressed Jackie that she asked Shikler to paint JFK's official White House portrait as well as her own.

Jackie was determined that someday Bobby's portrait would hang at 1600 Pennsylvania Avenue as well. She was, according to Arthur Schlesinger Jr., "quite simply Bobby's single most important asset in the campaign. She said she was willing to swallow her pride and do anything for him, and she did." Yet not everyone was particularly appreciative of Jackie's slavish devotion to the candidate. When polls showed Bobby pulling ahead of his principal rival for the nomination, Vice President Hubert Humphrey, there was jubilation at the Kennedy compound in Hyannis Port. "Oh, Bobby," Jackie said, "won't it be wonderful when we get back in the White House?"

"What do you mean *we*?" Ethel barked.

Stricken, Jackie fled the room. She wanted John and Caroline to remain close to their Kennedy relatives—to share in their father's legacy—but she also knew that she needed to chart a separate course for herself and the children. It didn't help that the United States of the late 1960s seemed to be descending into chaos; wherever he looked, John saw gruesome photos of Vietnam casualties, violent antiwar street protests, and bloody race riots that swept the nation in the wake of King's assassination.

"I don't want them growing up afraid," Jackie said of her children. "They have a right to a carefree life, to the extent that I can make one for them." There were few men in the world who could provide a level of physical, financial, and emotional security befitting the children of President Kennedy. Aristotle Onassis, Jackie had to conclude, was certainly one of them.

The sheer size of Onassis's fortune was a major factor, to be sure. "As far as Jackie was concerned," Gore Vidal said, "the only thing better than a rich man was an obscenely rich man." Then there was the matter of Ari's undeniable charm. "He was short, ugly, but he had far more presence than far better-looking men," Taki Theodoracopulos observed. "He wasn't awed by women. He was extremely generous, and he was a great flatterer. Everything about him was bigger than life. He was a real-life Zorba the Greek."

Still, Jackie felt that before she committed herself to anything, the children would have to get to know this larger-than-life Zorba. That Easter, Onassis flew Jackie and John to Palm Beach on his private jet while Caroline stayed behind. Onassis made an overt effort to win the boy over with hugs and gifts; John warmed to the genial, panda-like grandfather figure immediately.

In May 1968, Jackie again left John and Caroline in their nanny's care and embarked on a four-day Virgin Islands cruise with Ari aboard the *Christina*. Torn between Bobby and Onassis, spent both physically and emotionally, Jackie crumbled. For most of the cruise she was locked in her cabin, trying not to succumb to seasickness.

Once back on home turf, Jackie did her best to throw the press off Onassis's scent by attending a series of high-profile functions with old standby escorts like Ros Gilpatric and Lord Harlech. On June 4, 1968— the day of the crucial winner-take-all California primary—Jackie made two afternoon campaign appearances for Bobby in New York, had a late dinner with Gilpatric at her apartment, and then waited for word from Los Angeles.

When Bobby got to his fifth-floor suite at the Ambassador Hotel in Los Angeles, he found flowers and a magnum of Dom Perignon waiting for him. "The flowers are for your room, and the champagne is for you after you win the primary. Jackie." Around 11 p.m. Eastern Time, George Plimpton, who had been with RFK on the campaign trail in California, called with the news: Bobby had won by a wide margin. "That's *wonderful*, George," Jackie said. "Tell Bobby I love him." Plimpton would later regret that, amid all the excitement, he never managed to convey Jackie's final message to Bobby.

———

JACKIE STAYED UP watching the returns on television for another four hours, and finally turned in around 3:15 a.m. A half hour later, the phone rang. Stas and Lee Radziwill were calling from London, where the BBC was reporting breaking news from the United States.

"Jackie, how's Bobby?" Stas asked.

"He's fine. He's terrific," Jackie replied. "You heard that he won California by fifty-three percent, didn't you?"

"But, Jackie," Radziwill said, "he's been shot. It happened just a few minutes ago."

They waited for what seemed like an eternity for Jackie to react. "No!" Jackie cried. "It can't have happened. No! It can't have happened!"

John and Caroline, tucked in their beds at the other end of the sprawling apartment, somehow managed to sleep through their mother's screams.

The most dire of Jackie's warnings had come true: After thanking supporters in the Ambassador ballroom, Bobby was leaving through the hotel's pantry when shots rang out. A young Palestinian named Sirhan Sirhan, angered over the defeat of the Arabs in the recent Six-Day War with U.S.-supported ally Israel, had lunged from the shadows and fired six shots at Bobby. Within seconds, Jack's little brother was lying on the floor in a pool of blood, his eyes open, while Olympic decathlon champion Rafer Johnson and pro football legend Roosevelt Grier pried the pistol from Sirhan's hand. Ethel knelt next to him, whispering, "Oh my God, oh my God," while a busboy pressed a rosary in Bobby's hand and cradled his head.

Jackie prepared to get on the first available flight to Los Angeles, but first she had to decide how to break the news to the children. She had relied on grandmotherly Maud Shaw to tell them when Patrick and Jack had died, but this time she could not bring herself to burden Marta Sgubin or anyone else with the responsibility.

Before leaving for the airport, Jackie woke the children up gently and brought them into her room. "Something has happened to Uncle Bobby," she told them, "and I have to fly out to California to be with him."

"What happened to Uncle Bobby?" Caroline asked as John wiped the sleep from his eyes.

"A very bad man shot him," Jackie answered. "The doctors are doing everything they can for Uncle Bobby right now . . ." Before she could finish her sentence, Caroline burst into tears and John quickly followed suit. At seven, he could comprehend the enormity of what had happened—and experience the loss in a way he had been unable to following his own father's assassination in Dallas.

John would spend the rest of his life wondering if he really remembered his father at all, but Uncle Bobby and this horrible day—those things would haunt him for the rest of his life.

Chuck Spalding was waiting for Jackie when she stepped off the plane in Los Angeles. "She got off the plane wearing those dark glasses," he said, "but she seemed very calm, very much in control." At this point, Jackie only knew what the rest of the world knew—that Robert F. Kennedy had been shot in the head, neck, and right side, and that he had undergone four hours of surgery at Good Samaritan Hospital.

"How is he doing, Chuck?" she asked. "Give it to me straight."

"He's dying, Jackie," Spalding replied. "He's dying."

At the hospital, Jackie joined Ethel, Ted Kennedy, Spalding, Plimpton, Pierre Salinger, longtime Kennedy advisor Richard Goodwin, and several other members of RFK's inner circle in keeping vigil outside his hospital room. They were brought into the room two by two to visit him as he lingered for hours, kept alive on a respirator. In remembering this grim scene, Plimpton recalled that he was most impressed by the fact that "Bobby looked *huge*. He was on this very high bed, and he was up at an angle. His head was in this big white bandage. He looked like a medieval knight. It was like visiting a tomb at Westminster Abbey."

Eventually told by doctors that there was no hope for recovery, no one present was willing to make the hard decision and pull the plug. Ethel, in particular, refused. "I won't kill Bobby," she protested. "I won't." Taking control of the situation, Jackie signed the consent form authorizing doctors to turn off Bobby's respirator. "Nobody else," Goodwin said, "had the nerve to do it." With Ethel holding his hand, Bobby died on June 6 at 1:44 a.m. Pacific Time. He was forty-two.

Five minutes after Bobby's death was announced, Onassis called his closest friend, Costa Gratsos, in Athens. "She's free of the Kennedys," Onassis gloated. "The last link broke." Gratsos was not surprised at his friend's callous reaction. "As far as Aristo was concerned," Gratsos said, "his biggest headache had been eliminated."

Lyndon Johnson was no fan of Bobby, either, but out of respect for the Kennedy family and all that Bobby represented to the nation, he promptly dispatched Air Force One to pick up RFK's body and fly it back to New York. Just four and a half years after Dallas, Jackie was once again accompanying home the body of the man she loved.

Two days later, President Johnson led the two thousand mourners who crammed into New York City's St. Patrick's Cathedral to pay their last respects. Ethel, pregnant with Bobby's eleventh child, maintained her composure while the sole surviving Kennedy brother delivered his moving eulogy just feet from RFK's flag-draped coffin. "My brother need not be idealized," Teddy said, struggling to control his emotions, "or enlarged in death beyond what he was in life, to be remembered simply as a good and decent man, who saw wrong and tried to right it, saw suffering and tried to heal it, saw war and tried to stop it . . ."

Wearing a black lace mantilla, her face etched with grief, Jackie was, said Salinger, "in a trance, just completely in shock. It just defied belief that she—that we—would be reliving this nightmare."

John, proudly wearing his PT-109 tie clasp, took part in the requiem Mass with his sister and the other Kennedy children. While Caroline had cried when Mommy called with the terrible news that Uncle Bobby had died, John was clearly most worried about the obvious change in his mother. Throughout the funeral, he could be seen leaning forward in his pew and checking on Jackie.

As everyone filed out of the cathedral, Lady Bird Johnson reached out her hand to comfort her fellow first lady and even called out Jackie's name. "She looked at me as if from a great distance," Lady Bird recalled, "as though I were an apparition."

"It was just too much for her. Jackie was out of it—a zombie," said Spalding, who could see that John was now concerned for his mother's mental well-being. "John really was too young to see how Jack's death had really just flattened her, but now he got it. I felt so sorry for him, and for Caroline, too, of course."

Later, John joined his mother and sister aboard the twenty-one-car funeral train that carried Bobby's body to Washington for burial at Arlington. More than two million people—some with their hands on their hearts, others applauding or singing "The Battle Hymn of the Republic," many weeping openly—lined the 226-mile route as the train slowly made its way to the capital. As if to lend credence to the increasingly popular notion of a "Kennedy Curse," a passing train killed two of the spectators who had come to say farewell to Bobby, and badly injured six others. Later, as the funeral train rolled slowly through Trenton, New Jersey, a teenager watching from atop a freight car accidentally brushed against a power line and was critically burned. Before the train reached its destination, John heard all the grisly details from older cousins who witnessed both accidents.

It was dark by the time the train arrived in Washington, and the fifteen-minute graveside service at Arlington would be illuminated only by long, tapered candles handed out to the mourners. John, along with his aunts, uncles, and cousins, knelt to kiss the coffin before it was lowered into the ground.

When it was over, Ethel left alone, clutching to her breast the folded American flag that had covered her husband's coffin. Jackie remained behind with John and Caroline, all three bowing their heads in prayer beside the freshly dug grave. After a few minutes, Jackie took one of the floral pieces that had covered the casket—a small bunch of daisies—and led the children to their father's grave just twenty yards away. John and Caroline knelt there, too, and looked on as their mother lovingly placed Bobby's daisies on Jack's grave. "Oh Jack," John heard his mother whisper. "Oh Bobby . . ."

John's mother explained to him why
she's marrying a frog instead of a prince.
Because when he croaks, we'll all be rich!
—Classmate to John before Jackie's marriage to
Aristotle Onassis (resulting in John's
giving the classmate a bloody lip)

He comes spitting in my room, jabbing left and right,
Shouting, OK, Caroline, ready for a fight?
He is trying to blow us up with his chemistry set.
He has killed all the plants but we've escaped as yet.
—Caroline's poem about her brother,
a Christmas present to their grandmother Rose Kennedy

I don't want John to grow up to be
some "Screw you, Charlie" guy.
—Jackie

A Shoe Box Full of Diamonds

I hate this country," Jackie told Pierre Salinger the day after Bobby's funeral. "I despise America, and I don't want my children to live here anymore. If they are killing Kennedys, my kids are the number one targets. I have the two main targets. I want to get out of this country!"

Given the gossip swirling about her relationship with Onassis, it was no surprise that Ari was not among the two thousand people invited to Bobby's funeral. Lord Harlech, one of the ten pallbearers, felt it was obvious that Onassis's presence would have been "in very poor taste."

For the moment, taste was not at the top of Jackie's list of things to look for in a mate. She not only feared for the safety of her children, but she also craved privacy, seclusion—a life where all three of the people Jack left behind wouldn't be hounded by the press essentially around the clock.

It was becoming increasingly clear that Ari was the solution to all of Jackie's problems. No one, it seemed, was better equipped to provide for the safety of John and Caroline. The family's current four-man Secret Service detail paled in comparison to Onassis's machine-gun-equipped, seventy-five-member security force augmented by attack dogs. Privacy? Onassis offered that and much more behind the gates of his palatial homes in Athens, Paris, and Montevideo, Uruguay—not to mention aboard the *Christina*, in penthouse suites sprinkled across the globe, and on his own private island of Skorpios.

Just days after Bobby was laid to rest, Ari arrived at Hammersmith Farm with his daughter, Christina, in tow. "It was definitely a case of 'Ari to the rescue,' " said Jackie's columnist friend Aileen Mehle, better known as Suzy. "He showered jewels on her, he *wooed* her . . . He was repulsive, of course, but it wasn't just the money. He was *so* alive, so vibrant, and so vigorous. He was this life force."

For the remainder of the summer, Jackie led a charm offensive designed to persuade friends and family in New York, Newport, Hyannis Port, and Palm Beach that Onassis was suitable marriage material for JFK's widow. She failed miserably. "The term 'Eurotrash' hadn't been invented yet," Truman Capote said, "but that's definitely what they thought old Ari *was*."

Nor did it help that everyone knew Onassis was still carrying on his affair with Callas. "Everybody here knows three things about Aristotle Onassis," he told Johnny Meyer. Those three things: "I'm fucking Maria Callas, I'm fucking Jacqueline Kennedy—and I'm fucking rich." In the end, he had no illusions about ever being accepted by the Kennedys, the Auchinclosses, or any of Jackie's Social Register crowd. "They hate," he told Gratsos, "my Greek guts."

Onassis understood that, in addition to Jackie, there were only two people whose opinion mattered—one was ten years old, the other, seven. In Jackie's eyes, Bobby was the perfect surrogate father and male role model for her son. Now she was particularly anxious about what impact Bobby's death would have on John, and Ari faced the formidable task of convincing her that he could fill the void.

"When Ari wanted something," his friend Doris Lilly said, "he stopped at nothing to get it. And he wanted Jackie's kids to love him, especially John." Onassis waded into the surf with both children, went on long walks with them, bought them ice cream, and even spent hours with Caroline and John hunched over board games and puzzles. It certainly helped that, whenever he came to visit, he was trailed by servants carrying armloads of toys purchased from New York's premier toy store, FAO Schwarz.

Ari pulled out all the stops with John. "You know what you and I are, John?" he would ask the little boy. "We are *filaracos.*" *Filaracos,* Ari hastened to remind him, is the Greek word for "buddies."

Wherever they went, John and Onassis were difficult to miss—the stocky, dour-faced, pinky-ring-flashing mogul and everyone's favorite, tousle-haired all-American son. Shadowed by a half dozen hulking bodyguards, this odd couple turned heads in baseball stadiums, movie theaters, and amusement parks. On Cape Cod, Onassis even took the boy fishing. "Here," he said, handing John two crisp hundred-dollar bills. "Go buy some worms."

It also helped that Ari clearly made Mummy, as John called her, happy. "Jackie bounced back much more quickly after Bobby's death," Gilpatric said. "There wasn't that element of doubt about what she would do next. Onassis was right there with the solution: him."

Ari's spectacular wealth was a big part of the equation. For the first time in her life, she would no longer be treated as the poor relation. "The Kennedy women had always flaunted their money and power," George Smathers said. "This was Jackie's opportunity to say to them, 'Okay, what are you going to say now that I can buy and sell you?'"

As important as the money undoubtedly was, it was equally true that Jackie and Ari behaved for all intents and purposes like two people very much in love. Whether she was in New York or Hyannis Port or London; Jackie always awoke to a bouquet of orchids or roses and the note J.I.L.Y. (for "Jackie I Love You").

According to Larry Newman, the Kennedys' longtime next-door neighbor in Hyannis Port, they appeared to be "a far more romantic couple than Jack and Jackie—at least that's the way it looked early on."

Indeed, until that final year leading up to Dallas, Jack and Jackie seldom showed tenderness toward one another. "Jackie could be very playful, try and give Jack a hug or a kiss," Newman remembered, "but he'd turn very stiff . . . I felt sorry for Jackie when that happened." With

Onassis, on the other hand, things "were totally different. They'd hold hands, or they'd have their arms around each other. Sometimes they'd do these cute little dance steps, or they'd be *whistling . . .*"

Older and of a more naturally analytical nature than her brother, Caroline took a cautious approach toward the new man in her mother's life. After all, she still cut pictures of her father out of newspapers and magazines to add to the collection she started on November 22, 1963. By this point, they papered the walls of her bedroom. The loss of her uncle had left her feeling even more lost and vulnerable. "She had been so close to Bobby," Plimpton said, "that it took maybe a little longer for her to warm up to Onassis. But she liked Ari, absolutely. It was impossible not to when he turned on the Greek charm."

John was no less loyal to the memory of his dad. Whenever another child was visiting, he would inevitably ask, "Would you like to hear my father?" Then he turned to a small stack of records and selected one to play—usually JFK's inaugural address or his rousing "Ich bin ein Berliner" speech. "Jackie played these for him to keep the connection alive in John's mind," Tish Baldrige said. "I think it became a ritual for him. He was also proud. Why *wouldn't* the other boys want to hear his famous daddy?" After a few respectful minutes listening to Jack intone "Ask not what your country can do for you," John returned to the floor to play.

Onassis was savvy enough to listen attentively when John played his daddy's speeches, and to praise the late president as a great and good man, someone he deeply admired and respected. Jackie's wily lover stressed to John that no one could replace Jack Kennedy in their lives—certainly not him, although he would do his best to try to make John's mother happy.

It would turn out to be an expensive undertaking. Notwithstanding all the joy Ari seemed to bring her, Jackie enlisted Teddy's help in negotiating a prenuptial agreement with Onassis. That August, they made a special trip to Skorpios to hammer out the details. But when the Massachusetts senator made a spectacle of himself after getting drunk on ouzo, Jackie turned instead to her no-nonsense financial adviser, André

Meyer. In the end Meyer succeeded in getting Ari to ante up $3 million in cash for Jackie up front and a $1 million trust fund for each of her children.

As the juggernaut rolled on, John and Caroline were kept completely in the dark about their mother's intentions. Not once did their mother mention the word *marriage* when discussing Mr. Onassis; as far as the children were concerned, he was, like Lord Harlech, Gilpatric, and the rest, just one in the passing parade of well-dressed older gentlemen Mummy had spent time with since Daddy's death.

While the grown-ups continued to make wedding preparations in secret, another drama was unfolding at Jackie's Bernardsville, New Jersey, country estate. One weekend, members of the Secret Service Kiddie Detail followed the wrong car out of the driveway and allegedly "misplaced" John and Caroline. For the next two hours, a frantic search for the children was under way as Secret Service higher-ups in Washington feared the worst—that John and Caroline had been abducted.

The sun had already set by the time Jackie's New Jersey neighbor Peggy McDonnell drove up with Jackie's kids in the backseat. They had been playing with her children, and when no Secret Service car came to pick them up, she decided to drive them over herself. Understandably, Jackie was furious when told of this shocking security breach. If she needed another reason to marry into the heavily guarded Onassis family, it was hard to beat the day the Secret Service lost JFK's children.

John seemed oblivious to all the premarital intrigue swirling around him, in part because he had so many other things on his mind. When his teachers at St. David's told Jackie that her son lacked maturity and would have to repeat the first grade, she yanked him out of the school and enrolled him in the prestigious Collegiate School on the other side of Central Park.

This was another abrupt change for John, who had made so many friends among the students at St. David's. Since John loved hansom cabs, Jackie took him for a ride around Central Park, and broke the news to him then. This had one advantage: "I couldn't go anywhere—I couldn't escape. I had to sit and listen to her," John said. From that point on, "that's what she did. After a while, if we got in a horse-drawn carriage I would wonder what the big news was going to be."

Jackie obviously wasn't going to be walking her son to school anymore, but that didn't mean John could climb aboard Collegiate's yellow school bus and ride with his friends to school, either. Each morning at 7:50, a battered tan-and-cream Oldsmobile driven by JFK's crusty personal driver Muggsy O'Leary pulled up to a side entrance at 1040 Fifth and a Secret Service agent held open the right rear passenger door.

Five minutes later, Marta Sgubin and John emerged. Wearing Collegiate's blue blazer with its gold, orange, and purple crest, John clutched a large brown leather briefcase covered with travel stickers as he strode purposefully toward the car. The Secret Service agent then took his place in the front seat, next to Muggsy. Cutting straight through Central Park using the Eighty-fifth Street transverse, John usually arrived at 241 West Seventy-seventh Street seven or eight minutes later—in plenty of time to blend in with the other shaggy-maned sons of privilege as they streamed through Collegiate's high wooden doors.

Inside, Collegiate resembled any other school—public or private—in the city. John's home room had forest green carpeting on the floor, fluorescent lights, cinder-block walls, pull-down maps, wooden desks, and chalkboards. Mornings were devoted to the usual subjects: reading, spelling, geography, math, English, and a foreign language—in John's case, French.

Early on, John showed an interest in the theater, writing a short pantomime about kite-flying that his class performed during a special after-school assembly for parents. Following John's script, one of the boys tugs too hard on the string and it drifts away—a metaphor, the teacher later explained, for love and loss. A collective sigh was heard among the mothers in the audience. "Everyone knew what John had already gone through," said the mother of the boy who tugged too hard. His little pantomime struck her as nothing less than "charming and poetic."

Still, John was easily distractible and not exactly a stellar student—he later claimed it was clear that he suffered from attention deficit disorder (ADD)—but he did excel at athletics. After lunch, he and the other boys either went to the gym to play basketball or headed for Central Park to play soccer, baseball, or football.

John was still quick to make friends, and was not above angling for an introduction when it seemed the other boy outclassed him. Such was the case of Hans Hageman, one of the few African Americans at Collegiate and the school's star ten-year-old wrestler and runner. "At Collegiate," said journalist Nancy Moran, "being a good athlete is more prestigious than being the son of a president."

His own athletic skills notwithstanding, John still had to cope with teasing from the other kids. It didn't help that Jackie, clinging to her own notions of propriety, insisted John continue to wear shorts even though all the other boys his age were in long pants.

Unfortunately for the boys who taunted John, members of his Secret Service detail had been giving him boxing lessons. Anyone who called John "John-John" or made fun of his short pants could expect to collide with John's tiny fists of fury. "He socked me in the nose the very first day of school," a classmate said. "I wasn't the last one he gave a bloody nose to, either."

———

TAUNTS OF AN entirely different nature would soon be giving John new reasons to lash out. Doris Lilly was booed and heckled when she predicted on television's popular *Merv Griffin Show* that Jackie was about to marry Onassis. Leaving the show's Times Square studios, Lilly was then pushed, kicked, and cursed at as she walked down the street.

The rest of the Kennedys were no less outraged. When Pierre Salinger, who had been let in early on Jackie's plans, confirmed to Kennedy family spokesman Stephen Smith that she was indeed going to marry Onassis, Smith could only manage a two-word response: "Oh shit."

Jackie grew tired of hearing friends beseeching her to find someone less controversial, more . . . American. "I can't very well," she sighed to Truman Capote over lunch at La Côte Basque, "marry a dentist from New Jersey." Another friend warned her that marriage to Onassis would topple her from her pedestal. "It's better than freezing there," Jackie answered.

Jackie's only real concerns were religious. She was marrying a divorced man in a Greek Orthodox ceremony, and she knew that several of her Kennedy in-laws were pressuring Cardinal Cushing to threaten her with excommunication. Jackie made a special pilgrimage to Boston and promised Cushing that John and Caroline were to keep their Kennedy name and be raised Roman Catholic. Cushing declined to give Jackie and Ari his blessing, but he wasn't about to denounce them publicly, either.

On October 15, 1968, the *Boston Herald-Traveler* broke the story on its front page, tipping Jackie's hand. Before telling anyone else, Jackie piled the kids in a hansom cab for a ride around the park. John would always remember the clip-clop sound of horse hooves on pavement when Jackie told them she was marrying Onassis and that they were getting a stepfather.

Once she had told her children, Jackie frantically worked the phones, calling relatives on both sides of the family with the news. Janet Auchincloss was furious and accused Jackie of marrying Ari just to get back at her for divorcing Jackie's beloved rogue of a father, Black Jack Bouvier.

John's Grandmother Rose was the only family member to give the union her blessing. "Stunned" by the news, her thoughts "awhirl," the Kennedy matriarch wondered aloud if such a union would be accepted by the church, and if John and Caroline would accept Onassis as a stepfather. But she conceded that Jackie was not the sort of person who "would jump rashly into anything as important as this, so she must have her own very good reasons."

"She of all people was the one who encouraged me," Jackie later said. "Here I was, I was married to her son and I have his children, but she was the one who was saying, if this what you think is best, go ahead."

Rose's motives may not have been entirely altruistic. "I'm sure she did encourage Jackie to marry Onassis," said Smathers, who pointed out that Joe Kennedy's office was still taking care of Jackie's expenses. "She was tired of paying all those bills!"

"How could she do this to me?" Lee Radziwill shrieked over the phone to Truman Capote when she heard the news. Lee had had her own designs on Onassis back when Jackie was still in the White House. "How could this happen?!"

Onassis's own children, twenty-year-old Alexander and eighteen-year-old Christina, were devastated. They had clung to the hope that someday their parents would reconcile. "It's a perfect match," Alexander told his sister. "Our father loves Jackie and Jackie loves money."

No one felt the sting of betrayal more than Maria Callas, whose relationship with Onassis gave new dimension to the word *stormy*. Ari's friend Doris Lilly said the couple "fought like cats and dogs. Callas was a proud woman. She never said anything about the beatings, no matter how savage, and always wore makeup to conceal the bruises. As I heard Ari say many times, all Greek men beat their wives." More precisely, the Onassis mantra, which his friends knew by heart, went like this: "Every Greek, *and there are no exceptions,* beats his wife. It's good for them. It keeps them in line."

Callas made the ultimate sacrifice in 1966 when Ari demanded that she abort their son—the child she desperately wanted to keep—or risk losing him forever. She went ahead and had the abortion, but never forgave him for it.

The *diva divina* had also faithfully guarded his many secrets—among them, his passion for dressing in drag. Guests aboard the *Christina* as well as lovers like the Norwegian shipping heiress Ingeborg Dedichen, Gloria Swanson, Paulette Goddard, and Callas all remembered how Onassis loved to slip into lingerie, nylons, earrings, jangling bracelets, and high heels before parading around as "Arianna."

Swanson, who later learned that Onassis was in fact bisexual, couldn't help but be impressed. "He was an ugly man," Swanson said, "but as a woman he was, well, unforgettable."

Callas had endured many humiliations at Ari's hands. When her magnificent voice began to falter with age, he needled her mercilessly. "What are you?" he demanded. "Nothing. You just have a whistle in your throat that no longer works." This time, Lilly said, Callas was "destroyed" by the news that he was marrying Jackie. "But she wasn't going to give anyone the satisfaction of seeing the pain Jackie and Onassis were costing her."

Away from the press, Callas reacted by throwing the kind of seismic tantrum for which she was famous—opening the windows of her Paris apartment and screaming into the night. Officially, she projected an aura of benign, even benevolent, acceptance. Callas wished the love-birds well, then blithely remarked to the press that Jackie "did well to give a *grandfather* to her children."

No one was prepared for the global orgy of outrage that followed the wedding announcement of Jackie Kennedy and Aristotle Onassis. AMERICA HAS LOST A SAINT, screamed Germany's *Bild-Zeitung.* JACK KENNEDY DIES TODAY FOR A SECOND TIME, proclaimed Rome's *Il Messagero,* while the *Stockholm Express* asked, JACKIE, HOW COULD YOU? As far as the editors of *France-Soir* were concerned, the union was nothing less than "sad and shameful."

The venerable *New York Times* acknowledged in its front-page story that Americans were reacting with "anger, shock, and dismay." As far as the world was concerned, Doris Lilly observed, Jackie had gone "from Prince Charming to Caliban."

———

AT THE EPICENTER of the storm were John and Caroline, who were scooped up by Jackie and Ari and rushed to the airport bearing their father's name. There they boarded an empty Olympic Airways 707 (the plane's ninety-three passengers had been unceremoniously kicked off only moments before), where they were soon joined by Auchincloss and Kennedy relatives. With just eleven passengers aboard, the plane flew to Andravida, a Greek military base. There on the tarmac with its engines running was Ari's Piaggio seaplane, waiting to whisk them to Skorpios.

Jackie didn't want any reporters present at the wedding.

"Please don't bring them here," she begged her fiancé. But Ari was not about to let his ultimate moment go unrecorded. Over the objections of the entire world, he was about to make John F. Kennedy's beautiful, glamorous, and (until now) revered widow his wife. "Next to marrying the Queen of England," said the longtime dean of White House reporters, Helen Thomas, "he couldn't have done better. He wanted acceptance in the highest social circles, and he assumed this was a fast and easy way to get it. Or so he thought."

On the issue of press coverage, Ari persuaded Jackie to compromise. A small group of journalists would be permitted to cover the wedding party as it entered and left the whitewashed neoclassic Chapel of Panyitsa ("Chapel of the Little Virgin"). Hoping to keep the mayhem to a minimum, Jackie made her own plea to the press. "We know you understand that even though people may be well known," she wrote, "they still hold in their hearts the emotions of a simple person for the moments that are the most important of those we know on earth—birth, marriage, and death. We wish our wedding to be a private moment in the little chapel among the cypresses of Skorpios with only members of the family present—five of them little children. If you will give us these moments, we will gladly give you all the cooperation possible for you to take the pictures you need."

Shortly after 5 p.m. on October 20, 1968, Jackie appeared on the flagstone walk leading to the chapel. Cameras whirred and clicked as she and the groom made their way toward the chapel filled with twenty-two family members and friends. Once they reached the doorway, Jackie turned to the wall of photographers and said, firmly, "No. Not in here."

Five minutes later, John and Caroline flanked the bride and groom. Each stood ramrod straight and clutched a tall white candle. The flickering light revealed what one guest described as "an expression of worry and fear on their sweet little faces." They were not alone. Standing on the groom's side, Alexander and Christina looked as if they were attending a funeral, not a wedding. That day, said Ari's friend Willi Frischauer, both Onassis children "wept bitter tears."

Seemingly oblivious to the tensions simmering just beneath the surface, Jackie beamed throughout the short service. Everyone in the room agreed that the bride was stunning in a beige chiffon dress by Valentino—oddly, the same dress she had worn six months earlier to a friend's wedding in Virginia. She also wore flat shoes that matched her dress and Ari wore lifts—but Jackie still towered at least four inches above her betrothed. Callas liked to joke that Onassis "has all his suits made in London—unfortunately he is in New York at the time." But today Aristo looked undeniably dapper in a blue suit and burgundy tie.

To get to the chapel, guests had had to run through a light drizzle. As a result, everyone was wet—a good omen in his country, Polycarpos Athanassiou, the bearded Greek Orthodox priest who was conducting the ceremony, hastened to point out. It did not bode well, however, that Ari was clearly drunk. A Secret Service agent who made his own feelings about the wedding known by wearing a PT-109 tie clasp, pointed out that the groom was "unmistakably intoxicated."

Ari weaved noticeably as he and Jackie were crowned with wreaths of orange blossoms, placed wedding bands on each other's fingers, and then sipped wine from a silver chalice. The final ritual was the "Dance of Isaiah," in which the bride and groom walk around the altar three times, each trying to step on the other's first foot to determine who would call the shots in the marriage. To John's obvious delight, Jackie won.

As they left the church, the crowd outside tossed rice and—to ensure happiness, according to Greek custom—sugared almonds. "How are you feeling?" one reporter asked Ari.

"I feel very well, my boy," Onassis answered as Jackie looked on, smiling broadly.

"And how about you, John?" the same reporter asked. "How are you feeling?"

John studied the man's face for a moment before turning away.

Swallowed up by the mob of reporters, the new Mr. and Mrs. Onassis managed to make their way to a waiting gold-plated Jeep. With a grim-faced Caroline perched on her mother's lap, John sitting in the backseat, and a smiling Ari at the wheel, they sped off to the reception aboard the *Christina*.

As they drove off, John and Caroline looked "afraid, absolutely terrified by the circus," said *Washington Post* columnist Maxine Cheshire.
"Imagine how scary this all was to them," agreed Onassis's personal
secretary, Kiki Feroudi Moutsatsos. John and Caroline "had to be worrying about what would happen to them now that their mother was
marrying a man they hardly knew."

Undoubtedly adding to the fear factor were the Greek navy gun-
boats and cruisers patrolling the waters surrounding the *Christina,* not
to mention the bullhorn-equipped helicopters that kept swooping down
to warn reporters to keep their distance. "It was more like a war zone,"
Cheshire said, "than a wedding reception."

Sipping pink champagne, Jackie stepped out onto the deck with
Caroline to say hello to a select few American journalists, and then
returned to her guests gathered around the grand piano in the *Christina*'s glass-walled sitting room. After a few moments, the curtains were
finally drawn—and Jackie was finally able to light the first of several
L&Ms while Ari dispensed gifts to everyone in the room.

Out of concern for John and Caroline, Kiki Moutsatsos walked up to
them and started a conversation. "There was no doubt that the children
were overwhelmed by what was going on around them," she said. "Yet
it was also obvious they were polite, well-brought-up, adored children."

With Marta Sgubin sitting next to him, John sipped an orange soda,
while Ari lavished $1.2 million worth of jewels on his bride: an eye-
popping cabochon ruby ring and heart-shaped ruby-and-diamond earrings to match, two ruby-and-gold Capricorn ram's-head bracelets (she
was a Leo, he was a Capricorn), and two diamond Capricorn rings.
Not about to neglect his new in-laws, Onassis gave Lee and the Kennedy sisters diamond-and-gold rings with their particular sign of the
zodiac. For Jackie's mother, Janet, who despised Onassis, there was a
platinum-and-diamond pin.

Ari didn't forget the children, either. Caroline and her cousins
Sydney and Tina squealed with joy when he presented them with
sapphire-and-diamond bracelets. John perked up when he and Lee's son
Tony each got a thousand-dollar wristwatch.

As far as his new stepchildren were concerned, Ari's largesse would know no bounds. So that they wouldn't get bored on Skorpios, Ari bought Caroline a sailboat and a Shetland pony. John got his own Shetland pony as well, but Ari also bought the boy a jukebox, a red speedboat with his name written in large letters across the bow, and a mini-Jeep. When John wanted his pet rabbit flown to Greece aboard an Olympic Airways jet, the rabbit was not allowed his own seat in first class—Ari insisted that the pilot himself watch over it in the cockpit. And whenever Jackie or the children craved American hot dogs, as they frequently did, Onassis had them purchased in Coney Island and flown straight to Athens.

It was easy for John—or for that matter anyone—to understand why the *Christina,* christened after his adored only daughter, was Ari's pride. The yacht boasted a ballroom, a formal dining room, a private screening room, an El Greco hanging in the paneled study, an Olympic-size swimming pool, solid gold bathroom fixtures, several bars, a children's playroom decorated by Jackie's old friend, *Madeline* creator Ludwig Bemelmans, and mosaic floors throughout depicting scenes from Greek mythology.

To keep his guests amused, the yacht also carried on board a small sailboat, four speedboats, two kayaks, a Jeep, three dinghies, a glass-bottom boat, and a five-passenger Piaggio seaplane. A sixty-member crew, including two chefs and two full-time hairdressers, catered to the passengers' needs.

Aboard the *Christina,* John preferred to eat belowdecks with the crew. "He was such a curious kid—always asking about how the boat ran, how the engines worked, and always asking if he could help," a crew member recalled. While his mother and stepfather were entertaining upstairs, John "scrubbed pots and pans in the galley and loved it." John's favorite job aboard the *Christina*: donning the captain's hat and helping him steer the ship. "He was very serious about it. We all knew he'd make a hell of a sailor someday. Everybody on the *Christina* loved him."

When they weren't sailing to exotic ports of call, there was the seaside villa nineteen miles outside Athens at Glyfada, the gated mansion in Montevideo, his pied-à-terre on avenue Foch in Paris—and John's favorite: Skorpios.

Heavy with the scent of bougainvillea and jasmine, sprinkled with olive trees, fig trees, oleander, and cypresses, Ari's five-hundred-acre island paradise was suddenly the Kennedy kids' favorite playground. They spent weeks at a time there swimming, hiking, sailing, and for a time, horseback riding. When Caroline fancied a horse that the owners refused to sell, Ari did the next best thing and bought the horse's parents and siblings for his stepdaughter. Unfortunately, Jackie eventually called a halt to riding on the island; she felt the jagged, rock-strewn landscape posed too many dangers. No matter. Caroline was promptly given her own mini-Jeep so that she could keep up with John in his.

Despite the idyllic setting, cracks in the Onassis marriage began to appear early. When Jackie refused to meet Greek strongman George Papadopoulos or to accompany her husband to the formal announcement of his mammoth new Project Omega just days after the wedding, Ari was furious—even though she had made it clear before they exchanged vows that she was not willing to be used as a shill. "I didn't do it for Jack," she declared, somewhat disingenuously, "and I won't do it for you." At that point, Onassis was angry enough to tell Olympic Airways chairman Yannis Georgakis that marrying her may have been "the biggest mistake" of his life.

Ari's grumblings aside, Jackie seemed almost giddy as she settled into her new life as wife to one of the world's richest men. It helped that she was being waited on by a staff of more than seventy servants spread across three continents—not counting the *Christina*'s sixty-member crew. "I had never seen her in such high spirits," said her old friend Billy Baldwin, who arrived two days after the wedding to begin redecorating the *Christina,* the Skorpios house, and the Glyfada estate. "She had never seemed so free."

It wasn't *all* about the money, Jackie explained, or even what she insisted was her genuine affection for Ari. "It liberated me from the Kennedys," she said of the marriage, adding that simple ethnic prejudice was at the heart of most people's objections to it. "None of them could understand why I would want that funny little squiggly name when I had the greatest name of all. I like," she added with a wink, "seeing all those politicians dealing with Ari's squiggly name."

Unfortunately, during those first few weeks after the wedding, Jackie was left alone on Skorpios while her husband boomeranged from Athens to Paris and back again on business. Feeling abandoned, at least temporarily, Jackie dashed off a heartfelt letter to Roswell Gilpatric. "Dearest Ros," she wrote, "I would have told you before I left—but then everything happened so much more quickly than I'd planned. I saw somewhere what you had said and I was touched—dear Ros—I hope you know all you were and are and will ever be to me—With my love, Jackie."

Onassis somehow got wind of Jackie's note to Ros and dashed back to his bride's side. He spent the next three weeks honeymooning with Jackie on Skorpios. They swam, sunbathed, went for long walks across the island, snorkeled, and fed the miniature horses stabled on the island. They sailed the *Christina* to Rhodes, and when it was over, she joined John and Caroline in Manhattan.

With Jackie out of the picture, Ari began bombarding Callas with roses and phone calls. It was only when he showed up outside her Paris apartment at 36 avenue Georges Mandel and threatened to crash his Mercedes through the front door that she finally relented. Starting with discreet dinners in out-of-the-way restaurants, the couple rekindled their romance.

From this point on Ari and Callas, who now bitterly referred to Jackie as "the False Lady," saw each other almost constantly, according to Onassis's longtime chauffeur Jacinto Rosa. "Right up until a month before his death—for the truth is that Maria was the only true love of Onassis's life. She was his 'real wife'—even though they weren't officially married."

Yet even Rosa conceded that, in the beginning, Jackie and Ari behaved like a couple very much in love. Kitty Carlisle Hart was among the chosen few invited to 1040 Fifth for Thanksgiving that year—Ari's first. "We were all trying to explain to this foreigner the history of this purely American ritual," Hart said, "and to him it all sounded rather, well, silly." Eventually, Jackie just "threw up her hands and laughed." To Hart, "they seemed, at least in that first year together, to be very much in love with each other."

Ari called Jackie his "Class A Lady"—a line cribbed from the language on the packs of the L&Ms she chain-smoked: "20 Class A Cigarettes." But it was more than just pet names and public displays of affection. "Jackie must have said at least ten times to me, 'Isn't it weird that everybody thinks I married Ari for his money?'" Plimpton said. "I knew Jackie really, really well. She confided in me. If she had married Ari for money, she would have talked about it. Sure, the money was part of Ari's attraction, but only a part. She really loved him."

"There was a tenderness between them that was really moving," agreed society bandleader Peter Duchin, a close friend of Jackie's who spent time with the Onassises in New York and on board the *Christina*. "They really loved each other, and I think in a way that neither had loved anyone before . . . And they had fun! Ari took tremendous pleasure and pride in Jackie, and when she looked at him—well, there was obvious passion there."

Oddly enough, the marriage marked a sort of sexual renaissance for Jackie. Onassis, who had no qualms about discussing his prowess in the bedroom and sharing the details of his sex life, bragged that he and Jackie made love "five times a night—she surpasses all the women I have ever known." Salinger winced when he recalled "the graphic way Ari described their sexual relationship. Believe me, it was more than any of us wanted to hear." For her part, Jackie let it be known that, after a lifetime of following Catholic doctrine and not practicing birth control, she was placed on the pill at age thirty-nine. "Ari doesn't want any more children, and neither do I," she explained matter-of-factly.

"He was crazy about her," Moutsatsos said, "and, despite his appearance, she was just as crazy about him. They shared a great physical love," she continued, "one they enhanced by taking a variety of drugs Ari got from other people to increase sexual stamina and desire."

Ari's principal source was La Prairie, the Swiss clinic founded by controversial longevity pioneer Dr. Paul Niehans. Soon Jackie and Ari were being injected with a serum of live sheep cells that Niehans billed as both a powerful aphrodisiac and an elixir of youth. Not one to come to the party empty-handed, Jackie brought along what Doris Lilly described as "her own bag of goodies. She got Ari to start taking shots from Dr. Feelgood"—the same amphetamine-steroid mixture that Dr. Max Jacobson had given both Jack and Jackie Kennedy to get through their most stressful times in the White House.

The newlyweds also spiced things up by making love in less-than-conventional settings. They ripped out all the seats in the first-class cabin of an Olympic Airlines jet and turned it into their own airborne boudoir. Crew members of the *Christina* came upon the couple in the throes of passion beneath the canvas covering a lifeboat, and on another occasion in the dinghy that was tethered to the yacht.

Yet, with Ari often doing business in Europe and Jackie still rooted in Manhattan, the Onassises also spent long stretches of time apart. John and Caroline did not see their stepfather for weeks, even months at a time. Ari explained, unconvincingly, that this was all for the sake of John and Caroline. "Jackie is often at the other end of the world with her children—whom I should say I love very much," he said. "But they need time to get used to me, and I want to give them that time."

Not that he always made himself emotionally available to them—even when he was in the same room. Shortly after Thanksgiving of 1968, he joined Jackie and the children at her Bernardsville, New Jersey, farmhouse. Even before Ari set foot on the property, he put up barricades to block the road leading to the house and had a French photographer arrested for trespassing.

Once there, Onassis stayed inside, spinning more business deals over the phone while Jackie and the kids went riding to the hounds. At the end of the day, John came rushing into the house with the news that he had almost been thrown from his mount when it caught its hind leg on a fence. By that time, Ari had already departed for Paris.

Onassis continued to insist that maintaining a little distance from his new family was a good thing. "They need time," he said of John and Caroline, "to understand that their mother has remarried and that I want to be their friend, and not replace their father, whom I admired so much. A father cannot be replaced, especially one like John Kennedy. I only desire that they consider me a best friend."

Undeniably, John delighted in Jackie's newfound happiness, as well as in Ari's seemingly limitless largesse. Onassis did more than just shower his stepson with luxuries and pricey toys. From the very start, he worked hard at being a role model and father figure for John—a better one, he insisted to Salinger, than even Bobby had been.

Ari often canceled business plans just to spend time with the children on Skorpios. According to Moutsatsos, Ari made it seem as if "there was no other place he'd rather be" than with John and Caroline.

On fishing excursions, he kept John entertained with tales of his own rough-and-tumble boyhood, and when the fish refused to bite, Onassis made sure that a crewman slipped a fish on John's line so that he could still experience the thrill of a catch. Then there were the long, thoughtful strolls through the island's woodlands, with Ari patiently pointing out the island's animals and birds.

Now that he was spending more time in New York, Onassis did not want to disturb Jackie and the kids with his round-the-clock conference calls and endless deal-making. Instead, he operated out of an opulently furnished, full-floor suite at the Pierre Hotel, twenty-four blocks south of 1040 Fifth.

On the streets of Manhattan, Ari continued to pursue a genuine father-son relationship with JFK Jr. Jackie often looked down from the window of her apartment and saw Ari and her son walking hand in hand, Onassis leaning down to say something to John, then tilting his head to hear the boy's response.

"Just what is it you two talk about?" Jackie asked Ari after dinner one evening.

"I am teaching him," Onassis replied enigmatically.

Jackie looked at him quizzically. "Teaching him what?" she asked.

"To be a successful man," Ari said, as if the answer were perfectly obvious.

Later, she told Kiki Moutsatsos that she wondered exactly what her husband meant. "Probably how to act like a grown-up person," Moutsatsos answered with a shrug, "not a little boy. I wouldn't think twice about it."

Jackie was not convinced. "Oh, dear," she said, shaking her head. "I just hope he isn't spending all their time together telling John how to get a woman."

In truth, Onassis was doing most of the listening. During their marathon walks through Central Park and around the Upper East Side— usually punctuated with a stop for hot fudge sundaes at Serendipity— John chattered on about his schoolwork, his sports, his friends, basically anything that popped into his head. "John was a very talkative little kid," Plimpton remembered, "and Ari wasn't pretending—he seemed genuinely interested in what he had to say. It was important because, surrounded by so many famous adults like he was, well, a child could easily feel lost in the shuffle. Ari understood that."

There were times when John's running commentary proved especially valuable. When Ari took John to Shea Stadium to watch the Mets take on the Baltimore Orioles in the third game of the World Series, he relied on the boy to explain the rules of American baseball to him.

Following Jackie's lead—at Collegiate she was famous for being the only parent with a perfect record when it came to attending school events—Ari showed up at a number of soccer games and plays. "More than most of the other fathers, in fact," allowed another Collegiate mom. Where he used to search the stands only looking for Jackie's familiar face, John now expected to see Ari there as well. "It sort of shamed the rest of us, if you want to know the truth. What were *we* doing that could possibly be so important if Jackie Kennedy and Aristotle Onassis could make the time to be there?"

As the bond between them strengthened, Ari and his stepson felt comfortable enough for teasing and a little good-natured horseplay. When John's cocker spaniel, Shannon, lifted a leg and peed on Ari's shoe, they both dissolved in hysterics. Ari, meantime, took no small pleasure in chasing John around the deck of the *Christina* and then tossing him into the pool.

Each night at bedtime, Jackie tucked in both children, but only after Ari crept into John's bedroom, tickled him, and finished off with a big Greek bear hug. "Ari seemed to enjoy both children immensely," Plimpton said. "They kept him young."

Because of John, Ari was also on the lookout for members of the press who chartered boats, hung from trees with telephoto lenses, and leaped out at them from behind trash cans and parked cars. Like Jack, Onassis did not wish to risk Jackie's wrath by letting photographers too close to her children. Placed in charge of John one weekend when Jackie jetted off to New York, Ari locked John belowdecks for four hours while press boats circled the *Christina*. On Onassis's orders one of the yacht's crewmen launched a speedboat from the stern and zigzagged among the press boats, propelling photographer after swearing photographer into the drink. Finally, John appeared on the deck and climbed onto Ari's Chris-Craft for a quick tour of the neighboring islands—but not before tossing towels to the journalists who'd been given a good soaking.

Notwithstanding the bond of affection that now existed between them, John always felt that an "invisible barrier" existed between him and Onassis. "He was too old, too foreign, too rich, too *much*," said a friend. It spoke volumes that John never stopped calling the man who married his mother "Mr. Onassis."

Nevertheless, John and Caroline now found themselves in the embrace of Ari's own family. As much as they despised Jackie (and Callas and any of Ari's other women, for that matter), Alexander and Christina instantly warmed to the Kennedy kids. A licensed pilot at twenty, Ari's brooding only son shared John's abiding love of aviation—more specifically, his fascination with helicopters. Over the next few years, Alexander would occasionally take the controls of his father's private chopper and invite John along for the ride. Lee recalled that her sister "was so thrilled to see John so happy and excited. She knew how much he loved flying, especially helicopters."

For the rest of the Kennedys, such positive signs of harmony between Jackie and her Onassis in-laws were of no consequence. They still treated the marriage with "abject horror," Pierre Salinger observed. "That made John and Caroline even closer and emphasized for all of them that they were three against the world: Bouvier-Kennedys, as opposed to their garden-variety Kennedy cousins."

That did not mean Jackie was willing to forgo their Kennedy birthright. Eventually, Jackie would invite Salinger to Skorpios for the express purpose of telling them all about their father. "I want you to come here and every hour or so tell them something new about Jack," she said. "They don't have anyone here to keep his memory alive, and they *need* to know about him, Pierre. John especially. Caroline remembers everything, but John was just too young."

JFK's former press secretary obliged. "I spent a month on Skorpios," he recalled. "We'd go to the beach or out fishing and I'd tell them all about their dad. I made certain to stress their father's wonderful sense of humor and his love of life—and especially his love of them," Salinger said. "I pointed out that even though he often had reason to be sad, he was the person who cheered up all the others in the room."

Salinger "wasn't sure at first if Jackie would approve, but I thought it was important that they not be spoon-fed all the Camelot stuff—that would just give them a warped, unrealistic view of President Kennedy." JFK was "a human being and not a myth—and Jackie wanted them to know that more than anything." In the end, John and Caroline both had a "healthy perspective on their father. All the credit," Salinger said, "goes to Jackie." For the rest of his life, JFK's old comrade and friend would treasure the memory of "those two innocent, beguiling faces turned up to me and listening with rapt attention."

In December, Ethel gave birth to Bobby's eleventh child. Jackie flew down to Washington alone, took a limousine to Georgetown University Hospital, and went straight to the nursery—bypassing Ethel's room altogether. After declaring that Rory Elizabeth Katherine was "very pretty," Jackie spent some time alone with Luella Hennessey, the Kennedy family nurse who had been there for the birth of all four of Jackie's children.

Before returning to New York, she stopped at Arlington, asking her two-man Secret Service detail to remain in the car while she visited Bobby's grave, then the spot where Jack, Patrick, and their stillborn daughter Arabella were buried. Stunned tourists remained respectfully silent, but Jackie was noticeably irritated by the incessant click and whir of their cameras.

No sooner was she back behind her Louis XV desk at 1040 Fifth than Jackie dashed off a blistering six-page letter to Secret Service director James J. Rowley complaining "there are too many agents, and the new ones are not sensitive to the needs of little children." She insisted that John and his sister "must think they lead normal lives, and not be conscious of a large number of men protecting them from further violence."

It was important, she continued, that her children "not be made conspicuous among their friends by the presence of numerous agents, or have the households in which they live thrown into turmoil by the intrusion of agents who do not care about them or understand their problems."

Jackie wanted the Secret Service detail cut in half, from eight agents to four. She agreed agents "should be with the children from the time they leave the house in the morning until they return at 5:30 for supper," but insisted there was no need for a late-afternoon or night shift since at that time the children were secure in their doorman building. In

Hyannis and in New Jersey, she had confidence that local police could help provide sufficient protection at night.

Even the Secret Service director could not argue with the fact that Ari's private seventy-five man army was more than enough to keep John and Caroline safe in Greece. What clearly rankled Jackie most was the way Secret Service agents behaved during the family's weekends in New Jersey. "Agents tramp outside the children's windows all night, talking into their walkie-talkies," she protested. Agents' cars were "piled up in the driveway so that our little country house," she said, "looks like a used-car lot."

Jackie claimed that the folks next door had every reason to be angry when one of the agents "either went to sleep or was listening to the radio so loudly in his car with the windows steamed up that he did not hear a neighbor's child locked in the car next to him who had been crying hysterically for an hour, and was finally found by her parents. Then there was the time "an agent went in and forcibly dragged my children home for supper though I had told his superior that they might stay, etc., etc."

Rowley sympathized with Jackie's frustration, which resounded in her final paragraph. "The children are growing up," Jackie wrote. "They must see new things and travel as their father would have wished them to do. They must be free as possible, not encumbered by a group of men who will be lost in foreign countries, so that one ends up protecting them and not vice-versa."

Jackie went on to say that "as the person in the world who is most interested in their security, and who realizes most what threats are in the outside world, I promise you I have considered and tried every way, and that what I ask you for is what I know is best for the children of President Kennedy and what he would wish for them. Thank you so much, dear Mr. Rowley. I hope you have a happy Christmas. Most sincerely, Jacqueline."

After spending Christmas 1968 on Skorpios, Jackie returned to New York with John and Caroline in tow. As soon as she was out the door, Ari flew to Paris for dinner with Callas at her apartment. As Callas waited for him to arrive, recalled their friend Baroness van Zuylen, she behaved "like a nervous teenager."

Blithely carrying on with both women, Ari then returned to New York before departing with the children on a cruise to the Canary Islands. Later, bringing Rose Kennedy along on an Easter cruise aboard the *Christina,* Ari presented John's grandmother with a gold bracelet studded with rubies and diamonds—her reward for sticking by them when the rest of the clan had tried to scuttle their wedding.

On that cruise, Rose talked excitedly about the family's newest hope for recapturing the White House—Uncle Ted. At about the same time, reporters traveling with Ted Kennedy aboard a Washington-bound plane overheard the drunk senator repeatedly say, "They're going to shoot my ass off the way they shot Bobby."

Ted Kennedy's dreams of advancing from the U.S. Senate to 1600 Pennsylvania Avenue ended on July 18, 1968, when he drove his 1967 Oldsmobile off the Dike Bridge on Chappaquiddick Island, part of Martha's Vineyard, drowning his attractive young passenger, Mary Jo Kopechne. The tragic accident and Ted's inept attempt at a cover-up added more fuel to the growing belief in a Kennedy Curse.

"It was unquestionably another blow for Jackie," Plimpton said. "Ted had stepped up after Bobby's death, and she and the children were enormously fond of him. It was just another painful twist of fate that seemed beyond belief." Yet Jackie, who might easily have stayed out of sight on Skorpios, stood alongside her embattled brother-in-law in a show of solidarity. She even asked Ted to take the place of Bobby as Caroline's godfather. "It was a special trust," he later said. "It meant a great deal, and so did the support she gave me at the time."

Just ten days after Chappaquiddick, Ari presented Jackie with a special present for her fortieth birthday: the 40.42-carat marquis-cut Lesotho III diamond. Along with it came a matching diamond necklace and bracelet, and to commemorate the realization that summer of JFK's dream of landing a man on the moon by the end of the 1960s, a pair of 18-carat gold-and-ruby "Apollo II" ear clips designed by Greek jewelry maker Ilias Lalaounis.

"Ari was actually apologetic about them," Jackie told Greek actress Katina Paxinou, one of the guests at her birthday party. "He felt they were such trifles." As it turned out, the "trifles" Ari gave to John's mother that year cost more than $2 million—the rough equivalent of $16 million in 2014 dollars.

Although White House photographs showed him playing with his mother's pearl necklace, John was in fact much more intrigued by Jackie's Apollo II ear clips. Each anchored by a large moon of hammered gold, the large globes dangled from links fashioned in the shape of a lunar capsule.

At first, Ari claimed not to be concerned about how much Jackie was costing him—over and above the gifts he bestowed on her, the new Mrs. Onassis spent more than $2 million on herself during their first year of marriage. "God knows Jackie has had her years of sorrow," he said. "If it makes her happy, she can have anything she wants."

Jackie was, by any definition, a shopaholic—a manic, insatiable consumer who splurged on herself without abandon. Her compulsive spending had gotten her into deep trouble with Jack, who felt that her high-living image would end up costing him votes; her shopping habit was one of the few things they quarreled about bitterly in front of friends.

Now, without an electorate to offend, she indulged her every acquisitive whim. Clothes remained Jackie's principal addiction. Frequenting Paris's top fashion houses, she scooped up entire collections by her favorite designers. St. Laurent, Dior, Valentino, Givenchy, Chanel, and Lanvin all made up mannequins to Jackie's precise measurements just so they could keep up with her orders. Ari's longtime confidant Costa Gratsos called her a "pointer"—someone who, without ever inquiring about the price, simply points to an object and asks to have it wrapped up. At one Fifth Avenue store, she purchased $40,000 ($320,000 in 2014 dollars) worth of handbags, scarves, and sweaters in less than fifteen minutes. The manager recalled that one salesman "had to be taken home in a taxi and put to bed with a sedative."

On many occasions, John was present to witness firsthand what he later called Jackie's "spending jags." She was, Tish Baldrige joked, a "world-class consumer. There was no stopping her when she got that look in her eye, and you have to wonder what that might look like to a child."

Apparently it wasn't much of a concern for John, who around this time went to a dress shop near Collegiate and bought his mother two $19.99 dresses for her birthday. Jackie wore them, but only around the apartment. "She was very convincing," he later said. "She said she loved them. She said they had style."

As it had with Jack, Jackie's profligate consumption would lead to friction within her second marriage—and heated exchanges with Ari. Only this time they were arguing in front of children who were old enough to understand what was going on.

By late 1969, Jackie and Ari were spending even less time together than they usually did. This arrangement suited Jackie just fine, although dealing with an increasingly aggressive press as she actively pursued her high-profile solo life in New York became more and more problematic.

Of course, Jackie also thrived on publicity, actively seeking coverage so long as she called the shots. At times she had her secretary alert newspaper and magazine editors that she was to be at a certain event. On other occasions, said *Women's Wear Daily* publisher James Brady, "she avoided us as from the plague." Brady and the others were willing to put up with Jackie's shifting moods, and for one simple reason. He confessed she was the ultimate "cover girl. There is a continuous and enthusiastic, and even perhaps morbid interest in Jackie, her life and loves."

Her son was no less a target—literally. Nicknamed "the Shadow" by Ari, Greek photographer Dimitri Koulouris tossed stones at John hoping that he could snap shots of the boy angrily throwing stones back at him. Another time, according to court records, Jackie was water-skiing off Skorpios when the Greek photographer cut across the stern of the boat that was pulling her, severing her line. As a startled Jackie sank beneath the surface, thrashing as she struggled for air, Koulouris reportedly kept taking pictures.

Koulouris was eventually sentenced to six months in jail for nearly causing a collision between his speedboat and the Onassis seaplane. Jackie and John were both on board. In what amounted to an eerie preview of Princess Diana's life and death nearly three decades later, Jackie and Ari were often chased through the streets of London and Paris by swarms of photographers on motorcycles. "They are reckless, and someday they will kill someone," Jackie told Kitty Hart. "But it's not going to be me. I'm always telling the driver to slow down. A few pictures aren't worth getting killed over."

Notwithstanding Jackie's many brushes with the paparazzi abroad, no one irked her more than Ron Galella. The relentless New York photographer stalked Jackie and her kids on their home turf, turning their lives, John later said, into "one big and extremely annoying game of hide and seek."

Jackie proved more than a match for Galella, whose modus operandi involved leaping out from behind a car or bush, then making odd grunting noises as he snapped away. One Christmas, she would testify in one of two trials, he hired a man in a Santa suit to corner her outside her apartment—"pushing, trying to get next to me, pushing, scuffling . . ." The *National Enquirer* had hired Galella to take the picture of Jackie and Santa for the cover of its holiday issue. Instead, Jackie swiftly maneuvered past both of them and darted down the block. "She's fast," Galella allowed, "and Santa was slow."

Not one to give up easily, Galella hoped a photo of Jackie and the kids sledding in Central Park would meet the tabloids' holiday cover needs. Before he could capture the moment on film, two members of the family's Secret Service detail bulldozed him into a snowbank.

On Mother's Day, Jackie returned to 1040 Fifth after having brunch with John and Caroline. As they walked from their limousine to the building's canopied entrance, the photographer pounced. Quick-thinking Jackie swiftly thrust the Mother's Day flowers John had given her in front of her face, blocking Galella's camera and ruining the shot.

Even Jackie acknowledged that Galella had a certain . . . flair. On Capri, she would later tell a judge, he dressed up in a "white sailor suit with a little white sailor hat. He yelled at me, 'Hiya, Jackie. Are you surprised to see me here? How do you like me? I've joined the navy!'"

Then there was the dinner with Ari and architect I. M. Pei at a Chinese restaurant, when Galella popped out from behind a coatrack, and the time Jackie managed to ditch Galella in front the '21' Club by pretending to get out of her car, then hopping back in and speeding off.

Jackie was in no mood to play games when it came to John and Caroline, however. In the late summer of 1969, Jackie was leaning against a tree in Central Park watching Caroline take one of her weekly tennis lessons when Galella leapt onto the court and started taking pictures. "I'm not making you nervous, am I, honey?" he asked, crouching down in front of her.

"Yes, you are," Caroline replied, turning toward her mother with tears in her eyes. At that point, Jackie sprinted across the park with Galella in hot pursuit. Galella kept shooting, and even caught Jackie running past a police car with two officers dozing inside. Confident that she had successfully lured Galella away from Caroline, she put on speed and lost him in her tracks.

That fall, Caroline transferred from the Convent of the Sacred Heart to Brearley, an exclusive girls' school on New York's Upper East Side. At a school carnival, Caroline was mortified when Galella suddenly materialized and began bobbing and weaving around her, making his weird grunting noises.

Galella struck again thirteen days later, when Jackie and John were bicycling through Central Park. Mother and son were merrily pedaling along when the paparazzo leapt in their path, causing John to swerve. "Smash his camera!" Jackie ordered the Secret Service agent who accompanied them. "And arrest him for harassment."

Once the criminal harassment charges against Galella were dropped for lack of evidence, he sued Jackie for $1.3 million, accusing John's mother of assault, false arrest, malicious persecution, and "interference with my livelihood as a photographer." She countersued for $6 million, later testifying that Galella's "reign of terror" had left her feeling like "an absolute prisoner" of Galella.

To shore up her claim that Galella's actions were causing her entire family "grievous mental anguish," Jackie enlisted John's help. "Mr. Galella has dashed out at me, jumped in my path, discharged flashbulbs in my face, trailed me at close distances—generally imposed himself on me," John said in a written deposition that had clearly been prepared by his mother's legal team. John added that incidents like the one on his bicycle left him feeling "threatened."

Ari financed Jackie's legal pursuit of Galella, but he warned her that the case could backfire if she began to appear like a spiteful, imperious celebrity persecuting a hardworking photographer. Besides, Galella allowed only the most flattering pictures of Jackie to be published—his candid photographs of her were among Jackie's all-time favorites.

The case dragged on for years and would cost Jackie $300,000 in legal fees before U.S. District Court judge Irving Ben Cooper ordered Galella not to come within 150 feet of Jackie or within 225 feet of John and his sister. On appeal, those distances were reduced so that he was allowed to come within 25 feet of Jackie and within 30 feet of the children.

———

EVEN THOUGH HE had to dodge a pushy photographer from time to time, John was none the worse for wear. At Collegiate, he continued to scrape by at his studies and to excel at sports. By now most of the teasing had stopped ("They just got bored with me, I guess," he later said), and John's naturally respectful, unspoiled demeanor and generally sunny disposition earned him points with peers and faculty alike.

Between weekends at Hammersmith Farm and Hyannis Port—not to mention languid summer idylls on Skorpios—John realized even then that he had little to complain about. "It was a wonderful time," he later said. "Let's face it, I was a very, very lucky little boy." As for his relationship at the time with his stepfather: "Mr. Onassis was very nice to me. I was just this little kid, but he took the time to tell me things, to listen to what I had to say. I liked him a lot, and I like to think he liked me, too."

As lucky as he may have felt he was, the fact remained that JFK Jr. had already been to too many funeral masses for a boy his age. He added another to his list on November 18, 1969, when Grandpa Joe Kennedy died at the age of eighty-one. Just days before his ninth birthday, John marched to the front of Hyannis's St. Francis Xavier Church and confidently recited the Twenty-Third Psalm before seventy mourners who had come to pay their respects to the Kennedy patriarch. Caroline, wearing a large white bandage on her forehead after falling off a horse in New Jersey, was impressed. "John did an awfully good job," she was overheard telling a cousin. "I was sure he'd mess it up."

Two days later, John and nearly all his Kennedy relatives were back at St. Francis Xavier Church. This time, John served as an altar boy at a Mass commemorating the sixth anniversary of his father's assassination. Ari had not attended Joe Kennedy's funeral Mass, and John voiced surprise that the man he still called "Mr. Onassis" was once again nowhere to be seen.

Jackie and the children spent Christmas that year with the Radziwills at their Queen Anne mansion in England's Berkshire Hills. They decorated the tree, dined on goose and mince pie, drank eggnog, sang carols, and opened gifts. Ari, however, was not part of this festive holiday scene, either. Instead, he remained behind in Greece, cooking up deals and, it was rumored, trysting with his old flame Callas.

Although cracks in the relationship had already begun to show, it was a single indiscretion that signaled the beginning of the end for the Onassis marriage. In February 1970, five of the highly personal letters Jackie had written to Roswell Gilpatric—four written while she was married to Jack as well as the note she dashed off during her honeymoon with Ari—fell into the hands of Manhattan autograph dealer Charles Hamilton.

Ari didn't mind being portrayed as an uncouth cretin, a pirate, a dirty old man, or even a crook. But the idea of being cuckolded in public—and by a woman who had just spent $60,000 (nearly $500,000 in 2014 dollars) on two hundred pairs of shoes—was a blow to his manhood. "My God," he told Costa Gratsos. "What a fool I have made of myself."

By way of retaliation, on May 21, 1970, Ari dined openly with Callas at Maxim's in Paris—and made certain photographers were there to capture the moment. Like everyone else, John saw the story splashed across the front pages of the *New York Post* and the *Daily News*. But he also had a ringside seat for his mother's characteristically swift and inspired reaction.

On the morning of May 22, Jackie phoned Ari with the news that she was headed for Paris. The very next night, Ari was back at Maxim's— only this time with Jackie, and sitting at precisely the same table he shared with Callas just twenty-four hours before.

"For Jackie it wasn't so much a supper," said Ari's aide Johnny Meyer, "as a sock in the eye for Maria."

Three days later, Jackie was in Athens spending thousands on hand-woven rugs and stopped to sip ouzo at a bistro. She was quickly spotted by reporter and asked if the rumors of the Ari–Maria Callas story were true. "Oh my God," Jackie said, smiling, "what will they think of next!"

Unbeknownst to Jackie, at that moment paramedics in Paris were frantically working to save Callas, who became so despondent over the photo of Jackie and Ari at Maxim's that she tried to kill herself with an overdose of sleeping pills. The diva survived, and would soon be back at Ari's side.

Less than three weeks after hosting a forty-first birthday party for Jackie in New York, Ari helicoptered to the Aegean island of Tragonisi and surprised Callas as she sunned herself on the beach. Strolling up to her with a poodle in his arms—his gift to the dog-loving opera star— Onassis then kissed Callas under a beach umbrella. They both made certain that the entire touching scene was captured on film. Once again, Jackie raced to Ari's side to squelch rumors.

If nothing else, John's mother was determined not to be made an object of pity. She had an image to uphold—an image that was still rooted in the myth of Camelot. Once the portraits of JFK and Jackie were completed, first lady Pat Nixon contacted Jackie and asked if she was interested in attending a public unveiling.

Jackie declined, saying that she didn't "have the courage to go through an official ceremony and bring the children back to the only home they both knew with their father under such traumatic conditions." Describing the press and the attention as "things I try to avoid in their little lives," Jackie went on to explain that a public unveiling would "be hard on them and not leave them with the memories of the White House I would like them to have."

Jackie eventually caved in, agreeing to bring the children along for dinner with the Nixons on February 3, 1971. President Nixon sent Air Force One to New York to pick them up, and on the flight down to Washington, Caroline bet her little brother that he couldn't get through dinner without spilling his milk or having his shirttail come untucked—something, John said years later, "that used to happen with great frequency."

Pat Nixon greeted her guests at the front door, and Jackie was surprised at how warm and engaging she was—especially with the children. While the two first ladies chatted, Nixon daughters Tricia and Julie showed John and Caroline their old rooms. Although both rooms had been redecorated to suit the new occupants' tastes, Jackie said Caroline's face "just lit up" when she walked into her old bedroom.

After touring the "High Chair Room," where Maud Shaw used to preside over their meals, and the solarium that once housed the little "White House School" Caroline had attended with the children of family friends and White House staffers, President Nixon took John and Caroline to the Oval Office. Caroline remembered it well, and reminded John that he used to hide beneath his father's desk. John really didn't remember that, although he seemed vaguely aware that this room was where "Daddy used to work."

The visit turned out to be memorable for John, mostly because of the bet his sister made with him on the flight down. Years later he recalled that he managed to get through most of the dinner "and my shirttail was in and the milk was upright." But once dessert arrived, "something caught my attention," he said. The milk went flying—right into the president's lap. "He just didn't even blink," John said, impressed at how comfortable Nixon appeared to be around young children. Acting as if nothing had happened, the president "just kind of wiped it up."

Once she returned to 1040 Fifth, Jackie wrote Pat an effusive thank-you note. "Thank you with all my heart," Jackie said, pointing to the fact that this marked her first White House visit with the children since Dallas. "A day I always dreaded turned out to be one of the most precious ones I have spent with my children."

What touched the Nixons most, however, was the thank-you letter John wrote them, misspellings and all.

I don't think I could rember much about the White House but it was really nice seeing it all again. When I sat on Lincolns bed and wished for something my wish really came true.

I wished that I have good luck at school.

John was especially fond of the Nixons' dogs—Vicky the French poodle, a Yorkshire terrier named Pasha, and King Timahoe, an Irish setter. "They were so funny," John wrote. "As soon as I came home my dogs kept on sniffing me. Maybe they rember [sic] the White House."

JFK's Senate friend-turned-campaign nemesis made another thoughtful gesture when he decided not to upstage Jackie at the September 8, 1971, opening of the John F. Kennedy Center for the Performing Arts. Instead, he turned over the presidential box to Jackie and the Kennedy family. According to her brother Jamie, "whatever bitterness there had been during the 1960 presidential campaign was completely a thing of the past. In the end, she was very fond of Nixon."

By then, John had already experienced one of the most memorable summers of his young life. That July, he joined his cousin Tony Radziwill at Drake's Island Adventure Center off the rugged southwest coast of

Great Britain. For two weeks, the boys climbed, canoed, sailed, hiked, and camped—an experience that proved so exciting Jackie vowed that each year John would be treated to at least one such adventure.

One of John's early guides in this new world of exploration was Peter Beard, the charismatic photographer, African wildlife conservationist, and Lothario. Staying on Skorpios that entire summer, Beard was now able to indulge what had been a lifelong obsession with the Kennedys—especially the Kennedy women. "Peter was Jackie's biggest fan," said his friend Porter Bibb, who described Beard's interest in John's mother as "almost a fixation with him. What I saw from Peter when he was around Jackie was that he was coming on to her, and I thought she was amused."

Beard's athleticism, intellect, and boyish good looks ("half Tarzan and half Byron," wrote one wag) greatly appealed to Jackie's sister Lee. They carried on their affair under the noses of not only her husband Stas and Jackie, but fellow house guests David Frost and Diahann Carroll as well. (Lee and Stas would divorce in 1974.)

What Beard brought to Skorpios—and into John's young life—was what Bibb called his "ferocious energy." With Ari losing interest in her and the children, Jackie now bluntly told friends that she worried John was going to "wind up a fruit" without a man to "show him the ropes."

Beard certainly fit the bill, doing "the kinds of things Bobby used to do with John," Jackie said—water-skiing, swimming, exploring the island's rocky terrain with John, wrestling with him on the beach. The time was no less magical for Beard, who described Jackie as being "like a dormitory roommate, completely casual. Great meals, fantastic picnics. It was lush—nonstop Dom Perignon and O.J."

Beard was also impressed with Jackie's son, whom he called "a totally inspired person." Among other things, Beard noted in his diaries that John was already proving himself to be a gifted mimic—a talent he carried into adulthood.

The following spring, Beard led Caroline and John on a snake-hunting tour of the Everglades. Unfortunately, word was leaked to reporters, who staked out the hotel where they were staying. Up early,

John noticed a photographer who was fast asleep in the hotel. As he walked past, Jackie's son broke into his own rooster-strut imitation of Mick Jagger singing "Jumpin' Jack Flash." Startled awake, the photographer reached for his camera, but too late. John had vanished. (Along with his talent for impersonation, John was a rock aficionado who from this point on would be a passionate fan of the Rolling Stones.)

Ari, predictably, was no fan of Peter Beard. After he suggested to Beard that he might have overstayed his welcome, the handsome interloper merely shrugged. When Beard, always seeking to make an impression, accidentally cut himself and then dipped a pen in his own blood to make a diary entry, Ari left Skorpios in disgust.

Onassis had plenty of other reasons to be upset. During the small dinner party he hosted on Skorpios to celebrate Jackie's forty-second birthday, he got word from Las Vegas that his adored twenty-year-old daughter, Christina, had just married Joseph Bolker, a twice-divorced American real estate developer who happened to be twenty-seven years her senior. Ari simply "went ape," recalled Johnny Meyer. "I'd seen him fly off the handle plenty of times but never like that."

Onassis was jolted again by the secret marriage of his archenemy and business rival, Stavros Niarchos, to his ex-wife, Tina. Niarchos's former wife, Tina's sister Eugenie, had died under highly mysterious circumstances; at one point authorities indicted Niarchos for "involuntary homicide." Now Ari and his children feared Tina might meet a similar fate. "Ari was," said Meyer, "positively apoplectic." Christina was even worse. "It was a very emotional time," Bolker recalled. "A lot of yelling and screaming. A really bad scene."

Over the years, Jackie had developed a series of compulsions to help cope with stress: chain-smoking, nail-biting, nonstop exercise, marathon shopping—just to name a few. Now that she was being exposed to the more Levantine aspects of the Onassis family temperament—the volcanic eruptions, the black moods—she had to come up with something new: compulsive dieting.

Obeying the Duchess of Windsor's dictum that you can never be too rich or too thin, Jackie survived—barely—on a daily diet that consisted of a half grapefruit, yogurt, two and a half ounces of meat, three and a half ounces of green vegetables, and one apple. In ten days, she dropped twenty-four pounds.

Anorexia nervosa and bulimia had not yet found their way into the medical lexicon, but many of those close to Jackie believed she suffered from both. "Jackie starved herself to stay thin," said Roy Cohn, the controversial New York lawyer who first gained notoriety as Senator Joe McCarthy's counsel during the televised Army-McCarthy hearings of 1954. Cohn knew the Kennedys and Onassis, and later went to work as Ari's hired gun. "Sometimes she would go on a binge and eat everything she really liked—hot fudge sundaes, hot dogs, nothing fancy but the things she really liked—then that night before she went to bed she'd stick her finger down her throat and throw it all up. Ari never saw it himself, but one of the crew members on the *Christina* accidentally caught her in the act. At first they just assumed she was seasick, but then they figured out what was going on."

Jackie's eating disorder was rooted in her chubby adolescence, her mother's constant carping about her weight—and sibling rivalry. "There she was, the most famous, glamorous woman in the world, married to one of the richest men in the world, and she was *starving* herself," Doris Lilly said. "And for what? So she would look as chic as her sister Lee." Jackie admitted that she had always been jealous of Lee's delicate features and size-four figure. "She's always been the pretty one," Jackie said, "so I guess I'm the smart one."

RIDDLE OF JACKIE'S ILLNESS, read the headline of the British weekly the *People*, while *France Dimanche* concluded unequivocally that "Jackie is ill. Her eyes give the impression of deep suffering."

Even Jackie was worried, as it turned out. Startled at the suddenness of her weight loss and an unfamiliar lack of energy, she sought the opinion of France's leading cancer specialist, Dr. Georges Mathé of Paris's Villejuif Clinic. JACKIE SAID TO HAVE CANCER, screamed the front-page headline in the Athens *Akropolis*. HAS JACKIE GOT CANCER? chimed in the afternoon newspaper *Ta Nea*.

The children were understandably concerned, and Jackie reassured them that there was no truth to the rumors that she was ill. Caroline took her mother's word at face value, but John was worried enough to ask his nanny if she thought Mummy was "too skinny."

———

NOW THAT CAROLINE was away at Concord Academy in Massachusetts, John was left alone with a ringside seat to the Onassises' marital dysfunction. "He would always say, 'The Widow wants this' and 'The Widow wants that,'" recalled Aileen Mehle. "She tried to keep up appearances, but it was obvious that he was mad at her. And I mean all the time."

Ari made his displeasure known in other, not especially subtle, ways. "Jackie had a charming little rule," Costa Gratsos told columnist Jack Anderson, "that Ari had to bring back a present from every part of the world he visited. Once, all he brought her was a simple apron from Africa. She was livid. I suppose she expected a shoe box full of raw diamonds."

Ari did show up with Jackie for John's stage debut as a member of Fagin's gang of underage pickpockets in Collegiate's Christmas production of the musical *Oliver!* John felt at home on the student stage; every year on Jackie's birthday, Marta Sgubin staged a family production of one of Molière's classic farces with John in the starring role.

This evening at Collegiate, however, there was no mistaking the tension between Mr. and Mrs. Onassis—even as they sat in the audience at a school play. "Jackie was all smiles," another parent recalled, "and Onassis looked like he wanted to reach over and strangle her."

Looking to make his own getaway, John pleaded with Jackie to send him on another manly adventure. This time she agreed to let John join his friend Bob Cramer at Camp Androscoggin, a summer camp in a wilderness area north of Portland, Maine.

John was almost out the door when Jackie called an abrupt halt to the trip. In July, Greek authorities announced the arrest of twelve terrorists—four members of Germany's infamous 20 October Movement and eight Greek leftists—who were plotting to kidnap John and hold him for ransom.

Robbed of his annual adventure away from Mummy, John divided the summer of 1972 among Hyannis Port, Newport, the weekend house in New Jersey, Greece, and of course New York. On Skorpios and aboard the *Christina,* the atmosphere was different now. Alexander and Christina were still surprisingly warm toward John—especially Alexander, who continued to take John on spins around the island aboard his helicopter.

John's Greek stepbrother, who had just undergone rhinoplasty to rid himself of the prominent Onassis nose, cared enough for John not to expose him to any unnecessary risk. When the boy begged to take a flight in Ari's Piaggio amphibious plane, Alexander refused. Ari's son believed that particular aircraft to be a "death trap," and had already convinced his father to replace it with another helicopter.

Not that Ari spent much time with either Alexander or John. On those increasingly rare occasions when he was around, Onassis made his feelings toward John's mother painfully clear. "After a certain point," Aileen Mehle said, "I never saw love on his side when it came to Jackie. Now *she* was sweet and warm and affectionate. He was aloof." What made it worse was that "this is the way Ari treated Jackie in public. I can't imagine how awful he was toward her when nobody was around."

In such close quarters on Skorpios and aboard Onassis's floating Xanadu, John was exposed to the angry shouting, the hurled epithets, and the sound of crockery smashing—all part and parcel of marital disharmony in Greece.

"How confusing it must have been for this little boy," George Plimpton said, "to have Ari be a big part of his life one minute and then gone the next." As for the way he witnessed Onassis treating his mother: "Of course Jackie was everything to John and Caroline. As young as he was, John must have wanted to sock Ari in the eye for the things he did and said to Jackie."

Onassis was not above holding John's mother up to ridicule,

especially if it might teach her a lesson. Fed up with hearing Jackie complain about the press and no longer willing to finance her costly invasion-of-privacy lawsuits, Ari hatched a plan to embarrass Jackie to such an extent that there would be nothing more that the press could do to hurt her. As an added benefit, it would deeply hurt the woman he continued to deride as "the Widow."

In November 1972, ten photographers put on wetsuits and slipped into the waters off Skorpios. With detailed maps of the island, the dates, times, and places where Jackie was expected to be—all provided by Ari—they snapped scores of color photos of Jackie sunbathing and strolling around in the altogether. The full-frontal images caused a sensation when they ran in the Italian skin magazine *Playmen* and were then picked up by Larry Flynt's *Hustler*. Solely on the basis of the nude Jackie O shots, *Hustler* went from sales of a few thousand copies to over two million—launching Flynt's publishing empire overnight.

Needless to say, Ari's ill-conceived plan did not have the desired effect. John and Caroline cringed with embarrassment over having to see photographs of their mother—even censored photographs—displayed on every newsstand and supermarket counter in New York. Despite John's popularity at school, the teasing from classmates over what one magazine trumpeted as Jackie's "Billion Dollar Bush" was merciless and unrelenting.

Jackie, unaware that her husband was behind the whole fiasco, was livid. Instead of backing down, she demanded that Ari sue every photographer and every publication involved. Instead, Ari went straight to Roy Cohn's Upper East Side townhouse and informed him he was divorcing Jackie. Mindful of the fact that Jackie wasn't about to settle for the $3 million spelled out in their prenup, Onassis agreed to fork over an extra $1 million. "That's all the Widow gets," he said. "Not one penny more."

Not even Onassis believed Jackie would ever settle for such a trifling amount. He had recently learned that she was secretly selling her designer fashions to raise cash, and that concerned him. "He knew how greedy she was," Cohn said. "Onassis was really worried that Jackie would try and hold him up for a huge amount—$100 million or more—and that scared him shitless."

"The Widow" was completely in the dark about Ari's plans when, in January 1973, he flew to Paris and broke the news to Alexander over dinner. Ari's son was overjoyed, and promptly informed his sister. That same evening, Ari also reconfirmed his intention to eventually sell the Piaggio. In the meantime he asked Alexander, a seasoned pilot who had flown the Piaggio countless times, to take it up just once more, merely for the purpose of checking out a pilot he had just hired.

Less than three weeks later, at 3:12 p.m. on January 22, the Piaggio was taxiing into position with the new pilot at the controls and Alexander seated next to him. Fifteen seconds after takeoff, the plane banked sharply to the right and plummeted to earth, crashing into the tarmac.

Jackie and Ari were both in New York—she at her apartment, he at his Pierre Hotel suite—when they got the news that Alexander's plane had crashed. Although both he and the pilot were badly hurt, only Alexander's injuries were critical. Young Onassis's head wounds were so severe, in fact, that airport personnel at the scene had to rely on his monogrammed silk handkerchief to identify him.

Jackie wasted no time calling Caroline at Concord Academy. Since leaving home, John's sister had decided that she, too, wished to take to the skies. "People always think of John running up to welcome his father's helicopter," Pierre Salinger said. "They forget Caroline was on the White House lawn waiting for Daddy, too." Moreover, JFK's campaign plane was named after her—something she took considerable pride in as a little girl. "Caroline had been flying for years before John was even born," George Plimpton said. "Flying was second nature to her, and it made perfect sense that she'd want to give it a try." As enthusiastic as John was about aviation, it was their stepbrother who took them up in planes and helicopters whenever they visited Greece. Alexander's passion for flying was "infectious," Salinger said. "That may have rubbed off on them as well."

For several weeks Caroline had been taking flying lessons aboard a Cessna two-seater not far from Concord Academy, at Hanscom Airfield. No longer. With this latest reminder of just how dangerous flying could be—something the Kennedys knew all too well—Jackie forbade Caroline to pursue her pilot's license.

Alexander's untimely accident also forced Jackie to reconsider John's fascination with planes. An alarming number of Kennedys and extended family members had perished in plane crashes, and the crash that nearly killed Teddy in 1964 was still fresh in Jackie's mind.

Jackie herself had been nonchalant about flying in small planes; now it occurred to her for the first time that they might pose a real threat to her children. From this point on, she would do all she could to discourage John's dream of becoming a pilot.

John and Caroline stayed in the United States while Jackie and Ari flew to Athens. There Alexander, suffering from irreversible brain damage, lingered for hours before Ari made the gut-wrenching decision to end life support. Alexander was only twenty-four.

Onassis would never recover from his only son's death—not because he had been a loving father, but because he was consumed with guilt over *not* having been one. Just as important, Onassis's vast empire represented his bid for immortality; in highly patriarchal Greek society, Alexander was the embodiment of that future. Now Onassis would have to groom Christina (Ari's *Chryso Mou*—"My Golden One") for power. She would prove herself more than equal to the task—but things would never be the same.

Jackie, having experienced more than her share of grief, did what she could to ease Ari's pain. Two days after Alexander's funeral, she asked Pierre Salinger and his wife, Nicole, to fly to Dakar, Senegal and join them aboard the *Christina*. Onassis "loved" the intellectually challenging Pierre, Nicole said. "They went on for hours and hours, pacing up and down the deck, talking and arguing"—mostly about American history.

"Ari and I got along marvelously," Salinger said. "But his mood changed whenever Jackie started talking about Jack. Nerves were frayed, and you wondered how much of an impact this tense atmosphere was having on the kids."

At those times when John and Caroline saw Onassis lash out at their mother, Jackie patiently reminded them that their stepfather was still mourning the death of his only son. He was hurting, she explained, and not really responsible for his behavior. "They were two very sensitive, compassionate kids," Salinger allowed. "If Jackie told them he was just too overcome with grief . . . they'd understand that—to a point."

Salinger departed thinking the cruise "did seem to help," but he was wrong. Ari was becoming increasingly unhinged; Alexander's death had changed him forever. He was "no longer interested in life," Jackie said, and had become "a perfect horror to live with." Peter Duchin agreed that from this point on Ari was "moody, short with people"— what Mehle called Onassis's "endless blue funk."

Jackie kept trying to pull Ari out of this downward spiral of grief, distracting him with more travel—to the Caribbean, Mexico, Egypt, and Spain. None of it worked. Mehle ran into the couple in Florida. "I went down to the beach," she recalled, "and there was Ari curled up on the sand in a fetal position. Onassis was a mortally wounded man."

He was also becoming extremely paranoid, convinced that Alexander's tragic death was the result of an elaborate CIA plot. By July 1973, Ari was offering a $1 million reward to anyone who could prove that his son's plane had been sabotaged. A man possessed, Ari sat alone in the dark for hours, drinking Johnnie Walker Black Label and listening to the cockpit tapes of the doomed pilots as they desperately tried to regain control of their planes right before impact.

Duchin agreed that Alexander's death "knocked him out of the box. It completely changed Ari's personality . . . He felt fate had turned against him." Now Ari was "morose, nitpicking, critical—just extremely difficult to be in the same room with. All the spark he had was gone. Jackie got the worst of it."

Peter Beard recalled witnessing "the biggest fights between them you could ever imagine. He would blow up all the time—tantrums about everything. Yelling and screaming at her." Ari's rages became increasingly terrifying—until the inevitable happened. "They were having one of their screaming matches when Ari lost his temper and hit Jackie across the face," Cohn said. "She had a black eye, but since she wore dark glasses all the time nobody suspected a thing."

Jackie urged Ari to seek psychiatric help for his worsening depression. Instead, he found other ways to vent his rage. According to those who knew and worked for him, Ari carried on several short-term relationships with young men. In the aftermath of his son's death, these too turned violent.

Frank Monte, who worked as Ari's bodyguard in 1973, remembered that when he was in Rome, Ari saw "two Italian boys. One lived in Mr. Onassis's apartment and the other was always on call when Mr. Onassis wanted him. One was dark, the other was blond-haired but deeply tan. They were handsome, in their mid-twenties. Onassis would play around with them, making lewd jokes in front of me and the other bodyguards."

Ari, who frequently brought up the role of homosexuality in ancient Greek history, would "often talk quite openly about his two regular boys and other occasional boys," Monte said. But Ari's employees became concerned when these young men were subjected to violence. "He mistreated them, even beat them for pleasure. He'd often take one or the other to his bedroom and after a while, there'd be the sounds of punches and screams," Monte said. "Then we'd get a call from Mr. Onassis to fetch the poor kid and throw him out. Sometimes a boy would be yelling, 'No, no, I love you.'"

(Onassis apparently did not confine himself to pursuing sexual relationships with anonymous young men. Italian film director Franco Zeffirelli and Rudolf Nureyev claimed that Ari made passes at them aboard the *Christina*.)

Despite the ongoing strains in his mother's marriage prior to Alexander's plane crash death, John had always somehow managed to see the underlying good in his stepfather. Now that was impossible. Gone was the kindly father figure, supplanted by a sullen, bitter, increasingly deranged old man who did nothing to disguise that most of his rage was directed squarely at John's mother.

Onassis was never cruel to John or to Caroline. But he wasn't particularly kind to them, either. Gone were the long walks through Central Park, the trips to the playoffs, and the extravagant gifts. When he searched the bleachers at school events now, John would no longer see Ari sitting there next to his mother. "Onassis was in the middle of what amounted to a nervous breakdown," Tish Baldrige said. He had no way of comforting himself, much less make time for others.

Twelve-year-old John did what he could to cheer the old man up—asking Ari to join him at one of their neighborhood hangouts for ice cream, seeking his input for a school essay on Greek mythology. But Ari, according to one staff member, "was no longer interested in being a part of the Kennedys' lives. In a strange way, he blamed Jackie for what had happened to Alexander." Ari's longtime friend and lawyer Stelios Papadimitriou explained that "Greeks are very superstitious. I think ever since he married Jackie, everything went bad for him.

"Death and tragedy seemed to touch everyone *she* touched," Papadimitriou continued, "and he began to wonder if in some way he was being punished for marrying her." For years, Onassis had called Jackie "the Widow," but, said Ari's lawyer, "we called her 'the Black Widow.'"

Ari's rapidly deteriorating mental state aside, the stress also seemed to be taking a toll on him physically. He was losing weight. He suffered from debilitating headaches and fatigue, and for some odd reason his right eyelid drooped. In December 1973, Onassis checked into New York's Lenox Hill Hospital under the name "Philipps" and after a week of tests was diagnosed with myasthenia gravis, a rare, incurable muscular disease.

It would have taken a few minutes for Jackie to walk from her apartment to the hospital, but Ari had so alienated her that she refused to visit him. Christina rushed to his side from Paris, and would soon relocate to New York full-time so she could familiarize herself with the inner workings of Daddy's global empire.

Onassis kept the diagnosis to himself, but when he appeared in public with his right eye completely shut, the press speculated that he had suffered a stroke. Christina didn't help matters when she merely used white adhesive strips to tape Ari's eyelid to his forehead. The macabre result was soon featured on front pages everywhere, ramping up speculation that Onassis was grievously ill.

Jackie urged Ari to accompany her on a vacation trip to Acapulco, but when they arrived he realized the real purpose of their visit: to purchase a villa near the one where she and Jack had honeymooned two decades earlier. For Ari, this was the final slap in the face. He refused, and on the flight back to New York a shouting match ensued. Having put up with years of abuse from Onassis, Jackie now let loose with a torrent of insults. "Jackie could be understanding," Baldrige said, "only up to a point."

According to Johnny Meyer, Jackie took this opportunity to light into Ari for his "every lapse of taste and style," including what she called his "horrendous" table manners—"slurping soup, making animal noises while you chew, it's disgusting," Jackie told her husband. She did not spare Christina, either. "No man finds a fat girl with food on her chin attractive," Jackie said on the flight, "no matter how rich she is."

None of this came as a surprise to Jamie Auchincloss, who described his sister as "ferocious, once she was crossed." Agreed Gore Vidal: "She had a very sharp tongue indeed, and knew when to go for the jugular."

Christina was so incensed about "the Black Widow" that "the Singer" suddenly didn't seem so bad. Making a rare television appearance on the *Today* show in April 1974, Callas described Onassis as "the big love of my life." Did she resent Jackie Kennedy for marrying him?

interviewer Barbara Walters asked. "Why should I?" she answered with a shrug. "Of course, if she treats Mr. Onassis very badly, I might be very angry."

While the press was filled with speculation about Ari's mysterious illness—his speech was now slurred, he could barely hold his head up—tensions in the marriage, and the Jackie–Ari–Maria Callas love triangle, Onassis was plotting his revenge behind the scenes. In a new will, he left Jackie just $200,000 a year, and the children $25,000 each annually until they turned twenty-one. If they contested the will, neither Jackie nor Caroline and John would get a penny. He also named his ex-wife, Tina, the executrix of his will, leaving control of his empire and the vast bulk of his estate to Christina.

Ari went a step further, summoning journalist Jack Anderson to New York and asking him to unmask her profligate spending habits. Over lunch at New York's La Caravelle restaurant, which had been a favorite haunt of JFK and his father, Joe, Onassis "accused Jackie of embezzling millions from him. He explained the whole scheme in detail," Anderson said, "how she paid hundreds of thousands of dollars on clothes that she then secretly resold to used clothing stores in New York, pocketing the cash."

Anderson was told in no uncertain terms that Ari was about to file for divorce. "Once he had exposed her as this very greedy, voracious person," Anderson said, "he felt she'd be in no position to demand more millions in a divorce settlement."

———

NOT ALL THE salient details made it into the papers, but what did was enough to have an impact on John. "Caroline was away at school leading this protected life," Jackie's friend Cleveland Amory said. "But John was in the thick of it in New York. Jackie and Ari were in the papers every day, nonstop. It was the biggest story out there, and John couldn't get away from it if he tried."

Try to get away John did, taking every opportunity to break from the Secret Service detail that continued to shadow his every move. It was not uncommon for "Lark"—he was still known by his White House Secret Service code name—to be calmly pedaling through Central Park on his Italian ten-speed and then suddenly take off, leaving forty-something-year-old agents straining to keep up with him.

That April, while the world buzzed about Ari and Jackie, John slipped away from his bodyguards and, with two pals from Collegiate, sneaked into the Trans-Lux Theater on Broadway to see Mel Brooks's Western spoof, *Blazing Saddles*. Once again, headquarters in Washington was alerted to John's disappearance, every agency from local police to the FBI was notified, and for two tense hours Secret Service agents worked frantically to track JFK's son down.

They finally located John at the theater, catching up with him just as he and his friends came out, squinting in the bright light of midday. "A great movie!" John announced to the relieved agents. "Then," said the manager of the theater, "John seemed to take pleasure in telling the Secret Service guys about the film's famous campfire scene while his buddies collapsed with laughter."

A few weeks later, John vanished again. This time it was nearly three hours before agents found him, working on his serve at the Central Park tennis courts. Jackie was partly to blame for setting a poor example. Despite repeated pleas from friends like Nancy Tuckerman and Arthur Schlesinger, Jackie thought nothing of ditching her Secret Service detail at sunset and heading out to take a jog around the park reservoir alone. Tuckerman would "warn her of all the terrible things that could happen to her and, true to form, she never paid any attention. By nature," Tuckerman said, "she was fearless."

It was a trait both she and the notoriously reckless Jack passed on to their son. Even as an awkward adolescent in braces, John pushed everything to the limit—and sometimes beyond. "Everything with him," John's friend Billy Noonan said, "was an adventure, with an edge of danger thrown in."

When he was at Skorpios, John and his cousin Timothy Shriver would put on scuba gear and explore the coral reefs that ringed the island; defying orders to stay away from one particularly hazardous reef, the two cousins got stuck but managed to pull themselves free at the last minute. On Cape Cod, John liked to jump on his twelve-foot Sunfish with a couple of friends and play chicken with the ferries carrying a hundred or more tourists to Nantucket and Martha's Vineyard. John and his pals would see "how close we could get before we'd jump off, capsize, and save ourselves from bouncing off the ferry's steel hull," Noonan recalled. "John, inevitably, would be the last off the boat."

Jackie's seesawing love-hate relationship with publicity and the press that supplied it had dominated much of John's young life. "He had every right to be confused," Amory said, pointing to the fact that Jackie had actually met JFK when he was a U.S. senator and she was working as the Washington *Times-Herald*'s intrepid "Inquiring Camera Girl." Amory was just one of many writers Jackie called friends, and even Jack briefly worked as a journalist before entering politics. "She loved literature and gossip equally," Amory said, "and in the White House and afterward, she played the press like a Stradivarius. John saw all this."

So perhaps it shouldn't have been that surprising when he shared his career plans with journalist Beverly Williston. Williston was spending a weekend in New Jersey horse country when she bumped into Jackie and the kids. "So," Williston said, "what do you want to be—president?"

John's answer was immediate. "Nah! I want to write about politics. Everyone wants me to be a lawyer, but I want to be a reporter."

"That's what I do," Williston replied, taken aback by his answer.

"Do you get to travel a lot?" he asked. "Do you get to meet singers and actors?"

"Sometimes. It's a fun job," she went on. "You get to meet all kinds of people."

It soon became clear what John found most attractive about journalism. "So you don't have to go to college to be a reporter, right?" he asked.

John's shoulders slumped when Williston told him the horrible truth—that, yes, most journalists were college-educated. It was clearly not the answer he had hoped to hear.

With his pedigree, there seemed little doubt that John would wind up at an Ivy League school—although one would have never guessed it judging by his lackluster grades. Always a blur of nervous energy, he seemed more congenitally incapable of sitting still or concentrating than ever. Jackie wondered if all the stories about her imploding marriage were taking their toll on her son.

She also worried about substance abuse. When he was twelve, John and his Collegiate buddy Wilson McCray were caught swigging Johnnie Walker Black Label straight from the bottle while watching a Knicks game at Madison Square Garden. Perhaps it was significant that Johnnie Walker Black Label had always been Ari's drink of choice. It was also during this period that John developed a taste for red wine and strong Greek cigarettes.

Jackie might have done well to focus on John's growing fondness for alcohol and other unhealthy substances. Right now, she just wanted to know why her son wasn't the stellar student she and his sister had been—and what could be done to turn his academic career around.

John's mother sent him to a psychiatrist, Dr. Ted Becker, to see if there weren't psychological obstacles to his focusing and becoming a better student. "John is like a live wire, always in motion," Jackie told Salinger. "Maybe he can't calm down and focus on his schoolwork because of all the stress these horrible stories put him through." Jackie was concerned that it was garden-variety anxiety that kept John from earning better grades. If that was the case, she said, "I hope there's a pill for it."

For the time being, the consensus was that John was a normal adolescent male living under highly abnormal circumstances. Aside from his mediocre academic performance and an energy level that kept him more or less in constant motion—John was a world-class daydreamer and fidgeter—he seemed remarkably well adjusted and, for want of a more clinical term, happy. In the meantime, Jackie insisted that, during the summer months, John spend at least one hour each morning with his math tutor. "I was always terrible at math too," Jackie told Plimpton. "But," she added, betraying her decidedly traditional view of gender roles, "I don't think in today's world a man can afford to be."

In one area in particular, John showed a remarkable degree of maturity. Perhaps because he had already witnessed so much anguish, John was keenly attuned to the feelings of others. When Ari's assistant Kiki Moutsatsos was mugged outside Alexander's Department Store in midtown Manhattan, Jackie insisted that she recuperate at 1040. John's sister was away in Hyannis Port at the time, but he was there and promptly took over responsibility for nursing Kiki back to health. John, Moutsatos remembered, "was every bit as kind to me as his mother was"—maybe more so. It's doubtful whether Jackie would have cut strawberries up in the kitchen and fed them to Moutsatsos by hand.

At Collegiate, John no longer tussled with other students. One of the school's most-liked students, he crafted a persona that was part approachable, down-to-earth "regular guy" and part megacelebrity.

Anyone who was lucky enough to be invited to 1040—John's shorthand for home—was reminded of John's unique place in history the moment they walked into his large, Kennedy memorabilia-filled bedroom at the rear of the apartment. Models of Air Force One and PT-109 dangled from the ceiling, and framed photos covered every available surface—pictures of John hiding under JFK's Oval Office desk, mugging with President Kennedy and German chancellor Konrad Adenauer, sitting on his father's lap aboard the yacht *Honey Fitz.*

Then there was the president's extensive scrimshaw collection, and, propped up in one corner, the eight-foot-long bill of a rare narwhal. "Just a typical fifteen-year-old's bedroom," said his friend Billy Noonan.

Of course, John was anything but typical. The mindless teasing he had endured had made him far more empathetic than most self-absorbed teens. At Collegiate, he was widely regarded as a champion of the underdog. "If there was a new kid, John was the one who took him under his wing and introduced him around," a classmate said. "He knew what it was like to feel like an outsider, I think, so he recognized that in others."

Sadly, not everyone was so considerate. Shortly after 5 p.m. on May 14, 1974, John cruised into Central Park on his bike—unaware that a nineteen-year-old junkie named Robert Lopez was hunkered down in the bushes, waiting to pounce.

"Get the hell off the bike!" Lopez hollered as he lunged toward John. He was waving a stick at the boy. "Get off the bike or I'll kill you!"

John jumped off, but not quickly enough for Lopez, who shoved him to the ground anyway.

Grabbing John's tennis racket, Lopez hopped on the bike and rode north. He sold the racket and John's bike, then used the money to purchase cocaine.

The mugging of JFK Jr. was big news, and local TV anchors breathlessly reported that the police were searching for John's assailant. No one was more surprised than Lopez, who learned the identity of his victim while watching television with his pregnant wife, Miriam. "Oh my God!" Lopez yelled, leaping off the sofa and pointing at the screen. "That was me!" Police officials, under pressure in the 1970s to do something about the city's skyrocketing crime rate, were not exactly thrilled. "Six million people in the park that year," said one, "and they had to pick him."

It would be several months before Lopez confessed to John's mugging—and then only after he was arrested for another robbery. Lopez told his arresting officer, New York City detective Richard Buggy, that he targeted John not because he was a Kennedy—"Are you kidding? I had no idea who he was at the time"—but because John was simply "an easy hit." (More than two decades later, the lives of John and his mugger would intersect again, when Lopez signed up with a work program sponsored by the Robin Hood Foundation. By then, John was on the foundation's board of directors.)

Since Jackie herself had always been philosophical about the dangers lurking in Central Park, she preferred to look at John's mugging as a "blessing in disguise." Secret Service agent John Walsh wrote in a confidential report to his superiors that Jackie was "pleased that this had happened to John, in that he must be allowed to experience life." Walsh relayed Jackie's conviction that John "is oversheltered now with all the agents and unless he is allowed freedom he'll be a vegetable at the age of sixteen when we leave him."

Once again, Jackie spelled out precisely what she expected from Walsh and his colleagues. "She does not want us to inquire of the governess when John is going, or how he is getting there. We should be prepared for him to go in any one of a number of ways."

At the same time, Jackie insisted that the agents not crowd her son. "I don't want you on his heels," she said, repeating what had become a familiar refrain. "Secret Service agents are told to follow counterfeiters all over the place without them knowing they're being followed. Why can't you do it with John?"

While characterizing the Central Park assault as a much-needed wake-up call, Jackie was "displeased about all the publicity" because "people will think he isn't being accompanied by anyone and there is a danger in that."

So what was the solution? Walsh asked. Did Jackie want heightened security for her son, at least for the time being?

Absolutely not, Jackie replied. "No agent is to be in John's pocket," she ordered Walsh. "John is not to get in an agent's car and the agents are not to walk with him. They must follow him, hiding behind cars and bushes—whatever they need to do so he never sees them."

Not that she didn't want agents to be there if John needed them. "I want him followed," she explained, "but I don't want him to feel like he's constantly being guarded. It's not healthy."

At the same time, Jackie made it abundantly clear that she wasn't about to tolerate any more slipups. "If anything happens to John," she warned Walsh in a chilling reference to Dallas, "I will not be as easy with the Secret Service as I was the first time."

Jackie brought him up to be his own person,
not part of the Kennedys' tribal connection.
—FRANK MANKIEWICZ, LONGTIME KENNEDY FAMILY FRIEND

Jackie's mothering of John was complex.
She had an innate sense . . . of how to walk the
line between protecting him and giving him
the freedom to figure out his own way.
—BILLY NOONAN, JOHN'S FRIEND

John was simply not suited to lead the intellectual life.
He was always outside, always in motion. He did things.
—ALEXANDER THEROUX, JOHN'S TEACHER AT ANDOVER

7.

The Crown Prince

They were scuba diving forty feet below the surface of the Aegean, and Peter Duchin could see his diving buddy was in trouble. For some reason, John wasn't getting enough air; Duchin watched as John struggled with his face mask, then pointed to his oxygen hose. "By then," Duchin recalled, "John was a strapping teenager" of fourteen, but all Duchin could see was the toddler saluting his father's casket. An experienced diver, Duchin swam over and shared his mouthpiece with John while they swam slowly to the surface. John never panicked. In fact, Duchin said, he showed "amazing cool" even as he faced the very distinct possibility of drowning. Duchin, however, was anything but calm. "I kept thinking, 'I've got the son of the president of the United States here!'" Duchin said. "Jackie was very grateful, as you can imagine."

Duchin was one of the old friends Jackie had summoned to Greece to lighten the mood while Ari descended further into illness and depression. On February 3—before any divorce papers could be filed and before Jack Anderson's exposé of Jackie's spending could be published—Onassis collapsed in Athens with severe stomach pains.

Jackie rushed to her husband's side, and then flew with him to Paris, where surgeons at the American Hospital removed his gallbladder. For the next five weeks, he remained comatose in room 217—a first-floor suite in the hospital's Eisenhower Wing. Jackie was back at home in

New York with John on March 12 when Ari, fighting infection and the debilitating effects of his myasthenia gravis, slipped into a coma. Onassis's doctors told Jackie that her husband could die at any time, and prodded her to fly back to Paris. Jackie chose instead to remain in Manhattan.

Three days later, Ari died with Christina at his side. He was seventy-five.

Jackie had just returned to 1040 after an appointment at Kenneth's hair salon when Johnny Meyer called her with the news that she was now a widow for a second time. She immediately told Meyer that she would be flying to Paris with John and Caroline aboard Ari's Learjet. As she rattled off the details, Meyer could not help but notice that Jackie sounded "almost cheerful."

The first call Jackie then made was to John's uncle Ted, who had been instrumental in working out her original prenup with Ari. She would need the services of a powerful and well-connected U.S. senator to square off with Christina in negotiating a settlement now that Ari was dead. She then called her favorite designer of the moment, Valentino, and ordered a new black dress to wear to the funeral.

John was at a friend's house when the call came from his mother—he was third on her list. "I'm afraid Mr. Onassis has died," she told him matter-of-factly. John registered some small sadness at the news, but he could hardly be expected to react with an outpouring of grief. The outcome had been expected for weeks, and whatever bond Ari had forged with JFK's son had been irretrievably broken by Onassis's callous treatment of John's mother.

Meanwhile in Paris, Christina was so distraught over her father's passing—coming just five months after her mother Tina's mysterious death at age forty-five—that she slit her wrist. It might have been expected; the highly unstable heiress had tried to kill herself several times before, and would again. Reporters who spotted the white bandages on Christina's wrist as she left Ari's bedside were told it was "an accident, a bathroom slip," nothing more.

In Christina's mind, the Black Widow was to blame for everything that had gone wrong for the Onassis family in recent years—including the deaths of her favorite aunt, Eugenie, her brother, her mother, and now her father. "I don't dislike her, you know," Christina now said. "I *hate* her."

Getting off the plane in Paris, Jackie, wearing a black leather jacket and her trademark oversize shades, was greeted by hordes of photographers and reporters. No one from the Onassis family was there to greet her. Smiling incongruously, she issued a statement to the press. "Aristotle Onassis rescued me at a moment when my life was engulfed with shadows," she said. "He brought me into a world where one could find both happiness and love. We lived through many beautiful experiences together which cannot be forgotten, and for which I will be eternally grateful."

While Jackie went on to see Ari's body lying in state in the hospital chapel—his tan restored by mortuary cosmeticians, his arms clutching a large Orthodox crucifix to his chest—John flew on ahead to Skorpios. With him were Caroline, their uncles Ted and Jamie, and their grandmother Janet Auchincloss. Photographers waiting to catch Jackie's arrival on Skorpios made do with hounding her kids. John buried his head in a comic book, but to no avail. Fed up, he stuck his tongue out at his tormentors, providing them with one of the day's many perplexing images.

Jackie and Christina clung to each other for support as they were engulfed by the waiting press in Athens. But on the day of the funeral, the Onassises made it clear where they stood vis-à-vis Jackie. The funeral cortege was to wend its way to the fishing village of Nidri, where Ari's body was to be placed on a launch bound for Skorpios. Christina, Jackie, and Ted sat together in the back of the second car, behind the limousine carrying Onassis's three surviving sisters.

Just a few minutes into the journey, Ted, briefed on Ari's plan to leave Jackie with precious little, leaned over to Christina and said, "Now it's time to take care of Jackie."

"Stop the car!" Christina shouted at the driver. Leaping from the limousine before it could come to a full stop, she ran ahead to join her aunts in their car.

It quickly became clear that Jackie and her family were not welcome. On Ari's private island, a half dozen pallbearers carried his casket up the winding, rock-strewn footpath to the Onassis's private chapel. But rather than being allowed to walk directly behind the coffin as she had done during JFK's funeral, Ari's widow was elbowed to the rear by Christina and her aunts. "It was a deliberate move to block Jackie off— to isolate her," Johnny Meyer said. Even Greek Orthodox archdeacon Stylianos Pirounakis was shocked. "In all my years in the church," he said, "I don't recall another funeral where the widow was pushed into the background this way. Mrs. Onassis was made to feel as if she did not really belong. I find this extremely tragic."

Putting on a united front, Jackie and her mop-topped son clung to each other as they brought up the rear of the funeral procession. "Jackie was humiliated and hurt," Arthur Schlesinger said, "and John certainly knew it. Just look at the photos taken at the time. The look of dismay in both their faces, especially John's, is extraordinary." The moment harked back to that day years earlier when he tried to shield Jackie from the taunts of his St. David's schoolmates. "From the very beginning," Salinger said, "John was his mother's protector."

––––––

UNFORTUNATELY, WHAT STAYED in the mind of many Greeks was the image of Jackie smiling broadly while Christina and other family members wept. "It was a defense mechanism," Tish Baldrige said. "No, obviously Jackie wasn't wiped out the way she was by President Kennedy's death. But what I saw in that smile was courage—and a lot of defiance."

Nevertheless, the Greek public was outraged. ONLY CHRISTINA CRIED, read the headline in the Athens *Acropolis*. JACKIE WAS COLD.

Mindful that she was being portrayed as a grasping gold digger by Ari's camp—"the Greeks," she called them—Jackie remained in mourning for weeks. In the meantime, John and Caroline were dispatched to fulfill several of her social obligations.

Just three days after Ari's funeral, Jackie's children substituted for her at a lunch given at the Elysée Palace in Paris. "You have the look and smile of President John Kennedy," French president Valéry Giscard d'Estaing told John, "and I am very pleased that his children are here."

That April, Jackie sent John along on a tour of Russia with his cousins Tim, Bobby, and Maria Shriver and their parents, Eunice and Sargent. Even by Kennedy standards, John was a bouncing, darting, nerve-fraying bundle of energy. When he got bored listening to Sarge Shriver make a speech, he climbed to the balcony and sailed paper airplanes over the heads of his uncle's audience.

Like her cousin Caroline, nineteen-year-old Maria was struggling to control her weight. She watched in envious disbelief as John wolfed down just about anything he wanted without ever gaining an ounce. John "ate everything—ice cream, caviar, anything," Tim marveled. "He was a garbage can."

Even among the fun-loving Kennedy kids, fourteen-year-old John was a standout. When the family posed for pictures, Maria threw her left arm around John—only to have him lift her hand off his shoulder and bite it. As she would so often do when John pulled one of his tricks, Maria shrieked with laughter.

Under other circumstances, Jackie, a devout Russophile, would have tagged along. But she was preoccupied trying to nail down her Onassis inheritance. At one point in May 1975 when Christina met with a group of bankers and oil executives in London, Jackie flew to England under the name "Mrs. Wyberg" in hopes of cornering her. Proceeding straight to Ari's permanently reserved hotel suite, she discovered that Christina had already canceled the suite and cleared out all of Jackie's clothes.

As much as she despised Jackie, Christina did not want to go through a drawn-out war in the courts. Yet over the next year and a half, the two women battled fiercely over what Jackie was actually entitled to. Christina was particularly offended by Teddy, who continued to pressure her even after the funeral. "I didn't need that big walrus sloshing around in my pool and telling me to do right by Jackie," Christina told

Aileen Mehle. "Of course I was going to do right by Jackie—but in my own good time."

Finally, the two women arrived at the IBM Tower in London to hammer out a deal—this despite Christina's refusal to meet Jackie face-to-face. "They sat in separate rooms," said Ari's longtime spokesman Nigel Neilson, "and legal papers were shuttled back and forth between them by the firm's clerks."

In the end, Christina agreed to pay Jackie $26 million in cash—a $20 million lump sum settlement and the additional $6 million to cover taxes. "There is not," Neilson said at that time, "a lot of love lost between them."

Indeed, Onassis's tight circle felt only contempt for the woman they still referred to as the Black Widow. "She's despicable," said Gratsos, who ran the day-to-day operations of the Onassis empire following Ari's death. "I can't bring myself to even think about her." As for Christina: "She can't bear the thought of that woman. She never wants to see her again, or hear her name."

Christina took small comfort in being the world's richest woman. Ricocheting from one disastrous affair to another, she never freed herself from her dependence on pills and booze. There would be several more suicide attempts and three more failed marriages before Christina's naked body was discovered in a half-filled bathtub on November 19, 1988—three weeks short of her thirty-eighth birthday. The cause of death: pulmonary edema, resulting from her abuse of barbiturates and other prescription drugs. Ari's only grandchild, Christina's three-year-old daughter Athina, inherited everything.

———

JACKIE WAS DETERMINED not to make the same mistakes as a parent that Ari apparently made. "If you bungle raising your children," she liked to say, "I don't think whatever else you do well matters very much."

An important first step was keeping her kids away from their problematic Kennedy cousins, especially Ethel's hell-raising brood. Unable or unwilling to discipline her own children, Bobby's widow presided over a household where chaos reigned supreme. At Hyannis Port, the Kennedy kids were notorious for vandalizing boats tied up on the pier, ambushing tourists with water balloons, firing BB guns at passing motorists, and lobbing lit firecrackers into neighbors' homes. At a party for one of the neighborhood children, next-door neighbor Larry Newman watched in disbelief as they pulled out a knife and robbed a young girl of her birthday gifts.

Matters only got more out of hand during the 1970s, when John's cousins began dabbling in drugs. Drifting from one college to another on the strength of his name, Joe Kennedy II, Bobby's eldest, smoked pot and partied hard. On Nantucket one weekend, Joe took a friend's Jeep on a joyride with his brother David and David's girlfriend, Pam Kelley, in the backseat. Their wild ride ended when Joe lost control and careened off the road and into ditch, ejecting all three occupants. Joe emerged unscathed, but Pam was paralyzed from the waist down.

Joe certainly wasn't alone. RFK Jr. and Bobby Shriver were arrested for marijuana possession. Shriver wasn't about to repeat his mistake, but the same couldn't be said for Bobby Jr. Along with his brother David and John's cousin Christopher Lawford, Uncle Bobby's namesake began dabbling in heroin.

Jackie tried to keep her children—John in particular—away from the gravitational pull of Hickory Hill. When Ethel called to invite John to spend two weeks there in the summer of 1975, Jackie's response was swift and unequivocal. "No way!" she told Ted Kennedy's aide Richard Burke. "With all the stuff that was going on at Hickory Hill—especially with the problems the boys were having—Jackie just didn't want Caroline and John there."

In truth, John was perfectly capable of getting into trouble on his own. He was only thirteen when he started smoking marijuana, and remained a frequent pot smoker for the rest of his life. At Collegiate, he was disciplined numerous times. "We were always getting caught," John's classmate Wilson McCray said, "for getting stoned." In addition, John smoked pot on the roof of his mother's apartment, and in the powder room at 1040 Fifth Avenue.

John was not above pulling potentially deadly pranks of his own under the influence of cannabis. During a family ski trip in Switzerland, John and McCray waited for Jackie to hit the slopes before stealing a Volkswagen van and taking it for a spin.

Between the warnings from school and the pungent aroma wafting from her powder room, Jackie must have known what John was up to. Apparently she had no idea, however, that Caroline was growing marijuana in Jackie's vegetable garden at Hyannis Port. Caroline and John both routinely availed themselves of this homegrown supply—until a local policeman just happened to glance over the fence and spotted Caroline's crop nestled between Jackie's lettuce and zucchini plants.

Fortunately for JFK's kids, the Hyannis Port cop went straight to Jackie. Enraged, she threatened to ground them indefinitely unless they cleaned up their act. Jackie could be frightening when she wanted to. "Suddenly she'd drop the breathless little girl voice and, boom, you knew you were in trouble," Salinger said. "*Big* trouble."

Not that Jackie assumed they would just stop smoking pot because she ordered them to. For both John and his sister there was an abiding need to be accepted for who they were, not as the children of a martyred president and his impossibly glamorous wife. They would probably continue to break the rules, if only to fit in. So to strengthen her hand, Jackie ordered the staff to keep a closer-than-usual eye on them.

Mindful of the repercussions a JFK Jr. drug bust would have, Jackie's Secret Service detail turned something of a blind eye to John's pot smoking. In turn, he ignored the fact that, wherever he went, an agent was only a few yards away. At restaurants, one agent would usually be nursing a ginger ale at the bar while another was positioned near the front door. When John went to the movies, a quick scan of the surrounding few rows would yield one suspiciously clean-cut man in his late twenties or early thirties pretending that he was focused entirely on the screen. If John was riding with a friend, one of the agency's blue or black Ford Crown Victorias was never more than a few car lengths behind.

Their presence was welcome on several occasions that failed to make the news. There were several instances, usually at bars and clubs in New York, when an agent steered a belligerent drunk or a particularly annoying female fan in another direction. Once they stepped in when, on the stone front steps of the Metropolitan Museum, a chain-wielding street gang descended on John and his Frisbee-tossing pals.

Whatever John's transgressions were when it came to marijuana, Jackie was convinced that they paled in comparison to what the Kennedy cousins were up to—and she was right. "Jackie did not want her children *inhaled* into that frenzied macho world of the Kennedys," said her friend David Halberstam, the Pulitzer Prize–winning journalist and author. "She wanted them to be a part of their father's legacy, but she wanted them to develop the kind of self-control that many of their Kennedy cousins lacked. Jackie accomplished this very, very shrewdly, bringing them up in New York but letting them show the flag at Kennedy functions. She didn't want her children sucked in, and they weren't."

Peter Duchin agreed that, in terms of her desire to raise children JFK would have been proud of, "one of the big decisions Jackie made in her life was to get the children the hell out of Hyannis Port and away from the Kennedys. The cousins were left to their own devices, and she knew it could only spell trouble. It was something she worried about all the time."

Duchin recalled the summer when Jackie sent John on a diving expedition to Micronesia "just to keep him away from the Kennedy kids." Once she had outlined her plan, Jackie turned to Duchin. "Do you think," she asked, "that's far enough away?" Jackie "wasn't joking," Duchin said. "She was deadly serious."

Backed up by nannies Maud Shaw and Marta Sgubin, Jackie taught John and Caroline to be considerate of others—a lesson Ethel clearly neglected to impart to her offspring. "Jackie was all over John," Noonan said. "She wanted him to be a regular guy but also wanted him to be polite and dignified." Both of Jackie's kids were, Tish Baldrige agreed, "sophisticated far beyond their years—very much their mother's children." If there was one slice of pie left at a Hyannis Port picnic, John and

Caroline would never take it. Their Hickory Hill counterparts would "knock each other and the table over grabbing it for themselves," said Chuck Spalding, who went on to describe "pretty much all the other Kennedys" as a "loud and rowdy bunch. With them, manners pretty much went out the window."

Although he shared the Kennedys' competitive streak, John was reluctant to draw blood during the family's take-no-prisoners games of touch football. "Sometimes those games were a *bloodbath*," Larry Newman said. "From generation to generation—it never changed." People "really got injured during those games," Jamie Auchincloss agreed. "But John held back. He wasn't the kind of person who took pleasure in hurting people." According to his friend Billy Noonan, John preferred swimming, sailing, and tossing a Frisbee to team sports like football and baseball. "Football on the compound was a little too Kennedyesque— not just for me, but for John," Noonan said. John joined in, he later confided to another friend, only when he got "roped into it. He didn't want to seem like a snob."

In truth, the other Kennedys did view John differently—especially in the immediate aftermath of Aristotle Onassis's death, when it was falsely rumored that Jackie had been left up to $100 million. He and his sister "were already the stars—overshadowing everybody else," a former Hyannis Port household staff member said. There was a feeling among the Kennedys that John was "the crown prince of the family— and that somehow he didn't deserve it."

"John took the most heat because of the position he held in the family," his friend Rob Littell said. "He was something of an outsider . . . he had a slightly strained relationship with the tight-knit crew as a whole." According to his friend, these internecine resentments could be traced to a single emotion: envy. "This didn't bother him a bit," Littell went on. "He had the best of many worlds and he knew it."

———

WITH CAROLINE ALREADY looking at colleges and John headed for prep school, Jackie was about to become an empty-nester at forty-six.

Viking Press was Tish Baldrige's publisher at the time, and Baldrige suggested that the former Washington *Times-Herald* Inquiring Camera Girl consider going back to work—this time as a book editor. Over lunch at Manhattan's Le Périgord Park restaurant, Jackie broached the idea with Viking's publisher Tom Guinzburg, an old friend.

In September 1975, Jackie started her new job and was instantly dismissed by many as a bored socialite seeking a new diversion—a rank amateur with no particular qualifications for the job.

"I'm not the worst choice for this position," she fired back at her critics. "It's not as if I've never done anything interesting."

The first thing she had to do was convince her colleagues that she belonged there. Viking's editorial staff was "stunned by the news" that Jackie would be joining them as a junior editor, Guinzburg recalled. "Everybody wondered, 'What's this giant celebrity doing in our midst?'"

Ironically, the world's most sought-after personage was given the task of luring big-name celebrities to Viking. In her own case, Jackie voraciously devoured every syllable that was written about her, going so far as to instruct her maid Provi to purchase tabloids like the *Star* and the *National Enquirer* so that she could peruse them. Jackie circled all mentions of her name in red, and at times scrawled her own editorial comments—usually "HA!" and *"REALLY?"*—in the margins. Her secretary was then instructed to file the clips away.

At the same time, she harbored a fascination with the rich and famous that rivaled that of any schoolgirl. "She was always sidling up to you and asking 'What is Liz Taylor *really* like?' or 'Is it true that so-and-so is having an affair?'" Capote said. "Gossip was Jackie's drug of choice."

Within a few months of joining Viking, she tried and failed to land the authors whose memoirs would have put all those rumors about her being an amateur to rest: Queen Elizabeth, the Duchess of Windsor, Princess Margaret, and her old friend Frank Sinatra all turned her down. The Duchess of Windsor was particularly cutting in her reply. A member of her staff wrote to Jackie stating flatly that the Duchess was not about to discuss her life story with any "publisher's assistant."

Eventually, Jackie gravitated to Viking's Studio Books division, focusing her attention on editing lavishly illustrated coffee table volumes. One, about fireworks, was by her old pal George Plimpton. "She was a wonderful editor—*very* meticulous," said Plimpton, who marveled at how the job seemed to have infused Jackie with a new sense of purpose. "It must have been an extraordinary thing for her to be on her own," he said. "She was always somewhat diminished by the men around her." Now, Plimpton added, Jackie was "much more like the girl I first knew who had a sense of fun and enthusiasm."

Jackie still fretted about John's poor academic performance, and nagged Caroline incessantly about her weight. In fact, Jackie held both of her children to the same exacting standards. "Everyone knew the pressure on John to become a great man was tremendous," a prep school classmate said. "But he used to say he felt sorry for Caroline because to a certain extent people expected him to screw up along the way, while she was expected to be perfect—all the time."

Things nearly took another tragic turn for the Kennedys that October in 1975, when Caroline graduated from Concord Academy and began a yearlong internship with Sotheby's auction house in London. While she searched for her own apartment, Caroline stayed as a guest in the home of Conservative member of Parliament Hugh Fraser, JFK's longtime friend and a vocal critic of the Irish Republican Army.

Each weekday morning, Fraser drove Caroline to her work-study program at Sotheby's in his red Jaguar sedan. They were heading out the door on the morning of October 23 when Fraser's phone rang and he went back inside with Caroline to take the call. At 8:53 a.m., a bomb detonated beneath Fraser's car, flipping it on its roof before it exploded in flames. The eminent cancer research specialist Gordon Hamilton Fairley just happened to be walking by with his dog at the moment the bomb went off. The married father of four and his dog were killed instantly; Fairley's legs were blown off and his torso flung into Fraser's garden. Fraser was cut by flying glass from shattered windows and Caroline was thrown to the floor, but neither was seriously injured.

"That call saved my life—and Caroline's," Fraser said of his last-minute decision to return to the house and answer the ringing phone. "Thank God for the telephone. Had it not been for that call, we would all have died."

Jackie was awakened in New York at 7 a.m. by a call from the U.S. Embassy in London informing her of the IRA bombing and assuring her that Caroline was safe and unharmed. Not wanting John to wake up to televised footage of the carnage outside Fraser's London home, Jackie went into his room and told him what had happened.

"Mummy was shaking when she told me," John later recalled. The fact that the IRA had come so close to killing one of the world's most famous Irish-Americans, the only daughter of a man revered by all the world's Irish, struck John as "totally insane. It was so crazy. We were in complete shock."

Jackie called Caroline and urged her to consider coming home. John telephoned his sister as well, and told her that he was concerned about her safety. In the end Caroline decided to stick it out "like I knew she would," John said. "Nothing rattles her."

From this point on, John brooked no defense of the IRA or its terrorist tactics. When his pal Billy Noonan defended the IRA during one of their many political debates, John shot back, "Hey, your boys almost blew up my sister!"

There were other safety issues that concerned Jackie—the kinds that face most parents of hormone-driven teenage boys. After Ari's death, John had somehow managed to have Alexander Onassis's motorcycle shipped to the United States and stowed away in a friend's garage. John took the motorcycle out on remote roads where he wouldn't be spotted, but it wasn't long before Jackie learned about his new toy and confiscated it.

Aware of John's appetite for speed and his passion for taking risks— she admonished him for playing chicken with the Nantucket ferry, although he never stopped—Jackie held off on getting him his own car. Instead, she encouraged his older friends to do the driving, and at times even lent them one of her top-of-the-line, high-performance BMW sedans.

In New York, Jackie was ferried about town in limousines or, just as frequently, grabbed a cab. Upper East Siders were accustomed to the sight of "Jackie O" stepping off the curb and thrusting out her arm to hail a taxi like any other New Yorker. But outside the city, she drove herself everywhere. "She loved to drive," Dave Powers said, "just like Jack." There was one important difference. "Jackie was a terrific driver," Spalding said. "She knew how to handle a car, she didn't take chances. Jack was a madman behind the wheel—all the Kennedy men were."

Still, Jackie occasionally had her brushes with the law. Although Jackie was stopped a few times for exceeding the speed limit, no policeman or state trooper ever dared give her a ticket. John thoroughly enjoyed such moments, watching the reaction on each cop's face as he looked at Jackie's license, then bent down to stare squarely into the eyes of the world's most famous woman. Once when this happened, Tony Radziwill and Billy Noonan were along for the ride. After she received the usual warning and pulled cautiously back onto the road, her passengers roared with laughter. "*Okay*," Jackie said with a smile, "enough, you guys."

It was around this time that John and his friends found a new nickname for John's mother—a code word that was suitable but known only to a select few. For a time, Jackie employed an irascible Chinese butler who insisted on referring to her as "Big Lady" even when he was having a temper tantrum. Jackie assumed he was being deferential—until the undecipherable word he was muttering *before* Big Lady became painfully clear. "Fucking Big Lady" was not what she wanted to hear from a servant, and the butler was promptly sacked. From then on, whenever John spoke of "Big Lady," his inner circle knew precisely who he was talking about.

It was September 1976—the year of America's Bicentennial—and John was finally leaving home. Just as important, he would be turning sixteen in just three months, and that meant he could finally jettison the Secret Service detail that had hovered over him his entire life. "Free at last!" John shouted, pumping his fist as he strode onto the campus of Phillips Academy in Andover, Massachusetts. "Free at last!"

PART TWO

John on His Own

8.

Just One of the Guys

I f her son was no longer going to be under the protection of the U.S. government, Jackie could take solace that he was firmly ensconced behind the ivy-covered walls of America's oldest and most prestigious prep school. Comprising 170 buildings covering 450 acres, coeducational Andover (as Phillips Academy is more commonly called) counted among its distinguished alumni the diverse likes of Samuel Morse, Oliver Wendell Holmes, George H. W. Bush, George W. Bush, and Jack Lemmon.

Rooming with twenty-one other boys at Stearns West Hall dormitory, John took pains to prove he was, as Wilson McCray put, it "just one of the guys." Dominating one corner of his dorm room was a ship's carved figurehead—a life-size, bare-breasted mermaid. Strewn about the room were the usual talismans of prep school life: Frisbees, sweatclothes, empty pizza boxes.

Other items tipped off visitors to the fact that this particular room was not occupied by just another Andover freshman: a silk-screen portrait of Chairman Mao inscribed to "John Kennedy Jr." by the artist Andy Warhol; a silk boxing robe from a heavyweight title bout, with "Muhammad Ali" sewn on the back; a framed portrait of JFK hanging directly above his desk.

Yet, in his torn jeans, sweatshirt, and Docksiders, John did look like any other preppy headed for class. At sixteen, he now had a girlfriend—a pretty, curly-haired senior named Meg Azzoni. Since Azzoni was two years older than John, friends like Billy Noonan viewed this as "a real coup . . . She had a raspy voice she used for comic effect . . . I liked her immediately."

For obvious reasons, Azzoni was the envy of every female student—and not a few faculty members—at Andover. A natural athlete with a taste for mischief and off-color humor of the "There was a young man from Nantucket" variety, John was also popular among the men on campus. "You couldn't help but like him," one said. "He had this aura of quiet confidence, but was never arrogant or self-important. He was just an easygoing kid who wanted to get a little fun out of life like everybody else."

Unlike most of his fellow students at a time when the legal drinking age was eighteen, John rarely drank to excess. "He couldn't really hold his liquor," an Andover dorm mate said. "Two drinks and he was wasted, and he told me the hangovers were terrible." Whenever he went out for drinks with his buddies, John, armed with a fake ID (at this point in his life he could easily go unrecognized), usually ordered a beer and then followed it with a ginger ale or a Sprite.

Marijuana was an entirely different matter. "John smoked grass," said Holly Owen, the head of Andover's drama department, "but it didn't appear to affect him." Owen, who doubled as John's soccer coach, concluded John's "drug escapade was part of the rite of passage."

There would be countless close calls and embarrassing moments, like the time he intended to plant his own crop at the Kennedy compound in Hyannis Port—this time in Rose's cutting garden—and stuffed the coat pockets of his blazer with cannabis seeds. When he left the blazer at the home of Billy Noonan's mother, she called to tease him about finding "something" in the pockets. "She is so fucking funny, Billy," John said. "So fucking funny, your mother."

Where John's Secret Service agents and the parents of his friends chose to overlook his drug use, Andover's campus police were less accommodating. Late one night a security guard followed the unmistakable odor of marijuana to a party where John and several rugby teammates were celebrating that day's victory. The guard's knock on the door triggered a mad dash to flush the evidence, but John made no excuses.

Andover followed its normal practice and called John's mother with the news that her son had been caught smoking pot. No action would be taken this time, but a second such incident might lead to a suspension or even expulsion. John was surprised by his mother's low-key response. "I said I was sorry and then waited for Mummy to tear me up," he said. "But instead she was very calm and accepted my apology and told me not to do it again."

Jackie's rationale was simple. "He wants to fit in and for obvious reasons it's harder for him," she told Spalding. "If it becomes a problem, then I'll come down hard on him. But I don't think it will." Holly Owen, who doubled as John's soccer coach, agreed. "When John experimented with drugs," she said, "it was only to be one of the boys, not because he was out of control. That makes a huge difference."

John had already impressed Jackie with his strength of character. In July 1976, just two months before registering at Andover, he joined his cousin Timothy Shriver and seven other Peace Corps volunteers working to rebuild homes in earthquake-ravaged Rainal, Guatemala.

Sleeping on the earthen floor of a tent barracks and surviving on a diet of tortillas and black beans, John "wanted to be treated just like one of us," said Tom Doyle, a fellow volunteer. Toward that end, John built outhouses, hauled sand for bricks, and dug trenches in the stifling tropical heat.

Unlike his mother, John was not particularly proficient in languages. Still, his earnest attempt at speaking Spanish charmed his hosts. So did his determination not to be shown any special treatment—this despite the fact that, even here, two Secret Service agents were watching over him at all times.

Midway through his stay in Guatemala, John suddenly doubled over with sharp, stabbing pains in his abdomen. Soon he was shaking and sweating profusely—all symptoms of dysentery. His Secret Service detail insisted on driving him to Guatemala City so he could be treated by a specialist, but John told project director Luis de Celis that he wanted to stay. "He was a very strong-willed and dedicated young man," De Celis said. "He didn't want people to think of him as special or pampered. Everybody was impressed with how down-to-earth he was, and I have never seen anyone work harder than John Kennedy did."

During this time, Jackie was also striving to prove that she, too, had value in the workplace. In this, she seemed to be making considerable progress. "She's become more independent," Tish Baldrige said. "Now she realizes she doesn't need a dominating man to lean on. Jackie is looking radiant. Work is good therapy for anybody."

Her celebrity still got in the way. In early 1977, for example, she had her hands full trying to debunk rumors that newly inaugurated President Jimmy Carter was about to appoint her Ambassador to the Court of St. James's. "Every time someone is hard up for news they throw in my name as ambassador to some place or other," she said. "And then my phone rings all day." Now she picked up the phone and answered, "Meesus Onassis *no está aqui*." Jackie told Rose Kennedy's personal secretary, Barbara Gibson, that she had to "do that to get rid of people."

Around the same time, Jackie had to deal with Viking's decision to publish *Shall We Tell the President?*, a suspense novel by British author Jeffrey Archer (later Lord Archer) about an imaginary plot to assassinate Jackie's brother-in-law Ted Kennedy after he is sworn in as president in 1981. Jackie was widely criticized for continuing to work at a company that would publish such a book, and when it was published in the United States in July 1977, *Shall We Tell the President?* was panned by the critics. In a sly reference to Jackie, John Leonard of the *New York Times* wrote, "Anyone associated with the publication of this book should be ashamed of herself."

Stung by such criticism, Jackie abruptly quit Viking and headed over to rival Doubleday. Once there, she had to win the respect of her skeptical coworkers all over again. Doubleday's chief, John Sargent, had been a friend of Jackie's for twenty-five years. He hesitated to tell her that she would have to work out of a tiny, windowless cubicle. "Oh, that's all right, John," she replied, taping a ballet poster on the wall to brighten things up. "I've lots of windows in my home."

Words like *clueless* and *dilettante* swirled around her at Doubleday, but Jackie pretended to be blissfully unaware of any nasty watercooler gossip among her envious coworkers. "No, I've never felt that kind of resentment," Jackie told Sargent when he asked if all the carping was getting to her. "Perhaps it's just that the people who resent my working say it to everyone else—but not to me."

Sargent felt that Jackie "did everything she could to put people at ease. She knew people were afraid to talk to her, that they were awe-struck in her presence, but she did everything she could to get past that." Most of her coworkers eventually came to respect Jackie as a professional, but there would always be holdouts. "Even after all that she's been through and everything she's accomplished, my mother still takes a lot of crap from people for no particular reason," John said. "But she never lets it get to her. She's the strongest woman—the stron-gest *person*—I know."

Yet Jackie was ill prepared for the stone wall of resistance she en-countered every time she tried to sign up a megastar's memoirs. It was certainly not for lack of trying. Over time she was turned down flat by, among others, Katharine Hepburn, Brigitte Bardot, Bette Davis, Prince, Ted Turner, Barbara Walters, Elizabeth Taylor, even her old pal Rudolf Nureyev.

"It was a fantasy of hers that everybody else's life was much more interesting than her own," said her friend John Russell, chief art critic for the *New York Times*. According to Russell, Jackie would look down on the lunchtime crowd from her balcony table at New York's Four Seasons restaurant and say, "Think of the plots that are being hatched down there!"

"You'd think that nobody could impress Jacqueline Kennedy Onassis," John Sargent observed. "On the contrary, she was *fascinated* by people."

Like most people, John knew far less about his mother's work than he did about her social life. For the first time she was dating a younger man—New York *Daily News* columnist Pete Hamill. This came as a rude surprise to actress Shirley MacLaine when she read about their affair in the papers, since she and Hamill had been living together for seven years.

In July 1977, Hamill helped land Caroline a $156-a-week summer job as a *Daily News* copy girl. When he flew down to Memphis to cover the shocking death of Elvis Presley that August at age forty-two, Caroline tagged along. Although Caroline interviewed Presley family members and spent time by his open coffin ("His face seemed swollen and his sideburns reached his chin," she wrote), she quickly discovered that her own celebrity was getting in the way of her covering the story.

Jackie's affair with Pete Hamill generated mountains of copy for months, but at sixteen John was still relatively free to fall in love without having it make the evening news. At this point, Meg Azzoni was history. John had fallen for a golden-haired California surfer girl, but in the end it was she who turned him down—for another woman. One classmate recalled John sitting on the front steps of his residence hall and muttering to himself, half in jest, "Did I do that? Did I turn her off guys?"

John rebounded quickly, and was soon in love with Jenny Christian, the slender, blond, sixteen-year-old daughter of a New York surgeon. She claimed to have no interest in his celebrity. "He was extremely handsome, nice, and sweet," said Christian, who would remain John's steady girlfriend for the next four years. "It was a great romance. If he had fallen out of a pickup truck, he would have still been irresistible to me."

As irresistible as he was, John didn't consummate their affair until he and Jenny had been together for a year. "I lost my virginity in high school like most other people," he said. "I was kind of a late bloomer, actually."

Most of John's encounters with girls during this period were predictable. "He sucked up all the female energy in the room," a classmate said. "They came up to him and you were invisible." Not that every girl who encountered John—still skinny and slightly awkward at fifteen—had a firm grasp on his place in history. At a party, one young woman pointed at the monogram on John's shirt. "JFK," she said. "Isn't that an airport?"

John was able to forge one platonic friendship with an intelligent young woman at Andover that would last a lifetime. Alexandra "Sasha" Chermayeff met John during his freshman year and they soon became inseparable. They went to movies and dances together, but never became romantically entangled. "He was fond of Sasha," said Marta Sgubin, who stayed on as Jackie's housekeeper and cook after the children were grown, "for what she was." Sasha and JFK Jr. would attend each other's weddings, and he would become a doting godfather to her two children, both of whom would be named in his will. For twenty years, neither spoke of their friendship, in part because he did not wish to disrupt Sasha's peaceful family life. "For John," Sgubin said, "it was a very private thing."

John was hoping that he could keep his grades private as well. He flunked math and merely scraped by in his other subjects. It was well known around Andover that John spent hours working out at the gym with his friends. "These were just punishing workouts John would do," one said. "He was a total animal. We'd leave after two hours and he'd stay behind for more."

One of his teachers, Alexander Theroux, urged him to get his priorities straight. "I asked him to spend less time weightlifting," Theroux said, "and more time reading his Strunk and White book on grammar."

Theroux actually turned out to be one of John's most ardent defenders among the Andover faculty. "One of the great myths is that he was dumb," said Theroux. "In a kind of reverse snobbery, that's what everybody expected him to be." In fact, he went on, John was intelligent, but not a genius. John was a very plucky, very quiet student."

It was not hard to see why, Theroux explained. All his life, people had always come to John; he did not have to make an effort to extend himself. "He never had to work hard because people always met him more than halfway."

Perhaps, but the rest of the faculty and administration weren't interested in excuses. At the end of the eleventh grade, his grade point average was low enough to warrant expulsion. With its reputation for academic excellence, Andover rarely allowed students to remain under these circumstances. "They threw you out on your ear," one Andover alumnus said. *"Period."*

A pleading phone call from JFK's widow, however, was a powerful thing. John was allowed to stay—but he would have to repeat the eleventh grade. John, cognizant of his reputation for being intellectually lacking, was embarrassed when news of his being held back a year hit the papers.

"Are you a poor student?" a reporter asked point-blank.

"Well, I don't know," John answered blithely. "That depends on what you call a 'poor student.'"

There was one area at Andover in which John did make an effort to excel. Seriously bitten by the acting bug after he sang and danced in *Oliver* at Collegiate, John now signed up for Andover's production of *Petticoats and Union Suits*. Lured by the prospect of watching John embarrass himself, the theater critic for the *New York Times* wrote that "one can't help be aware of the fifteen-year-old John Kennedy in his role, although like the others in his celebrated family, he seems to be trying painfully to avoid special attention."

Undaunted, John went on to act opposite his girlfriend Jenny Christian in Megan Terry's *Comings and Goings,* and later in Shakespeare's *The Comedy of Errors.* His toughest acting assignment at Andover would be taking on the lead role of McMurphy in Ken Kesey's frightening look at life inside a mental hospital, *One Flew Over the Cuckoo's Nest.* Knowing his mother was in the opening-night audience—and hearing her gasp with every harrowing turn in the plot—made John "slightly crazy," a fellow cast member said. "But at the same time, he was obviously proud of what he was doing, and happy that she was there."

Given Jackie's packed social schedule, John was not entirely sure she'd show up. There was the usual run of galas and openings, and the faces of many of Jackie's dates were familiar: financier Felix Rohatyn, Peter Duchin, Metropolitan Museum director Thomas Hoving, and Karl Katz, the Met's special project director alternately described as a "confirmed bachelor" and Jackie's "intellectual boyfriend." David Halberstam remembered the Byzantine manner in which Jackie went about picking her escorts. First, she would make an offhand comment to one of her closest confidantes that she was interested in a particular man. That information would then be passed down the social grapevine and eventually "word was relayed to you and you'd call her up and you'd go out."

John thought it was particularly amusing that, after Senator George McGovern escorted Jackie to two or three functions, the country was abuzz with rumors that the 1972 Democratic presidential nominee might leave his wife, Eleanor, for Jackie. Jackie was also linked during this period to Alejandro Orfila, the dashing former Argentine ambassador to the United States, after he escorted her to a bicentennial gala in Washington. "Jackie swept into the Kennedy Center on Orfila's arm," wrote one columnist, "in the manner of a beloved queen returning from exile."

In the late 1970s, Jackie would be rumored to be romancing, among others, Saudi tycoon Adnan Khashoggi, NBC executive Carl Killingsworth, and heart transplant pioneer Christiaan Barnard. John paid little attention to these unlikely candidates, but when his mother was photographed arm in arm with Frank Sinatra, he asked her if anything serious was brewing.

Jackie described her relationship with Sinatra as nothing more than two old friends getting together to reminisce; Ol' Blue Eyes had, after all, been JFK's chief Hollywood backer—until Jack and Bobby, fearing Sinatra's ties to organized crime might tarnish the administration, dumped him.

In truth, Jackie and Sinatra continued to meet secretly, usually in the early-morning hours at various restaurants and watering holes around

Manhattan—P. J. Clark's, '21,' Jimmy Weston's, and Patsy's among them. In the end, Jackie decided that Frank, who was the same age as Jack, was simply too old for her now. "Jackie," Truman Capote observed, "had lost her taste for domineering older men. She didn't need any more sugar daddies in her life telling her what to do."

It was then, in mid-December 1976, that Jackie turned to Pete Hamill. For the next ten months, Jackie and the columnist, who was five years her junior, were virtually inseparable—until an unpublished column of his about Jackie surfaced. In it, he excoriated Jackie for exploiting her position as "some national object of veneration. She was not, of course, a victim of that veneration," he wrote. "She encouraged it, indulged it, created the desire for more knowledge by cultivating the image of aloofness." He went on to say her spending habits were "outrageous" and "obscene." The *New York Post* pointed out in its article on the couple that it was Hamill who wrote of Jackie: "No courtesan ever sold herself for more."

John shared his mother's taste for gossip, and when he read about Hamill's comments in the *New York Post* he called his mother up to comfort her—and to share his less-than-charitable view of Hamill with her. He needn't have worried about Hamill. Throwing her social schedule into overdrive, Jackie reverted to old standbys like John Sargent, New York City Commissioner of Cultural Affairs Henry Geldzahler, and *New Yorker* writer and author Brendan Gill—as well as younger men like Halberstam and documentary filmmaker Peter Davis.

Soon one contender would emerge from the pack—someone who clearly had no interest in the limelight and whose quiet, dignified demeanor belied a fierce devotion to Jackie. John would later say he had been rooting for Maurice Tempelsman from the beginning.

Born into an Orthodox Jewish family in Antwerp, Belgium, Tempelsman fled the Nazis for New York in 1940. Skipping an opportunity to attend college, he went straight into his father's diamond-importing business, Leon Tempelsman & Son. Maurice shrewdly hired former Illinois senator and two-time Democratic presidential candidate

Adlai Stevenson as his lawyer, and Adlai—a close friend of Jackie—promptly linked Tempelsman up with the powerful Oppenheimer diamond-mining dynasty. Soon Maurice was a "Sightholder," one of only 160 people on the planet permitted to buy diamonds direct from the De Beers cartel (and then only ten times a year).

Casting his lot with the Democrats, Tempelsman contributed heavily to the party and was soon fast friends with young Senator John Kennedy and his captivating bride. Frequent guests at the White House, Maurice and his wife, Lily, were even invited to the first state affair hosted by JFK and Jackie—the spectacular candlelit dinner for Pakistan's President Mohammed Ayub Khan on the lawn at Mount Vernon.

Jackie had one of her earliest dates following Ari's death with Tempelsman, a figure virtually unknown to the American public. On August 20, 1975, they caught the new Broadway musical *Chicago*, followed by an after-theater supper that lasted until 3 a.m. As had been the case with so many of her other lovers, Tempelsman was still very much married. To further complicate matters, he and the devoutly Orthodox Lily had three children, ranging in age from fourteen to twenty-one.

No matter. Jackie made no attempt to conceal her budding romance. In the coming months, Jackie and Maurice were spotted murmuring to each other in French at upscale restaurants like Lutèce, the Four Seasons, La Côte Basque, and '21.'

After years spent in the company of such commanding figures as Jack and Bobby Kennedy and Aristotle Onassis, it seemed odd that Jackie would fall for the portly, balding, comparatively drab diamond merchant. "Husbands did not always treat her the way she deserved," said Jackie's friend Vivian Crespi. Tempelsman, on the other hand, "worshiped the ground she walked on. He did not dominate her, she did not dominate him. They were equals."

Lily Tempelsman, meanwhile, kept the home fires burning at the couple's apartment on Riverside Drive. Far more devout than her husband, Lily refused to divorce him under New York law but did grant

Maurice a *get*—an Orthodox Jewish divorce—after he moved into 1040 Fifth in 1982. When asked in 1977 what she thought of Jackie dating her husband, she fired back, "Why don't you ask her?"

That summer of 1977, John's visits to Hyannis Port were few and far between—by Jackie's design. Meanwhile, the Kennedy cousins grew increasingly "wild and undisciplined," according to Rose Kennedy's secretary, Barbara Gibson, "taking what they wanted, feeling above moral bounds." Whenever Ethel's kids visited their grandmother Rose Kennedy on Cape Cod or in Palm Beach, Gibson added, "It was like a horde of rampaging Huns was descending on us." John, on the other hand, was "perfectly respectful and polite" whenever he came to visit. He was, Gibson added, "clearly the product of his mother's love and concern."

John's "perfectly respectful and polite" attitude did not always extend to his friends. Perhaps out of a feeling of entitlement, perhaps merely due to absentmindedness, Jackie's son was chronically late for everything. If there was something to be done, he invariably did it at the very last possible minute. He expected to be admitted to any party, theatrical event, sports event, or concert whether or not he had ticket, an invitation, or a pass. He seldom carried cash or credit cards, expecting whoever he was with to pick up the tab.

If he suddenly became tired, bored, or distracted at a social event, John simply picked up and left—sometimes leaving his friends behind without a way to get home. Billy Noonan wrote in his memoir, *Forever Young,* that years later, when John had his own apartment in New York, he would invite friends for the weekend "and forget to leave them the key. There they'd be, left on John's stoop, fending for themselves while he was off who-knows-where."

"Marcel Proust said that in every relationship there is one who kisses and one who extends the cheek," Alexander Theroux said. "John extended the cheek." Apparently John understood on some level that he might appear to be arrogant rather than just impulsive and forgetful. To dispel that notion, Theroux said, he "had to work at trying hard. John Kennedy was like a salmon swimming upstream."

I

2

John's fascination with aviation could be traced to moments like this, when he and his mother watched as Daddy's helicopter took off from the South Lawn in 1962. Later that year in Palm Beach, John and Caroline, dressed up as angels for the local Christmas pageant, cozied up to Mom in front of the fireplace.

4

3

6

5

7

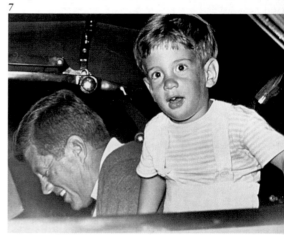

8

White House Pals: "Is there a rabbit in there?" JFK asked when John hid beneath his desk. As JFK's friend Paul "Red" Fay looked on (top), the president reacted in mock surprise to one of John's many shared secrets. Above, John tagged along when the president headed out for a round of golf at Hyannis Port in August 1963. Daddy offered John candy as they strolled along the West Wing Colonnade in early October 1963.

John was clearly amused by something when he and his mother arrived at church near their weekend home in Middleburg, Virginia, on October 23, 1963—less than a month before Dallas (top). As JFK's casket passed by, Jackie bent down and told John to say goodbye to Daddy—with history's most famous salute (center). In June 1964 (bottom), John and his mom walked hand in hand up the front steps of their new home in Georgetown.

9

10

11

12   13

Besieged by photographers and tourists, Jackie grabbed the kids and fled to New
York. At the New York World's Fair in 1965 (top left), John met Mickey Mouse.
A month later, Uncles Bobby and Teddy looked on as John met two more icons—
Queen Elizabeth and an English bobby—at the dedication of his father's memorial
at Runnymede.

15

Vacationing with Uncle Bobby in Sun
Valley, Idaho, John rubbed noses with
a Samoyed pup. A month later, he was
sledding down the slopes with his mom
and sister, Caroline, in Gstaad, the Swiss
ski resort (below).

14

16

"Behave yourself, young man." During a King Kamehameha Day visit to Honolulu's Iolani Palace, a stern Jackie warned John to calm down—or else.

17

18

A stunned Jackie attended RFK's June 7, 1968, funeral at New York's St. Patrick's Cathedral with John and Caroline. That fall she shocked the world by marrying Aristotle Onassis.

19

After lunch at one of her favorite restaurants, Trader Vic's, Jackie, John, and Ari headed home to 1040 Fifth Avenue.

20

21

22

Whether it was stopping at the refreshment tent between riding events in New Jersey (top), pausing to chat while vacationing in Capri (center), or fussing with John's collar as they strode toward Ari's yacht *Christina* in Greece (bottom), Jackie took John "everywhere," George Plimpton said. "Unlike a lot of boys, he wasn't embarrassed to be with her. John was always very proud of her."

After a tennis lesson like this one in 1974, John was mugged in Central Park (top). Jackie was "pleased" that it happened. "I want him to experience life," she said. The next year, John supported his mother (below) as the Onassis women forced her into the background at Ari's funeral.

23

"John's a good boy," Jackie said, "but he's always getting himself in a jam." He poked fun at himself in this photo that ran in the Andover yearbook in 1979, the year he graduated (top). That same year, he joined Caroline and a beaming Jackie at yet another black-tie affair in New York (center). John struggled throughout his academic career with undiagnosed ADD and dyslexia, so Jackie was justifiably overjoyed when he graduated from Brown University in 1983 (bottom).

25

26

27

John had just begun his six-year affair with actress Christina Haag when they attended a Metropolitan Museum gala in 1985 (top). Not long after, Jackie and John met the Reagans at a reception to benefit the Kennedy Library, held at Ted Kennedy's McLean, Virginia, home (center). A poised and confident speaker, John electrified the 1988 Democratic National Convention in Atlanta when he introduced his uncle Teddy (bottom).

28

29

30

In 1991, John, having by then passed the New York State bar exam on his third try, showed up at his cousin Willie Smith's rape trial to provide moral support—in direct defiance of Jackie.

John and his then-love Daryl Hannah caused a near riot when they arrived for the wedding of Edward Kennedy Jr. in Rhode Island (above). Bill Clinton was sixteen when he famously shook hands with John's father. In 1993 he joined Jackie and John on the dais during rededication ceremonies at the Kennedy Library.

Although he was
still very much
involved with Daryl
Hannah, John
was photographed
watching the
New York City
Marathon in
November 1993
with "mystery
woman" Carolyn
Bessette.

34

35

36

John helped his sister
make her way through
the mob of reporters and
onlookers who gathered
outside Jackie's apartment
after her death (above).
The next day at her
funeral in New York,
Jackie's "two miracles"
clung to each other, their
faces etched with grief.

"Ladies and Gentlemen, meet *George*." Going ahead with his plans for the first "*People* magazine of politics," despite the odds and his late mother's skepticism, John unveiled *George* magazine on September 7, 1995.

Action Man. Like his athletic mother, John was, in one friend's words, "congenitally incapable of standing still." When he wasn't Rollerblading, biking, or tossing a Frisbee in Central Park, he was kayaking, swimming, or running on the beach in Hyannis Port.

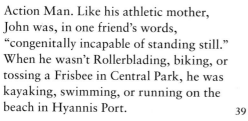

39

42

Backed up by his dog Friday, John had a rare confrontation with the paparazzi in late 1996 (top). Despite problems in their marriage, John and Carolyn "couldn't take their hands off each other," said friend James Rubin. They unabashedly proved Rubin's point on the streets of Lower Manhattan (center) and at a charity event in Manhattan (below).

43

44

45

As John got older, Plimpton observed, "Jackie used to complain that he was constantly on the move, and that he didn't always stop to consider the impact his actions would take on others. She also used to say 'Jack was like that too.'"

As part of her ongoing campaign to "toughen up" John and keep him away from his cousins in the process, Jackie enrolled him in Outward Bound's survival training program on Maine's rockbound Hurricane Island. To graduate from the program, John had to spend three days alone on an island surviving only on three gallons of water and whatever edible plants he was able to find in the wild. John loved it.

Once back at Andover, however, John quickly grew bored. He kept getting into mischief on campus, and his grades continued to stagnate. On a weekend home from school, John was caught pouring glue down the building's mail chute—a stunt that was serious enough to prod Jackie into action.

She was casting about for something to occupy John when a Wyoming congressman who had been a friend of JFK recommended that she send her son to the Bar Cross Ranch to work as a wrangler. "She wanted John to get out and around," ranch owner John Perry Barlow said, "to get in closer contact with the salt of the earth, and get his hands on something real."

Jackie was pleased that the experience wasn't going to cost her anything—John would bunk with the other ranch hands and was to be paid what they were paid. Although his share of the Kennedy fortune already amounted to more than $5 million, it was enough that Mummy wasn't footing the bill this time. This was John's first paying job.

When he arrived at the Bar Cross Ranch in the summer of 1978, John was "like a giant Labrador puppy," recalled Barlow, whose own varied resume included a stint writing songs for the Grateful Dead. "Lots of energy, little focus. But he was amenable to *being* focused. He knew he had to measure up, and he loved the challenge."

The rest of the hired hands weren't exactly thrilled. "Aw, come on," they told Barlow, "you're not going to do this to us." Yet, said Barlow, "almost immediately John won everybody over."

No one could argue with John's work ethic. He dug post holes for a corral fence "with ravenous intensity," Barlow said. "He went at it as if he was killing snakes." Later, while rounding up cattle on horseback, he admitted that there were others in his immediate family who were better suited to the task. "You really need my mother and my sister up here!" John cracked.

During those six weeks in Wyoming, "John never once complained about anything," Barlow said. "It took no time at all for him to be totally in his element—working hard and learning the ropes and just loving it, completely loving every minute of it." When he returned to 1040 weather-beaten and ten pounds lighter, Jackie was thrilled. "They kept saying I was a miracle worker," Barlow said. "But he was already a miracle when he got here."

Jackie had a profound sense of responsibility—
not obligation—and she managed to impart that
to her son. She was one of the great human beings.

—JOHN PERRY BARLOW, FAMILY FRIEND

The single most important thing
in John's life was his mother.

—PETER DUCHIN, JACKIE'S FRIEND

"My Mother Will Be Frantic"

JFK's son returned to Andover in 1978 with a renewed sense of purpose. Academically, he continued to falter, but now he took pride in
the work he was doing for the school's community outreach program.
For two days each week, John taught English to immigrant junior high
school students in nearby Lawrence, Massachusetts.

John also took the time during this period to rekindle memories of
his father. One day Chuck Spalding dropped in on John while he was
listening to a tape of one of his father's speeches—a tribute to Eleanor
Roosevelt—for a history class at Andover.

"Listen!" he told Spalding, his voice filled with excitement. "Right
in here is where I crawl under the desk and Dad kicks me. It's coming
up now. Here it is. He was talking on the radio and I crawled under the
desk and grabbed him."

Such moments were rare. The only other memory he claimed as his
was of that time they all sat on the Truman Balcony to the bagpipes and
drums of the famous Black Watch Regiment. John remembered squirm-
ing in his mother's lap, straining to get a better look over the balcony
rail. It was nine days before the assassination—the last time they were
photographed together at the White House.

John later admitted that, for the most part, he viewed his father
"through the color of others and the perception of others and through

photographs and what I've read." In the course of his life, John looked at photos and film of his famous salute to JFK's coffin thousands—tens of thousands—of times, trying to trigger some flicker of memory in his brain. He always came up dry. "Do you really remember things that happened to you when you were two years old?" John would sometimes ask. "Do you? Really?"

Meanwhile Caroline, who did remember, was also making her mother proud by never falling off the dean's list at Radcliffe College. To celebrate Caroline's twenty-first birthday and John's eighteenth, Jackie invited 150 people to New York's chic Le Club on November 26, 1978. All the Kennedys were there, as well as friends of the birthday boy and girl, and more than a few luminaries from the worlds of society, show business, and politics. (President Jimmy Carter couldn't make it, sending Secretary of State Cyrus Vance in his stead.)

"The 'passing of the torch' theme was pretty obvious," said one guest. Indeed, the invitation actually showed an angel holding two torches. It had been fifteen years since JFK was shot to death, and now his only surviving brother stood to toast John and Caroline. "I shouldn't be doing this tonight," Ted Kennedy said, his voice quavering. "By rights, it should have been the father of these two children. Jack loved his children more than anything else. Young John and Caroline bring new life to the family."

Christina Haag, who years later would become John's lover, chatted with the host. "It's all going *so* well, don't you think?" Jackie asked. They both watched John in the middle of the dance floor and agreed he was having fun. Watching Jackie's face light up, Haag thought, "Remember this moment, that one day you might be forty-eight and filled, as she is, with this much joy and wonder."

Bunny Mellon, Arthur Schlesinger Jr., Gill, Plimpton, Vance, Tempelsman, Jackie's distant cousin Louis Auchincloss, and the rest of Jackie's crowd sipped Dom Perignon while John's Andover pals guzzled beer and tequila and smoked cigars. Most of those over thirty drifted off by eleven, and a little after midnight Ted, Eunice, Ethel, and Jackie headed home.

Once they were gone, John and his friends lit up joints, drank Hennessy stingers from wine goblets, then danced to the disco beat of the Bee Gees, Gloria Gaynor, and Donna Summer. At 4 a.m., Billy Noonan stuck his head out the door and snarled at the pack of photographers who had been gathered for hours. "I'm giving you fair warning," he told them, "don't start any shit."

Within seconds, John emerged wearing a black jacket, a long white scarf, and sunglasses. The paparazzi lunged forward, and Noonan bolted for them as promised. As Noonan got ready to throw the first punch, John not only tried to hold his friend back but put his hand over his mouth to shut him up.

It was too late. A donnybrook ensued and John was knocked to the pavement. "Stop!" he yelled, pleading with everyone to back off as he struggled, sunglasses in hand, to pull himself up on the rear fender of a parked car. That didn't work, either. As his friends and the photographers wrestled outside the club, John grabbed Jenny Christian's hand and sprinted to the corner. There they flagged a cab that took them straight to 1040.

Newspapers the next day were filled with photos of the brawl—the most memorable images showing John spread-eagle on the sidewalk while his buddies clenched their fists and spewed epithets. Mortified at his behavior, Billy Noonan wrote a long letter of apology to Jackie. She responded by inviting him to the Kennedy family birthday party, although she was not about to let them forget this lapse in judgment. From now on when she saw John and his friends headed out the door wearing sunglasses, she delivered the same line: "Oh, dark glasses. Are you boys going out looking for a fight?"

John and Jackie faced the press together at his Andover graduation ceremony, when they had to make their way through a mob of photographers just to reach the buffet table. John was visibly angry. "Look," he said, "I just want to spend some time with my mates and enjoy my graduation."

An old hand at moments like these, Jackie merely ignored the interlopers. "Oh Ted," she told the senator within earshot of reporters. "Can you believe it? My baby, graduating!"

By this time, John was making ample use of the apartment his father kept on Bowdoin Street in Boston. Sparely decorated, it served as little more than a crash pad for John and his Andover buddies. Between visits to local pubs like the Black Rose and the Bull & Finch (famous as the inspiration for the bar in the television series *Cheers*), John continued his work with troubled teens. At the Massachusetts State House, located just up the street from the Kennedy apartment, John showed groups of juvenile offenders *Scared Straight,* the graphic documentary about life behind bars. Even the most incorrigible delinquents watched in shocked silence. "Jesus," John said after screening several episodes. "It should have been called *Scared Shitless.*"

Jackie was scared, too—scared that, left to his own devices after prep school graduation, John would now fall prey to Ethel's Hickory Hill mob. "Jackie was hearing one horror story after another," Duchin said, "and she was more determined than ever that John not be sucked into that."

Just how far Jackie was willing to go surprised even John. With a half dozen others, he spent the summer of 1979 trekking through the wilds of Kenya as part of a ten-week course run by the National Outdoor Leadership School.

Confident that her son was in the hands of trained professionals, Jackie was blissfully unaware of the fact that John's party got hopelessly lost on its first week out. A vote was taken, and his fellow survivalists agreed that John had the requisite skills to lead them back to their base. As they hacked their way through dense undergrowth with John in the lead, all he could think of was how upsetting this all was for Jackie. "I just hope the press doesn't get wind of this," he told the others. "My mother will be frantic."

Not surprisingly, course officials began to panic. In a spare-no-expense effort to locate JFK Jr., search planes were dispatched along with scores of Masai warriors who scoured the region on foot. After two full days, a lone Masai tracker stumbled upon John and his team. They had wandered into a village in the remotest part of Kenya, where, on the wall of one family's hut, hung a photo of John's father.

Jackie was nonplussed when she was informed that her son had been rescued. "Rescued?" she asked. As it turned out, no one had bothered to tell her about John's ordeal until *after* he had been found.

There was no time to dwell on the tragedy that might have been; Jackie was far too immersed in getting her son into just the right college. John was accepted by Harvard, his father's alma mater, but didn't want to go. "He knew he hadn't earned it," John Perry Barlow said. "John knew it was strictly because of who he was, and that he didn't have the grades, so he didn't go there."

John wanted to chart his own course, and Jackie understood completely. "It's hard enough being in his father's shadow out in the wider world," she told Arthur Schlesinger. "Can you imagine the expectations at Harvard, what a burden that would be?"'

John had his pick of schools like Princeton, Yale, Dartmouth, and Columbia, but he was also realistic about his chances of ever measuring up academically. Founded in 1764, Brown University had by 1979 become the school of choice for wealthy prep school graduates for one reason: it provided the Ivy League experience without the rigorous academic demands. For starters, Brown had no core requirements for graduation, and each student was encouraged to devise his own academic program.

A cluster of white clapboard and redbrick buildings perched on a hill in the middle of Providence, Rhode Island, Brown offered John little protection from the press. When he showed up to register, photographers caused such a scene that he promised to pose in front of the Brown University sign at the campus entrance if they just left him alone long enough to enroll.

As accustomed as he was to such attention, John hated being embarrassed in front of the other students. "Half the time he was sort of saying under his breath, 'Okay, have you had enough?'" one photographer recalled. "'I feel really dumb doing this. Can we stop now, guys? Guys?'" According to Bob Littell, one of John's closest friends at Brown, John just "wanted to be a college kid, not a freak show."

One time-honored way to gain immediate acceptance with one's peers, of course, was to join a fraternity. John happily endured the indignities of Hell Night at Phi Psi, going through an initiation ritual that included wallowing in animal entrails, guzzling a pitcher of beer, swallowing a goldfish (of course), being paddled, and picking up an olive by clenching his derriere—all topped off by streaking naked across the campus.

John was soon impressing his fraternity brothers with, among other things, his ability to attract beautiful coeds. Fairly typical was the time Billy Way, who had been a friend of John's at Andover, burst in the front door trailed by several coeds. The minute one of them realized John was sitting on the couch, she walked up to him and demanded that he prove he was really JFK Jr. and not a look-alike. Once John produced his wallet, the young woman thrust her hand down the front of his pants, then led him off to one of the bedrooms.

John's frat brothers weren't above taking advantage of his star power. When they hung a sign outside saying he was in residence, there was a line of attractive coeds waiting to get in.

"When you're eighteen years old," Bob Littell said, "you can get into a lot of trouble when people respond to you like that. An astounding number of women wanted to sleep with him . . . but he almost always resisted the sexual opportunities that came his way, preferring real relationships."

At Brown, perhaps some of those relationships were *too* real. By this time, John realized that he would spend his life constantly in the crosshairs of young women, not all of them completely sane. One young lady showed up carrying an album of photographs with cutouts of John's face pasted into every picture. "Here are John and I at the beach," she said, proudly turning each page, "and here we are at my birthday party." Rob Littell was John's roommate at the time, and when the strange young woman ("Miss Crazy") tossed out Littell's things and declared she was moving in, Brown security was finally called.

Not long after streaking across the campus to howls from ogling Brown coeds, John delivered his very first public speech, at the October 29, 1979 dedication ceremony for the I. M. Pei–designed John F.

Kennedy Library outside Boston. Not yet nineteen and already standing a broad-shouldered six feet one inch tall, the skinny adolescent who had scuffled with the paparazzi just the year before was now a strikingly handsome cross between the Kennedys and the Bouviers. Looking out over an audience that included President Jimmy Carter and dozens of familiar faces from JFK's New Frontier, John held the crowd spellbound with his reading of Stephen Spender's poem "I Think Continually of Those Who Were Truly Great."

As they filed outside after the ceremony, John and Jackie paused by JFK's sailboat *Ventura,* which is displayed outside the library. "You know," he whispered, "I don't even remember him. Sometimes I think I might, but I don't."

Jackie put her hand on John's shoulder, and then, slowly, led him toward their waiting car.

At Brown, he tried to conjure up those lost memories, studying his father and his policies like any other student, taking an American history seminar on the Kennedy administration and the war in Vietnam. "I had heard John was a dummy, that he was more interested in sex than in school," said Steve Gillon, who taught the course on JFK's presidency. "But he was very articulate and intelligent. He contributed things to the discussion that went beyond the textbook." Gillon went on to say that John, who referred to his father in class simply as "the president," actually "dominated the discussion in certain areas, such as civil rights and the role of the Supreme Court." John received a respectable B+ in the class—not enough to counterbalance his failing grades in other classes.

Spurred on by a desire to tackle the issues that had confronted his dad, John tapped several classmates for an informal debate society; they quickly discovered that, although he could debate both sides of an issue, he had strong opinions on everything from abortion rights to racism to nuclear disarmament. "We were all impressed by how much he knew, how passionate he was," said one student. "He wasn't at all reluctant to show his serious side."

According to the man John came to call his best friend, John's own passion for politics could be traced back directly to debates with Jackie and her intellectual friends over dinner at Hyannis Port. John used that setting as "theater," Billy Noonan recalled. "He pondered aloud his interests and concerns, gesturing with his hands, cutting the air to make his point . . ." This was where "John developed, like an actor, his love of debate and engagement."

As perfectly suited as he may have seemed for the world of politics, John's true passion wasn't world affairs or history. It was acting. When he appeared in March 1980 as the soldier Bonario in Ben Jonson's *Volpone,* the reviewer for the *Brown Daily Herald* gave John a five-star review—then publicly retracted it in a follow-up piece.

In his retraction, the student critic decided that "John doesn't move well—he's very inhibited and self-conscious on the stage. And his voice is off-putting. He sounds like a rich New York preppie."

So what made the *Daily Herald* reviewer change his mind? "I didn't think John was as good as I made him out to be," he explained. "But I was sitting next to his mother on opening night and I guess I was dazzled."

Undaunted—and encouraged by his mother not to give up—John went on as an undergraduate to have major roles in plays ranging from Shakespeare's *The Tempest* to Miguel Piñero's gritty prison drama, *Short Eyes.* Before going on in *The Tempest,* John was forced to deal with a wardrobe malfunction. As he left his frat house for the theater in elaborate Elizabethan costume and full makeup, John was hit by a volley of water balloons fired from a cannon set up across the quad.

"He kind of gasped," recalled Rick Guy, a fellow history major and a player on Brown's lacrosse team. "But he didn't yell or scream like a lot of other people would have." Instead, he shook his head and went back inside to clean up before his performance. "John took everything in stride because he wanted more than anything to be treated like an ordinary guy."

For everyone, the greeting was always the same: "Hi, I'm John." Guy pointed out that it was "never John Kennedy, always just John. He would totally disarm you by asking questions—and not in that artificial way people have of pretending to be interested in you. He really wanted to know about other people's lives." In the end, Guy said, everyone who met John walked away feeling he was "just a tremendously decent, regular guy."

There were plenty of reminders that John was anything but a regular guy. On the opening night of David Rabe's *In the Boom Boom Room*, another actor in the play, Rick Moody, was backstage waiting to go on when a hearty laugh boomed from the audience. "That's my sister," John said, grinning. "That's Caroline." Appearing for the first time in public wearing a crew cut, John even managed to upstage the coed who played his girlfriend. She had gone topless for the role.

Describing JFK Jr.'s acting style wasn't easy. "A little Brando, a little De Niro, a healthy dollop of Nicholson, maybe a dash of his dad's inaugural pluck," Moody said, adding that he was initially surprised that John delivered his lines "with uncanny reserves of charisma." Then he wondered, "What's the surprise in this? He'd been acting his entire life."

"All actors are hiding behind a mask," said Katharine Hepburn, who found John's interest in acting "perfectly logical. It's really the perfect way to cope with celebrity, because people are only seeing you play a character. They don't get to the real *you*." (Adding to the Freudian mix, John began collecting actual masks—from Asia, Africa, and the Caribbean. Eventually "there were scary ones and hairy ones, comical and mystical," Robert Littell said. "The implication, in a Psych 101 way, is that John was attracted to masks because he wore one himself for so long, figuratively speaking.")

Jackie dutifully came to nearly all of John's openings, and was invariably caught up in the moment whenever he set foot onstage. "Her reactions were pretty intense—especially if something bad was happening to John's character," a fellow student said. "She'd gasp and grab Caroline's arm. She was completely caught up in it."

"John's acting," Jackie told Robert Littell at one point, "is the thing that brings me the most joy." But when *Saturday Night Fever* producer Robert Stigwood offered nineteen-year-old John the chance to play his father in a feature film based on JFK's early years—a part John desperately wanted to take—Jackie vetoed the idea.

Caroline was proving easier to handle. After graduating from Radcliffe with honors in 1980, she went to work in the Metropolitan Museum of Art's Film and Television Department. There she met Edwin Arthur Schlossberg, founder of a small company that produced multimedia video projects for museums and businesses. The son of a wealthy textile manufacturer, Ed Schlossberg was thirteen years Caroline's senior and—like Maurice Tempelsman—Jewish. Soon Caroline was living in Schlossberg's million-dollar loft, and Jackie was breathlessly introducing him to her friends as "my daughter's new friend."

In the meantime, Jackie had asked Tempelsman to quietly arrange for John to spend the summer of 1980 in South Africa learning the ins and outs of the diamond trade. There was always the possibility, Jackie reasoned, that John might wish to join the Tempelsman family business. "This must have been to ingratiate herself with Maurice," Gore Vidal mused. "Yes, Jackie loved money and very rich men, but she wasn't about to see Jack Kennedy's son grubbing around in the jewelry business."

John was clearly not about to follow in Tempelsman's footsteps. But his South African sojourn did yield results of another sort. Having witnessed the evils of apartheid firsthand, he returned to Brown determined to take action. With Jackie's blessing and financial backing from Tempelsman, John set up a campus lecture series aimed at spreading the word about the dire political situation in South Africa. His first speaker was Andrew Young, civil rights pioneer, onetime Atlanta mayor, and former ambassador to the United Nations.

His social consciousness aside, John was digging a deeper and deeper hole for himself academically. Jackie rightly feared that John might drop out of college at any moment—or, even more likely, be pushed out. He had always been a less-than-conscientious student, but throughout his time at Brown, John flirted with expulsion. John was reminded that, in his first two years at the university, he had failed to pass four courses in any given semester. "Even with our modest graduation requirements," Professor Edward Beiser warned John, "you are skating on very thin ice."

"Neither I nor John will fail to be galvanized by your message," Jackie wrote back when faculty contacted her directly with the news that John was about to be expelled. Informed that her son was on academic probation, she wrote to the academic dean that the "vital lesson of how to allot every second of his time" would "sink in as he frantically tries to make up his work." A year later, as he did extra work to make up for unfinished assignments and poor test results, Jackie sat down in Hyannis Port and dashed off a letter to John's professor. "I look forward to hearing that he is off probation," she wrote, "and to never getting another notice that he is on it."

Yet John still yearned to be an actor, and sought out his ex-uncle Peter Lawford for advice. "If that's your dream," Lawford told him, "then do it." Jackie was anything but pleased when she found out, and wrote Lawford telling him not to interfere. "That, of course, made Peter even more determined to support John," said his widow, Patricia Seton Lawford, "in whatever it was *he* wanted to do."

If there were underlying tensions—and there undoubtedly were—John and his mother never let on. To all outward appearances, said John's fraternity brother Richard Wiese, theirs was a "very warm" relationship. Wiese got his first look at the Jackie-John dynamic when John had to do a last-minute errand and asked Wiese to look out for his mother. "You know what she looks like," John said. "Dark hair, big sunglasses . . ."

"Yes, John," Wiese interrupted, "I think I'll recognize her."

Later, Wiese escorted Jackie to John's room so she could use the phone. Unfortunately, it "looked as if someone had tossed a grenade in there." In search of the phone, Jackie waded through the sports equipment, clothes, pizza boxes, cans, papers, books, Styrofoam cups, and Coke bottles that covered the floor. Spotting a black cord, Jackie crawled through the debris until she realized it led to a stereo. "But where is the *phone?*" she asked, throwing up her hands. Wiese led her to the phone in his room.

John came by his sloppiness naturally. "He never hung anything up—just dropped it on the floor where he took it off," Wiese said. His mother ran a tight ship, but when left to his own devices, John opted for squalor. The interior of his battered gray Honda Civic was strewn with bags, beer cans, and fast-food wrappers. He was an eager participant in cafeteria food fights, and at one point drove out to the country and purchased a pig—not a small potbellied pig, but a farm-bred hog—that he intended to keep at the frat house as a pet. He named the pig Litpig, after Rob Littell, and kept it in the fraternity's basement for a week before returning it to its original owner.

John continued to smoke pot, and, perhaps driven by the need for acceptance, experimented with stronger stuff. At one party, he was present when his friends allegedly passed around a silver straw and an ashtray filled with cocaine. Each time someone took a hit, a little more of the design on the bottom of the ashtray was revealed.

Once the ashtray got to John, the face of John Fitzgerald Kennedy was staring up at them, with "1917–1963" printed below. Everyone paused. Then John, said one witness, "saw what was on the ashtray and took it anyway."

Every single day of his life, there was something there to remind John of the father he lost. It might have just been a passing mention of the airport, or of one of the countless highways and schools named after JFK. There was an unspoken rule among John's friends never to bring up his father's name, and certainly never to mention the assassination. But the event was so embedded in the nation's consciousness that it "came up all the time," said Rob Littell. And when it did, Littell added, "he didn't flinch."

JFK Jr. even seemed to take some solace in cultural references to his father. A die-hard fan of the Rolling Stones, John never hesitated to sing along to his favorite Stones song, "Sympathy for the Devil," when it was playing on the car radio or on the stereo at Phi Psi, putting special emphasis on the lines:

I shouted out, Who killed the Kennedys?
When, after all, it was you and me.

Given all that was expected of him, John was keenly aware that most people felt he had fallen short. Although most reporters agreed that John had already proven himself to be the most polite and down-to-earth of the Kennedys, their stories painted a very different picture.

When he was mugged in Central Park on the way to a private tennis lesson, John was portrayed as a clueless brat who lacked the street smarts of any other New Yorker. Newspapers ran story after story about his poor academic performance, and when John was held back a year at Andover, the press seemed to confirm that he was the dimmest bulb on the Kennedy compound's porch. The birthday party fracas that left him sprawled on the pavement didn't help much, either. Nor did photos that ran around the world of John in the foppish period costumes he wore for student productions like *The Comedy of Errors* and *Volpone*. Even his hairstyles over the years—from Little Lord Fauntleroy bob to Prince Valiant pageboy to pre-Raphaelite curls—conveyed an unflattering image of upper-class snobbery and entitlement.

John was the first person to acknowledge that this growing perception that he was a spoiled rich kid wasn't entirely inaccurate. "Well, aren't I all those things?" John conceded. "Let's be honest here. I've got it pretty damn good. I know that, and I'm very grateful."

Ted Kennedy knew that his favorite nephew didn't deserve his reputation as an aristocratic airhead. During the summer of 1981, John was earning a hundred dollars a week as an intern at former North Carolina Governor Terry Sanford's Institute for Policy Sciences and Public Affairs at Duke University. Ted begged Jackie to let her son give a press conference there. "People should see," Senator Kennedy reasoned, "that there is a lot more to John than what they've been reading in the papers."

The news conference gave everyone their first real glimpse of the media-savvy charmer John had become. One reporter couldn't resist teasing him about the ink stain on his white shirt. "I would wear one of those plastic pocket protectors," he shot back, "but they make you look like a Republican." He also informed the press that he was teaching himself the guitar.

Was he thinking of a political career? one reporter asked. "I'm not really thinking about careers at the moment," John replied offhandedly. "I'm not a big planner."

Uncle Ted was thrilled with the outcome of John's first press conference, and passed his feeling along to Jackie. "He is a natural," the senator told her. "He had them eating out of the palm of his hand, just like his father."

In his junior year, John decided to move off campus and into a house atop a cobblestone-paved hill at 155 Benefit Street. His new housemates were Rob Littell, tennis team captain John Hare, aspiring actress Christina Haag, and Christiane Amanpour—"Kissy" to her roommates—destined to become one of the most famous names in television news as a star correspondent for CNN and CBS.

By this time he had also broken up with Jenny Christian, who was at Harvard studying psychology. The two remained friends. As a matter of course, John would maintain warm and lasting friendships with all his former lovers; not a single one would go on record making even a mildly negative comment about him.

John's new love was a comely, chestnut-haired literature and history major named Sally Munro. Born and raised in Marblehead, Massachusetts, Munro so closely resembled John's sister that captions routinely misidentified Munro as Caroline. Moreover, Munro and Caroline had attended the same prep school, Concord Academy.

John's on-again, off-again romance with Munro would stretch over five years. During this time, John explored relationships with a number of other women. "John was not a womanizer like his father," one of his frat brothers said, "but his thing with Sally wasn't exclusive." As he grew to manhood, the number of women making a play for Jackie's son had grown exponentially. "His phone was ringing off the hook from girls he knew—and some he didn't know. Women were mailing him their panties . . . We all thought John showed remarkable restraint, considering."

Jackie showed restraint as well, never commenting on his romantic life and always warmly welcoming his main girlfriend-of-the-moment into the Kennedy household. Over dinners at 1040 and the Kennedy compound in Hyannis Port, Munro would learn, as Jenny Christian had before her, all about her host's little idiosyncrasies—how, for instance, Jackie picked up her fork as soon as dinner was served by her longtime butler Efigenio "Effie" Pinheiro and set it across her plate ("At the White House I learned nobody eats until the hostess picks up her fork"), how she rang a tiny silver bell to summon each course, how she moved the conversation along by deftly engaging each person at the table (managing, as one guest put it, to coax a witty remark out of the shyest person there).

John's girlfriends would also learn that, particularly when she was relaxing at Hyannis Port or on Martha's Vineyard, no one was to disturb Jackie between lunch and dinner. When one unlucky girl made the mistake of striking up a conversation with Jackie at 4 p.m., she was upbraided by John. "Why did you do that?" he demanded. "That is her time to be alone with her thoughts. Just don't do it again."

Yet such tense moments were rare. The same women who spoke so highly of John even after breaking up with him were no less in awe of what one called Jackie's "innate generosity of spirit that instantly put you at ease."

Not that Jackie was introduced to more than a tiny fraction of the women who drifted in and out of her son's life. In the early 1980s, the New York disco scene was at its peak, and no VIP guest was more highly prized than JFK Jr. Many weekends, John drove down to New York to dance and drink the night away at clubs like Xenon, the China Club, and Nell's. On Sunday night, John would drive his Honda Civic three hours north to the University of Connecticut, where he and his cousin Timmy Shriver taught English to the children of immigrants.

In keeping with family tradition, John racked up speeding tickets as he crisscrossed New York and New England—and then ignored them completely. Finally, in March 1983, Massachusetts branded him a scofflaw and suspended his license. John ignored the suspension as well, and kept right on driving. He also thought nothing of commandeering his friends' cars; on more than one occasion he "borrowed" a buddy's Mazda GLC or VW Rabbit, only to report the next morning that he had "crashed it."

He was especially fond of driving in Manhattan, where nearly all John's friends got around by cab, bus, or subway. His roommate and future girlfriend Christina Haag recalled the night they drank cheap red wine and then wound up driving from one end of Central Park to the other—three times. "My legs were bare, too close to his hand on the stick shift," Haag recalled. "He drove fast, and I leaned back in my seat, letting my fingers trail the air outside."

John's wider reputation as the Hyannis Port heartthrob gained traction when tabloids began running photos of John horsing around with friends on the beach, or getting ready to scuba-dive. "You'd be standing on a street corner and he'd just whip off his shirt for no apparent reason," one friend said. John, who then weighed 175 pounds but could bench-press 250 pounds, was "proud of the fact that he was in great shape," Rick Guy said. "It was no good trying to meet girls when Mr. Adonis was around," a classmate added. "They had absolutely no interest in you—unless somehow they thought you were the way to get to *him*."

Closing in on graduation, John capped off his college acting career essaying the role of the heavy in *Short Eyes*. "The gum-chewing, tattooed Kennedy throws his bulk around the set with infinite self-assurance," wrote campus theater critic Peter DeChiara, "and an air of stubborn defiance."

At last, a rave that the critic didn't retract. John decided that he wanted to go to Yale Drama School—an idea that was immediately nixed by the Big Lady. Jackie wanted him to go to law school, the logical next move in a course charted for Washington.

There were reports—all fallacious—that Jackie threatened to disinherit her son if he didn't play along. As crestfallen as he undoubtedly was, John did not put up a fight—not this time. "He was very protective of her," Duchin said of John's attitude toward his mother, "and wouldn't do anything to disappoint her—even if it meant giving up something that was important to him." He would not be going to Yale Drama School, but he wasn't rushing to enroll in law school quite yet, either.

On June 6, 1983, John marched onto the green at Brown University with the rest of the graduating seniors, all sweating in their polyester gowns beneath a blazing sun. John was seriously hungover from the party at his Benefit Street digs that had dragged on until seven that morning. Searching above the heads of his classmates as everyone filed to their seats, he finally spotted Jackie in the crowd and waved. "Hi, Mom!" John shouted loudly.

A cheer went up from the Kennedys, and Jackie pointed up at something in the sky. Everyone looked up to see the skywritten message she had arranged for her son—the same bungled inscription on a birthday cake that years earlier had them all howling with laughter: GOOD GLUCK JOHN.

They needed to laugh. The day before, Ted Kennedy had once again invoked JFK's name at a Brown forum on nuclear disarmament. "I know how much my brother Jack cherished John's future," Ted said, his voice trembling, "and how proud he would be if he could be here today." Later that night at a dinner held for John at Providence's swank Providence Biltmore hotel, it was John's turn to get emotional when Ted presented him with a framed copy of notes scribbled by his father at the height of the Cuban Missile Crisis.

The night of his graduation, John threw a party for fifty of his Brown classmates at Hyannis Port. The swimming pool next to Grandma Rose's house had yet to be filled for the season, so many guests, feeling the effects of alcohol and pot, simply slept on the bottom. Rose, needless to say, was not in residence at the time.

Jackie no longer worried that her son would end up a pampered weakling, that he needed more "toughening up." Ready for any physical challenge, Jackie's boy had proven himself over and over again to be a rugged, self-reliant outdoorsman.

That said, John was up for another summer adventure now that he had his bachelor's degree in history. For the young man who grew up on tales of the seven seas and whose mother had an affinity for pirates, it was hard to imagine anything more exciting than what his old diving buddy Barry Clifford had to offer.

Clifford had embarked on a quest to raise the pirate ship *Whydah*, a square-rigged, three-masted galley that had wrecked on the shoals off Wellfleet, Massachusetts in 1717. When it went down, the *Whydah* was said to have taken with it $200 million worth of purloined treasure—booty accrued by the infamous buccaneer Black Sam Bellamy.

Before he could join the crew aboard Clifford's research vessel the *Vast Explorer,* John had to dispel the prevailing notion that he was just another soft, coddled neophyte. "He's a good diver and a helluva athlete," Clifford told the *Vast Explorer*'s six-foot-ten, 325-pound captain, Richard "Stretch" Gray. "You can depend on him, believe me."

Maybe so. But before the *Vast Explorer* departed from Martha's Vineyard, Captain Gray put young Mr. Kennedy to the test. John was given the onerous task of swabbing out the lazarette, a nauseatingly filthy storage space at the extreme stern of the ship that is often referred to as the "glory hole." The cesspool smell emanating from the lazarette was so powerful that it caused even seasoned sailors to retch. John did the job perfectly, in record time, and—as always—without uttering one word of complaint. "John never complained about anything, ever," Clifford said. "He just did whatever he was told to do, period—and with a smile."

It was hard to imagine anything more perfectly suited to John than hunting beneath the sea for buried treasure. All the things he craved were there: danger, excitement, camaraderie, the thrill of discovery, and—during moments alone on deck or in the silent depths of the sea—solitude.

Diving six hours a day, unwinding with his mates at local Vineyard pubs, and then bunking with the rest of the crew belowdecks,

John quickly became one of the most valuable members of the salvage operation. He was also the *Vast Explorer*'s resident cutup, imitating Gray's squint and teasing Clifford for violating ship rules he himself had laid down ("Hey! Who left personal belongings in the dive room? Let's throw them overboard!").

"John was someone we all liked and appreciated," said Clifford, who would take two more years to finally locate the *Whydah*—the only pirate ship ever found. "I had the highest respect for him."

With good reason. At one point, Clifford's team decided to explore the inside of a World War I freight vessel that had sunk off the Vineyard. They were deep inside the bowels of the ship when one of the divers, John Beyer, suddenly couldn't breathe. Beyer's regulator had broken, Clifford remembered, and John "immediately gave him his regulator and they buddy-breathed."

The experience was similar to the time years earlier when John's breathing apparatus malfunctioned and Peter Duchin led him slowly to the surface—but with an important difference. This time the two men had to find their way through the decaying passageways of the ship. "It was like going through a maze to get out of the ship," Clifford said, "but John didn't even blink. There was no panic. It was just cool, calm, collected, business as usual."

(Incredibly, it was John who first spotted the *Whydah*'s cannons, but at the time his reports were discounted by experts. In 2007, divers found John's weathered, plastic compass with the initials "J.F.K." attached to one of the cannons—precisely where he said it would be.)

John's "cool, calm, collected" side masked a roiling inner turmoil over who he really was, where he fit in, what he really remembered about his father. One reason John kept in more or less constant motion—working out, running, biking, skiing, waterskiing, kayaking, swimming, roller-skating, hiking, even skydiving—was to avoid having to dwell on the historic events that shaped his young life, and where it all might lead in the future. "If I stop to think about it all," he told Rob Littell, "I would just sit down and fall apart."

Yet he did stop to think. There was an introspective side to John unknown to the public and even some of his friends. This was the side of John that found comfort in heading into the wilderness alone for days, or spending endless hours paddling a one-man kayak off the shore of Cape Cod. With college now behind him, John took more solitary walks at night atop the narrow breakwater that extended from Hyannis Port into Nantucket Sound. The wind was often howling and waves crashed against the rocks—it was often not the safest place to be. "What the hell were you doing out there by yourself?" Noonan would ask his friend.

"Pondering," John would answer.

It did not help that his birthday was just three days after the anniversary of Dallas (Caroline's November 27 birthday was also too close for comfort, and the proximity to Thanksgiving added to the jumble of emotions). "I just wish the two dates weren't so close," John would say to Littell and others. "The press just never lets up."

This year—the twentieth anniversary of JFK's murder—promised to be especially trying. Jackie dreaded the inevitable media frenzy, and what impact it might have on John at a time when he needed to focus on what direction he wanted his life to take. She was determined to take bold steps to remove John from the line of fire.

It had been twenty-one years since millions of Indians lined the streets of New Delhi shouting "Jackie Ki Jai! Ameriki Rani!" ("Hail Jackie! Queen of America!") during her visit to India and Pakistan as first lady. Now Jackie, who had always claimed a spiritual connection to the subcontinent, was sending John to India. There he would travel the country doing research on rural development—a nine-month stint under the auspices of the University of New Delhi.

Jackie's friend, the writer Gita Mehta, praised this bold move as an example of how "subtle and intelligent a parent she has been." John Kenneth Galbraith, who as U.S. ambassador to India had been Jackie's host during her famous visit, agreed. "She wanted to get away from the circus atmosphere at home, certainly," he said. "But that was a small part of it. India was worlds away from anything he had ever known—a place where he would be left alone to focus on the things that really matter in life."

There was an obvious element of risk—John no longer had his Secret Service protection, and would be traveling the remotest, most undeveloped regions of the country. As alien and daunting as it all seemed, Jackie still felt John would be safer there.

In another unexpected yet shrewd move, Jackie did not resist when John asked if he could bring his girlfriend, Sally Munro, along. "Why not?" she said with a shrug. "India is a very romantic place. Best to enjoy it with someone."

John, as was his habit, worked hard at making the most of his time in India. In addition to his studies and the research work that took him to villages in the most remote corners of India, John clambered over temple ruins, climbed mountains, made side trips to Sri Lanka and Nepal, hit the beaches with friends, bathed in the Ganges—and sampled the hashish that was in plentiful supply.

He also met Mother Teresa, and was surprised when she scolded him for walking in the street. "It is very dangerous. Did you not hear what I told you?" she barked. "Why don't you listen?"

Returning to New York in June 1984, John moved with his friend Robert Littell into a two-bedroom, two-bathroom sublet at 309 West Eighty-sixth Street. John went straight to work as deputy director of the 42nd Street Development Corporation, which his mother had co-founded, collecting an annual salary of just twenty thousand dollars. He also helped get two fledging charities off the ground: Reaching Up and the East Harlem School at Exodus House.

On any given day over the next fifteen years, John could be spotted weaving in and out of traffic on his $1,500 Univega bike as he headed to the next place he had to be. Sometimes he'd be wearing an Armani suit, other times only shorts and running shoes—wherever he ventured in the city, said a neighbor, "people might point, or even call out his name, but usually they just paid no attention." Either way, "John just looked straight ahead and kept right on going."

As dependent as he was on these expensive bikes, John made little effort to hold on to them. Out of impatience and absentmindedness, he seldom took the time to lock his bike or chain it to a stationary object. The results were predictable: John had a bike stolen every two or three months. "He could spend thousands for a bike," Billy Noonan said, "and have it stolen an hour later." Littell believed his friend "set some kind of record" when it came to bikes—and wallets. Once, John and Littell drove an hour back to a rest stop on Interstate 95 because John had inadvertently flung his wallet into a trash can at McDonald's. (Scores of frustrating incidents like this finally led John to chain both his wallet and his keys to his pants.)

As always, John left plenty of time for play as he weighed his long-term career options. He continued to frequent the clubs where he gained instant entree ("Doormen bowed and velvet ropes fell," Littell said). Monday nights were usually spent at sports bars around the city watching football with his friends, and he had courtside seats for Knicks games at Madison Square Garden.

And then there was the time John invited a dozen friends and their dates over to watch a World Series game, turned on the remote—and a XXX porn scene lit up the screen. Realizing that he'd left one of the many porn videos he owned in the VCR, he scrambled to turn off the set and then sheepishly offered to freshen everyone's drinks.

For a short time John, who made a special visit to see the erotic carvings at Konark and Khajuraho when he was studying in India, seemed fascinated by pornography. One midtown video store owner accused him of owing more than a thousand dollars in fines for neglecting to return dozens of X-rated tapes. Wearing shorts and carrying a backpack, John went unrecognized as he strolled through Times Square, stopping to sample the live sex shows that proliferated there at the time.

During this hedonistic phase of his life, John was also acquiring a reputation as a bit of an exhibitionist. He had already posed for a series of provocative, seminude photographs taken by a female friend at Brown—including one apparently making imaginative use of his mother's sable coat.

"He loves to walk around in the nude," said Couri Hay, who worked out at the Aspen Club in Colorado when John was there. "He walks around in the gym with his bathrobe open, and when he takes a shower he leaves the curtain open." On Cape Cod, Hay said, John was equally cheeky, skinny-dipping at a Hyannis Port pool party, then strolling around naked while waiters served guests drinks. In Edgartown on Martha's Vineyard, locals claimed he walked around town wearing only a towel, giggling when he coyly let it slip. Hay's verdict: JFK Jr. "could have been a porno star."

Several years later John caught the attention of vacationers at St. Barth's in the French West Indies. This time, New York travel agent Shelley Shusteroff captured John swimming and walking along on the beach in the altogether. Shusteroff, presumably mindful of John's privacy issues, turned down a six-figure offer to publish the photographs.

In 1984, Jackie was still doing everything she could to prevent John from being swallowed up by Ethel's unruly tribe. That became even more imperative after August 25, when Bobby and Ethel's heroin-addicted son David was found dead in a Palm Beach hotel after injecting himself with the painkiller Demerol, the tranquilizer Melaril, and cocaine. David was twenty-eight.

That Christmas eve, Jackie and John suffered another blow. After decades of alcohol and drug abuse, Peter Lawford died at sixty-one. Jackie, who remained close to her former brother-in-law, called Pat Seton Lawford and wept over the phone. John was upset, too; he had counted on Lawford's support in convincing Jackie that he belonged on stage and not in a courtroom.

John spent Christmas with Caroline and Jackie at 1040, then flew to Los Angeles the next day for Lawford's funeral. "Jackie was grief stricken—very emotional, and very kind," Pat Lawford said. "John was so sweet, and a little lost. Peter was one hundred percent behind his wish to become an actor. With Peter gone there was really no one else in the family who would back him." Indeed, all the Kennedys—including Caroline—agreed with Jackie that he should go to law school. Most of Jackie's friends felt that way, too, with the notable exception of Rudolf Nureyev. "Show some balls!" Nureyev told John with his usual Russian flair for the dramatic. "Do what *you* want!"

John found a new accomplice in his old Benefit Street housemate,

Christina Haag. The daughter of a wealthy marketing executive, Haag, like Caroline, had attended Manhattan's exclusive Brearley School. Growing up in the same Upper East Side circles, Haag had actually known John since they were fifteen. In March 1985, they both signed on to play the lead roles in *Winners* by Brian Friel, the Irish playwright who would go on to win a Tony for *Dancing at Lughnasa*. The drama, about star-crossed lovers named Mag and Joe who drown in a boating mishap, eerily foreshadowed events in John's own life.

Christina, who had spent a year studying acting at the Juilliard School, was taken aback by John's talent for mimicry—although, given his background, it seemed only logical that he'd be able to deliver a flawless Irish accent. When they got into a fight over the correct way for an Irishman to pronounce the word *God,* it was left to the Dublin-born director Nye Heron to decide—and he ruled in John's favor. "Humbled, I was grateful he didn't gloat," Haag recalled. "His ear, the gift of any actor, was superb." After that, Haag added, "I took my pointers from John."

Unfortunately, the play's opening was postponed a month after John somehow managed to fracture his right ankle while working out at the gym. It was one of many such mishaps that plagued the accident-prone John throughout his life. He actually embraced these minor failings that led to the broken bones, the lost keys, the stolen bikes. These were the shortcomings, one friend said, that "he knew made people feel more comfortable around him, that made him seem a little more like the rest of us."

Around the same time, Jackie was dealing with another family tragedy—one that the press paid very little attention to. John's aunt Janet—Jackie's half sister Janet Auchincloss Rutherfurd—had been undergoing treatment for lung cancer for six months. Jackie even donated bone marrow in a vain attempt to save her.

"Jackie really came through for our sister," Jamie Auchincloss said. "Jackie pushed aside everything else to be there for Janet. I think that was one of Jackie's finest moments, really." Yusha Auchincloss agreed. "The strength and concern and love she showed for Janet were inspiring. When the chips were down, Jackie was that kind of person. Totally loyal to her friends and to her family."

Jackie was holding her sister Janet's hand in March 1985 when Janet, thirty-nine and the mother of three, died at Boston's Beth Israel Hospital. Jamie was equally impressed with the way Jackie swung into action to handle Janet's funeral. "Jackie was so acquainted with death . . . When it came to funerals, she understood ritual better than anyone. She was like a priest."

John was among the mourners at his aunt's memorial service in Newport. Yet his focus was more on the cumulative effect all this grief was having on his mother. "Janet was so young," Yusha said, "and even though there was a big age difference she and Jackie were very close. She was devastated, of course. We all were."

John made his professional acting debut on August 15, 1985, at Manhattan's seventy-five-seat Irish Arts Center. Jackie had permitted him to do the play only if critics were barred from seeing it. "Jackie was terrified," her cousin John Davis said, "that the critics would come and see John in *Winners,* since rave reviews might encourage him to continue a career in acting."

To minimize the publicity, Jackie and Caroline boycotted the show entirely. It was just as well, John said. Their presence, he told the cast, would only "cause a fuss"—and guarantee front-page headlines in the next day's *New York Post.* "John just wanted to see if he could measure up as a professional," Davis said, "in something other than a college production."

John was hardly likely to get booed off the stage. This production of *Winners* would be performed only six times, and before an invitation-only audience of family and friends. Yet the words of praise from those involved in the production were effusive: "John is the best young actor I've seen in twelve years," proclaimed Nye Heron, who went on to produce such films as *In the Name of the Father, In America,* and *The Boxer.* The Irish Arts Center's Sandy Boyen called John "an extraordinary and very talented young actor. He could have a very successful stage and film career if he wanted it." But, Heron added, "evidently that's not going to happen."

Not unaware of John's star power, several producers offered to take

Winners straight to Broadway if John stayed in the cast. John declined. "This is definitely not a professional acting debut by any means," he asserted. "It's just a hobby." (Five years later he would flex his acting muscles for the first and only time onscreen, delivering just two lines as a "guitar-playing Romeo" in the indie film *A Matter of Degrees*.)

Winners did mark a turning point of sorts for John, who by this time had broken up with Sally Munro. He fell hard for the lushly beautiful, blue-eyed Christina, and after taking her home to Brooklyn on the back of his new motorcycle (which was stolen days later), told her so. Unfortunately, Haag had decided—for the time being at least—to stay with her longtime boyfriend, the actor Bradley Whitford. (Whitford would go on to fame playing Josh Lyman in TV's *The West Wing*.)

Not accustomed to rejection, John tried to make sense of why anyone would choose a struggling young actor with a pretentious name like Bradley Whitford over him. Not that he lacked for female companionship. Littell recalled the day six-foot-tall *Sports Illustrated* cover model Ashley Richardson showed up at their Eighty-sixth Street apartment looking for John, wearing nothing but a mink coat and Prada booties. On another occasion during this period between serious girlfriends, John failed to hang up the phone properly when he was in bed with one girl, giving an earful of noisy sex to another. The girl on the phone remained on the line long enough to scream at John, but forgave him the very next day.

"Is he sexy?" asked Clic model Audra Avizienis, who homed in on John's seldom-recognized capacity for introspection. "Oh yes, he has this quiet sadness. There's something pensive and sad about him."

John's mother, meanwhile, was having a difficult time trying to come to terms with the senseless death of her sister. "She was such a happy person, so much fun and just so *alive*," John said of his aunt Janet. "Watching her suffer like that was just too much for my mother."

Emotionally drained, Jackie decided to visit the place she had come to regard as her spiritual wellspring: India. By all accounts her fascination with all things Eastern—particularly Hinduism, Buddhism, and the mystics—bordered on the obsessive. She now made pilgrimages to the subcontinent on an annual basis. John joined her in India that fall, staying in the glittering palaces of Delhi, Jaipur, Jodhpur, and Hydera-bad. It became clear to John on this journey—the first time he visited India with Jackie—why she kept returning to the region. "The people of India," John Kenneth Galbraith said, "revered her."

Restored by their Indian interlude, Jackie resumed her mind-spinning social schedule in New York while John added Christina Haag to the guest list for his annual birthday bash. Within months, John and Christina began an intense affair that lasted a tempestuous five years. It was easy to see why she changed her mind. Beyond the obvious, John was an unabashed romantic. "I love your hair," he would tell Christina, cupping her face in his hands. "I love your neck. I love that other people see how much we love each other. I love when they tell me."

Yet from the very start, John also made it clear that, if Christina cheated on him, he didn't want to know. John admitted to having a strong jealous streak, and to being unable to cope with that sort of personal betrayal.

As time progressed, photos of street corner spats between John and his lovers would fill the tabloids, filling him with embarrassment and regret. One classmate conceded that John might "blow up and yell, or pound his fist against something—I even saw him stamp his feet like a little kid." But "three minutes later he'd regret it and apologize." John Perry Barlow chalked this up to John's being "a passionate person. He had a temper, no doubt about it. But he never let it get the best of him."

If he was angry about his mother's opposition to his acting, John never let on—not even to his closest friends. When Haag brought it up, he merely laughed it off and changed the subject. "Disappointed? Yes. Frustrated, certainly," Tish Baldrige said. "But it wasn't as if Jackie just put her foot down and threatened to cut him off. She very deftly steered him in the direction they both knew in their hearts was right for him—toward public service, toward politics."

Jackie was careful never to appear ham-fisted or intrusive—particularly when it came to her son's love life. She was "strong-willed and opinion-ated," Rob Littell said, but "careful not to overstep her bounds."

Even before their affair began in earnest, John repeatedly referred to

Christina Haag as "the girl I'm going to marry." Two years into their relationship, he called his mother to say that he had a big surprise for her and Marta and would drive out to the New Jersey house to fill them in.

When he got there, Jackie had broken her engagement ring out of the safe and informed him the moment he walked in the door that it had taken a while, but she had finally come to terms with the idea that her son was getting married. John's news, however, was that he had spotted an orange Karmann Ghia on the street with a "For Sale" sign in the window and purchased it on the spot.

"Isn't it great?" he asked his dumbfounded mother. "Don't you just love the color?"

"John, this is your big news? This garish old jalopy?"

Jackie eventually saw the humor in the situation, but Marta didn't. She had spent $1,300 on an Ungaro dress for the engagement party—a dress that could not be returned.

John would eventually marry, of course, and the bride would not be Christina Haag. But in 1986, twenty-five-year-old JFK Jr. was focused on finding a career path now that he had put his dreams of an acting career behind him. "Jackie didn't really have to pressure him to give all that up," George Plimpton said. "He always knew greater things were expected of him."

That winter, John took part in a roller-skating party to celebrate the twentieth anniversary of the Bedford-Stuyvesant Restoration Project, set up by his uncle Bobby. He strapped on a pair of skates, grasped the hands of two neighborhood children, and took them for a spin around the rink.

It was hard not to notice that the press was swarming all around John, the photographers recording his every move. "I think they're waiting for me to fall," he told his skating partners.

"I didn't know you were so famous," one of the boys said, perplexed by all the attention John was getting. "What's your name?"

"John Kennedy."

"John Kennedy! He was one of our presidents," the boy said.

"Yeah, I know," John replied. "He was my dad."

*All of these people have expectations of me
because of my father, but I believe he would have
wanted me to do whatever the hell I wanted.*

—JOHN

*The people who came in contact with him tended
to be surprised by his dignity and his quiet goodness.*

—JOHN PERRY BARLOW

10.

"I'm Not My Father"

It was the eve of Caroline's wedding to Ed Schlossberg, and Jackie wiped away a tear as her son stood up at the rehearsal dinner to give a toast. Ed had asked John, just named "America's Most Eligible Bachelor" by *People* magazine, to be his best man. It was the fourth time that summer John had served in that capacity. ("And I get better each time," he said with a wink.) This time, John talked about how close he, his sister, and their mother had been. "All our lives, it's just been the three of us. Now," he said, turning to Schlossberg, "there are four."

Caroline's wedding date—July 19, 1986—happened to be the groom's forty-first birthday. It was also the seventeenth anniversary of Chappaquiddick. Paying no heed to appearances, the wedding went on as scheduled, with more than two thousand spectators—hundreds of them members of the press—jamming the streets of Hyannis Port and nearby Centerville, where the ceremony was conducted at the Church of Our Lady of Victory.

The mother of the bride had meticulously planned every detail—except the wedding dress. "I am not going to get involved," Jackie told the designer, her friend Carolina Herrera, "because Caroline is the one who will wear it. I want her to be the happiest girl in the world." It was another example, Baldrige said, of Jackie's "knowing when not to interfere, when to step back and let her children be themselves."

No one was more famous than Jackie for maintaining a brave façade at all costs. But this time she wept unabashedly during the wedding ceremony. As Mr. and Mrs. Ed Schlossberg departed to the cheers of the crowd, Jackie stood on the church steps, eyes red and swollen, happy tears streaming down her cheeks. Still smiling, Jackie bit her lip and rested her head on Ted Kennedy's shoulder.

At the reception that night, John looked on with pride as Ted wrung even more emotion out of the moment. "We've all thought of Jack today, and how much he loved Caroline and how much he loved Jackie . . ." Then he raised a glass to the mother of the bride—"that extraordinary woman, Jack's only love. He would have been so proud of you today."

Doris Kearns Goodwin cornered Jackie later and praised her for raising two children who were so obviously devoted to each other.

"I want that kind of closeness for my sons," the author said.

"It's the best thing," Jackie replied without hesitation, "I've ever done."

Jackie would have even more reason to be happy that fall, when John enrolled in classes at New York University School of Law. With Caroline already attending Columbia Law School, both her children were now headed toward respectable careers in the legal profession— and, she hoped, lives spent in the political arena.

There were still a few loose ends to tie up. Over dinner in Hyannis Port, Jackie gently "suggested" to John and Rob Littell that it was time for them to "break up"—that living like frat brothers on West Eighty-sixth Street was not conducive to John's new life as a serious law student.

The move came none too soon, as it turned out. When they moved out of the apartment, John and Littell left the place in such a shambles that one friend of John's told writer Michael Gross it "looked like a herd of yaks had lived there." A neighbor claimed the carpets were so badly burned it "looked like they'd had cookouts on it," and the floors were so damaged that "every surface had to be sanded, spackled, and patched."

There were also holes in the walls. Some represented moments when

John, safely venting the anger he felt toward a girlfriend or his mother's efforts to kill his acting dreams, punched a hole squarely through the plaster. Other indentations were the result, Littell later explained, of "roughhousing gone bad."

After moving alone into the Surrey, a residential hotel not far from his mother's apartment on the Upper East Side, John buckled down to his law studies. Then, at Jackie's urging, he spent the summer of 1987 clerking for the Reagan Justice Department in Washington—a job for which he was paid $353 a week. "John actually liked Ronald Reagan," Littell said, "and took plenty of ribbing for it from the rest of his family."

Jackie also knew something about the law. In addition to her legal battles with author William Manchester and photographer Ron Galella, Jackie had waged war in the courts to save Grand Central Terminal and New York's Lever House, one of the world's first glass-walled skyscrapers. As part of her ongoing crusade to preserve New York's landmarks and halt overbuilding, she also blocked developers from constructing a high-rise over St. Bartholomew's Church on Park Avenue, and from throwing up two office towers at Columbus Circle that would have cast a looming shadow over the southern end of Central Park. "They're stealing our sky!" she protested at a packed news conference. (Years later, twin towers did go up on Columbus Circle: the glass-sheathed Time Warner Center.)

John was proud of everything his mother did, but as a dyed-in-the-wool New Yorker he took special pride in the fact she saved Grand Central. Eventually, a seven-foot-wide aluminum plaque went up inside the terminal. The inscription:

JACQUELINE KENNEDY ONASSIS LED THE FIGHT
TO SAVE THIS BEAUTIFUL TERMINAL. THE VICTORY
WON IN THE UNITED STATES SUPREME COURT IN 1978
ESTABLISHED THE PUBLIC'S RIGHT TO PROTECT LAND-
MARKS IN CITIES AND TOWNS ALL OVER AMERICA.

The year of her Supreme Court victory, Jackie made an important real estate deal of her own, quietly paying the Hornblower family of Martha's Vineyard $1.15 million for thirty-six acres (later expanded to 474 acres) along Squibnocket Pond in the Vineyard's Gay Head section.

Washington architect Hugh Newell Jacobsen was hired to design nothing more daring than a nineteen-room saltbox—more like a connecting series of saltboxes—and a separate barnlike two-bedroom guesthouse. A silo-like portion of the guesthouse—they would call it "the Barn"—was built expressly for John.

Jackie dubbed the estate Red Gate Farm—although guests would swear they never saw a red gate anywhere on the property—and moved in in the summer of 1981. The house and guesthouse boasted white oak floors. The rooms, all decorated in pastels and lined with books, looked out over the ocean through multi-paned windows made the old-fashioned way, with wooden pegs instead of nails. Not only were there heated towel racks in the bathrooms, but the toilets all flushed with hot water to prevent condensation.

The main house had eight fireplaces, and Jackie insisted on having the one in her bedroom lit by her butler every morning—even at the height of summer. The kitchen boasted a sixteen-burner Vulcan stove, and breathtaking views of the Atlantic and Squibnocket Pond. The price tag for what Jackie called "my wonderful little house" topped $3 million.

As a couple, Jackie and Maurice were happiest on Martha's Vineyard. "They had an intimate, loving relationship," said Marian Ronan, who worked as a maid at Red Gate Farm. "Maurice had his own bedroom next door to Jackie's—but he slept with her . . . There was a big hallway door that could be closed and locked, cutting them off from the rest of the house and giving them complete privacy."

Jackie stuck to her strict regimen of exercise—getting up at seven each morning, she slathered her face with Ponds cold cream and swam for two hours in Squibnocket Pond. In the afternoons, she compulsively ran, swam, biked, and rowed—all the while sticking to a diet of fish and vegetables that, said Ronan, wasn't enough to keep a sparrow alive.

She did satisfy her appetite for gossip, however, spending part of each day in the "little kitchen" next to the main kitchen in her bathing suit, her hair up in curlers, kibitzing with the help. Nothing delighted her more than a juicy piece of gossip. The first time Jackie read about Woody Allen's scandalous affair with Mia Farrow's adopted daughter Soon-Yi Previn, Ronan said, "She put her hand to her mouth to try to stifle her laughter." Later, she bombarded Mia with phone calls in an attempt to get her to tell her side of the story in a Doubleday book.

Although she cherished her solitude, Jackie welcomed visits from John. She was less enthusiastic about his being there with friends when she was not in residence. Whenever this happened, he reverted to his old frat house habits, having as many as sixteen guests at a time. After a weekend devoted to playing drinking games, roughhousing, and smoking pot, he and his pals invariably left Jackie's tranquil getaway looking as if it had been sacked by Genghis Khan.

Marta Sgubin upbraided John for leaving his mother's house a shambles. "You should have more respect," the normally soft-spoken Sgubin shouted, "for your mother's house!" Mortified, John limited the number of friends he invited to Red Gate Farm and admonished the ones he did invite to behave themselves. It wasn't long, however, before he reverted to his old, messy ways.

The staff kept a watchful eye on John whenever he visited, but they—and Jackie—were unaware that in February 1988 John had secretly begun taking flying lessons from local pilot Arthur Marx at Martha's Vineyard Airport. "I was impressed with him immediately," Marx said, "because he rode his bike to the airport from his mother's house at the other end of the island and it was freezing. That's how much he wanted to fly."

As a pilot, John was "full of enthusiasm," Marx said. "He really, really dug it, and he took flying seriously."

Marx took several flights with John at the controls. "He was always focused in the airplane," insisted Marx, who would take his last flight with John in 1998. "I never saw him as a pilot act in an impulsive way. In fact, John was probably better than he thought he was."

That June, John finally decided to tell his mother that he was taking flying lessons. He even brought Jackie to meet Marx. "This is my mother, Jacqueline Onassis," John told his flight instructor at the time. "As if," Marx laughed, "I wouldn't know who she was. If she had any problem with John's flying, I didn't see it. She was perfectly charming."

If nothing else, Jackie knew how to disguise what she was really thinking. She had always encouraged John to take risks—from rebuilding homes in earthquake-ravaged Guatemala to diving for sunken treasure in the Atlantic to trekking through the wilderness in such dicey corners of the world as India and Africa.

Yet Tempelsman confided in a friend that there was "just something about John piloting a plane that frightened her." Now Jackie, whose dreams were haunted by the memory of Dallas for years, was having nightmares about her son perishing in a plane crash. Jackie begged John to give up this one dream. "There have been too many deaths in the family," she told him.

Once again, John's devotion to his mother trumped his own desires. Not wanting to cause her any undue anxiety, he relented and put aside his dream of learning to fly—for now.

————

A COLLECTIVE SIGH went up from the delegates at the 1988 Democratic National Convention in Atlanta when John Fitzgerald Kennedy Jr. stepped to the podium to introduce his uncle Ted. Now twenty-seven years old and heartthrob handsome, John evoked such a response that *Time* magazine's Walter Isaacson worried that the roof of the Omni Coliseum might collapse "from the sudden drop in air pressure caused by the simultaneous sharp intake of so many thousand breaths."

What followed was the kind of reverential silence seldom accorded any speaker at a political convention. Even John's voice—polished yet devoid of any accent or his parents' distinctive quirks—took his countrymen by surprise; this was the first time most Americans had ever heard JFK Jr. speak.

"Over a quarter of a century ago," John began, "my father stood before you to accept the nomination of the presidency of the United States. So many of you came into public service because of him and in a very real sense it is because of you that he is with us today."

Millions were impressed with the remarkably poised young man making his debut on the national political stage—and none more than Jackie. Having waged her war of attrition against John's ambitions to become an actor, she was now ready to see him embrace the real-life role he was born to play.

The timing seemed perfect. John was spending the summer earning $1,100 a week at the prestigious Los Angeles law firm of Manatt, Phelps, Rothenberg, & Phillips, and that fall he was entering his final year at NYU Law School.

After his rousing convention speech, John returned to his summer job at Manatt, Phelps and to Christina Haag, who happened to be appearing in a play at the Tiffany Theater on Sunset Boulevard. This would be an idyllic time for the couple, who shared a clapboard cottage on Thornton Court in the Venice section of Los Angeles. John, who was in the habit of bestowing nicknames on just about everyone, began calling Christina "Chief" and "Puppy." She called him "King."

That summer, without telling his mother, John resumed his flying lessons—this time at nearby Santa Monica Airport. With her boyfriend flying the plane and an instructor sitting next to him, Haag tagged along on a trip to Catalina Island. Buffeted by strong winds as he descended toward a short, narrow runway, John offered words of reassurance before finally bringing the plane in safely: "Don't worry, Puppy. Don't worry . . ."

Since John was so fond of monikers (he called Billy Noonan "Chopper" or "Sylvester"; nieces Rose and Tatiana were "Lola" and "Lolita") his friends kept casting about for a nickname for JFK Jr. that would stick. Now that he had traded in his unruly locks for a sculpted, executive-boardroom-ready cut, John was continually ribbed about his perfect hair. John was dubbed "Helmut Head"—a name he rather enjoyed. Once his friend Hilary Shepard-Turner had him paged at the airport. "Mr. Head," the announcer boomed over the loudspeaker.

"Mr. Helmut Head. Please come to the courtesy telephone." John answered the page. From then on, John signed his letters to Shepherd-Turner and other pals "H. Head." (Another moniker would surface years later, when a particularly severe cut was described as John's "Eddie Munster look.")

Then, of course, there was the matinee idol face, the megawatt smile, the chiseled physique. John's looks, even his closest male friends had to concede, were exceptional. "I am a heterosexual male," John Perry Barlow said, "and there were times when he was sitting across me at the table and I would sort of be taken aback by how handsome he was. You'd sort of say to yourself, 'God, this guy looks *perfect.*'"

The editors of *People* agreed, anointing John as the world's reigning male sex symbol by putting him on the cover of its September 2, 1988, issue as "The Sexiest Man Alive." The story's cloying first paragraph: "Okay, ladies, this one's for you. But first some ground rules. GET YOUR EYES OFF THAT MAN'S CHEST! He's a serious fellow. Third-year law student. Active with charities. Scion of the most charismatic family in American politics and heir to its most famous name."

The magazine's "serious fellow" caveat aside, Jackie viewed John's new Sexiest Man Alive image as a crass attempt to exploit the Kennedy name—and a serious setback to his embryonic public-service career. After all she had done to steer her son away from the glitz of show business, Jackie also worried about the impact all this attention was bound to have on John's ego. "He already knows that he's gorgeous," she told her friend Bunny Mellon. "I hope all this doesn't distract him from what's really important."

John was determined to enjoy the moment, and poke fun at himself in the process. He put on a fig leaf and showed up at one Halloween party that year as Michelangelo's David. He went to another party as "the Golden Boy," attired in gold glitter and a loincloth. Later, he would offer the definitive answer to people who suggested all the attention was somehow beneath him. "Listen," he told ABC's Barbara Walters, "people can say a lot worse things about you than you are attractive and you look good in a bathing suit."

Now that he was a bona fide sex symbol, John's love life was fair game for the tabloids. Not that this in any way inhibited him. John was "sleeping with every hot chick on the planet," Billy Noonan said.

John liked to call his best friend and leave a taunting message. "Check out the cover of *People* [or *Vogue* or *Vanity Fair*]," John would say. "I banged her last night. Just thought you might like to know." Later, Noonan would get all the juicy particulars from John over the phone. "The possibilities were limitless," he said, "and John played them out."

The temptation to draw parallels between the Sexiest Man Alive and his womanizing dad was irresistible. Ever since the revelations about JFK's affairs began to emerge in the late 1970s—with Marilyn Monroe, Judith Campbell Exner, and others—Jackie and John just looked the other way. "Obviously," Gore Vidal said, "it's not the kind of thing a boy brings up to his mother. They just pretended none of it ever really happened. All the Kennedys are very good at that."

———

ONE UNWELCOME REMINDER of JFK's torrid affair with Marilyn— the affair that most troubled Jackie—arrived on her doorstep in the form of another blond bombshell by the name of Madonna. Already a pop icon, Madonna was best known at the time for her "Material Girl" video, an homage to Monroe's "Diamonds Are a Girl's Best Friend" number from the film *Gentlemen Prefer Blondes*.

The Material Girl and JFK Jr. met briefly at a party following one of her concerts at Madison Square Garden in 1985. Three years later, after the breakup of her stormy marriage to Sean Penn, she went after John. Beyond the obvious—stories of her sexual escapades abounded— Madonna was convinced that destiny was taking a hand in bringing together the undisputed heiress to Monroe's platinum persona with the son of JFK. She told friends she believed that her affair with JFK Jr. would be nothing less than "cosmic."

Like his mother, John was perfectly capable of being starstruck. "You could see it in his eyes that first time they met," said dancer Erika

Belle, one of Madonna's closest friends at the time. "John was totally in awe."

In a clumsy effort to avoid detection, the couple rendezvoused at the health club where they both worked out and shared the same trainer, venturing outside together only for a quick morning jog through Central Park. She quickly came up with her own handles for John; Madonna called him either "Johnny," or just "Kennedy." It wasn't long before John took Madonna to meet his mother.

At 1040, Madonna stepped off the elevator and signed the guestbook "Mrs. Sean Penn" (technically, she still was). Not surprisingly, Jackie was anything but thrilled with this particular liaison. There were many things about Madonna that rubbed Jackie the wrong way, not the least of which was her habit of thumbing her nose at Roman Catholic rituals. Madonna's use of crucifixes and other Catholic images was deemed sacrilegious by the Vatican, and across the globe she was being condemned as a heretic. Nor did it help when Jackie picked up a copy of *Life* only to see Madonna dolled up as Marilyn on the cover. "I imagine it was all hitting a bit close to home," Vidal said.

Had she been able to look past Madonna's brassy exterior, Jackie would have recognized an articulate, well-read young woman who could speak knowledgeably about art, dance, and fashion. Madonna also had a head for business. At that time, *Forbes* put Madonna on its cover as one of the wealthiest women in the entertainment industry, with a then-impressive personal net worth approaching $40 million (which would, according to *Forbes,* grow to over $500 million by 2013).

John, of course, wasn't interested in Madonna because of her head for business. One day while he was staying with Billy Noonan in Hyannis Port, John phoned New York to check his messages. On the other end, a woman with a familiar voice was calling from Rome. "Kennedy," she began, "I'm drunk and when I see you next I'm going to take your . . ." The rest was decidedly X-rated, and after John played it for Noonan, his friend asked to hear it again.

Unable to quite place the voice, Noonan begged John to tell him who it was. "Madonna," John answered matter-of-factly.

Noonan was speechless. "You are banging Madonna?" Noonan asked. "How do I not know this until now?"

So what was it like sleeping with Madonna? "Let me tell you," Kennedy replied, "she's a sexual dynamo."

The only place the superstar couple could let their guard down was in Hyannis Port, where they bundled up in sweaters and jackets and jogged on the beach. Inside the compound, they curled up by the fire, sipping daiquiris from Waterford crystal glasses marked "Caroline" and "John-John"—souvenirs from the family's first trip to Ireland after the assassination.

If John sought during this period of his life to emulate his skirt-chasing father by having an affair with the 1980s' answer to Marilyn, it was hard to think of anyone who fit the bill more perfectly than the Material Girl. Given the obvious and frequently drawn parallels between Madonna and Monroe, it was also difficult to imagine anyone whom Jackie would find more offensive or unacceptable as a love interest for her cherished only son. It is highly doubtful that John intended to hurt his mother, but his decision to carry on an affair with his generation's reigning blond pop goddess appeared to offer a way—however far-fetched or ill-advised—for John to connect with his father by experiencing something akin to what Jack experienced.

In New York, the JFK Jr.–Madonna affair stayed tightly under wraps. Amazingly, they managed to avoid detection largely by attending parties and plays separately, then getting together afterward.

Somehow, John was managing to keep this clandestine liaison from his steady girlfriend, Christina. "She hasn't a clue," he told Noonan. After another midday lovemaking session at a New York hotel, John rushed to meet up with Haag. She leaned into his chest and inhaled. "Whose perfume is that?" she asked him.

"Oh, that? I ran through Bloomies to get here," he said, using shorthand for Bloomingdale's department store. "I stopped at the perfume counter to get you something but all these salespeople ran up spritzing me, and it started attracting attention, so I just said to hell with it . . ."

Christina was dubious, but let it slide. Madonna's ex was less charitable. After a tribute to Robert De Niro at New York's American Museum of the Moving Image, JFK Jr. joined Jeremy Irons, Liza Minnelli, Sean Penn, and other celebrities at a party in De Niro's honor at the Tribeca Grill.

At one point during the festivities, John walked up to Penn, stuck out his hand, and introduced himself.

"I know who you are," Penn glowered back. He was clearly still incensed over reports that John and his wife were sleeping together while she was still married. "You owe me an apology." Aware of Penn's fondness for fisticuffs, John beat a hasty retreat. The next morning, a funeral wreath of white roses bearing the inscription MY DEEPEST SYMPATHIES arrived at John's front door. "Johnny," the card read, "I heard about last night. m."

Jackie, who became a grandmother for the first time when Caroline gave birth to Rose Schlossberg on June 25, 1988, was still rooting for John to marry Christina Haag. After running into Christina at a performance of *Macbeth* starring Christopher Plummer and Glenda Jackson one evening, she and Maurice Tempelsman offered Haag a ride home. As their limo passed the marquee for *Speed-the-Plow,* the David Mamet play in which Madonna was making her Broadway debut, Jackie grabbed Haag's arm.

"Oh!" Jackie said. "Have you seen it?"

"Not yet," Haag replied. Both Jackie and Haag knew about John's rumored affair with Madonna, but for now all Christina could do was accept John's fervent denials.

Jackie, of course, knew otherwise.

"The play was good, but Madonna was *terrible*," Jackie said, laughing between puffs on a cigarette (by this time she had switched to Marlboros). "I think you should go. I think you should go next week—and have John take you. And go backstage!"

Fortunately for everyone involved, Haag did not take the bait. But whether it was out of a desire to see Christina confront Madonna or simply to make her skirt-chasing son squirm, it was clear that Jackie did not approve of John's romantic entanglement with the woman who billed herself as the 1980's answer to Norma Jean.

———

EVEN BEFORE HE ended his affair with Madonna, John racked up other celebrity conquests. Returning from a trip to Los Angeles, John arrived at the Delta terminal at JFK Airport and was walking outside to find his waiting car when he heard someone call his name. The door of a limousine opened, and out popped Sarah Jessica Parker, who later became best known for television's *Sex in the City*. Taking her cue from swimwear model Ashley Richardson, Parker wore a mink, high heels, and—as a titillating flash of her coat revealed to John—nothing else.

The Kennedy-Parker affair, which John conducted while he was seeing Madonna, among others, lasted only a few months. "The body's beautiful," Parker acknowledged, but added that she found it impossible to deal with constantly being upstaged by him. "What you have is wrong," she joked with him. "It's not right. It's unfair, as a woman, to have to stand next to you."

Another of John's celebrity romances lasted longer; it would jolt along in a series of fits and starts for more than five years. John had actually met Daryl Hannah when they were both eighteen and vacationing with their families on St. Martin. The stepdaughter of billionaire Chicago financier (and major Democratic Party contributor) Jerry Wexler, leggy, blond Hannah was not about to go unnoticed. To make certain of this, she toted around a teddy bear on the beach, at restaurants and clubs—wherever she went.

By the summer of 1988, Uncle Teddy was trying to curry favor with Wexler by setting John up with Hannah. But it wasn't until that September that they finally met again, at the wedding of Lee Radziwill to director Herb Ross. Hannah no longer needed a teddy bear to be noticed. She was now a major box-office draw with such hits as *Splash, Wall Street, Roxanne,* and Ross's *Steel Magnolias* under her belt.

Hannah lived with rocker Jackson Browne at the time and John was still stringing Haag along. But within weeks they were spotted dining in a West Village restaurant, then shooting pool almost until dawn at S.T.P., a bar in TriBeCa. Hannah missed John's graduation from NYU Law School in May 1989—Christina was there alongside Jackie and Caroline—but it was Daryl, not Haag, who was chosen by John to accompany him aboard a forty-six-foot yacht cruising Virginia's Smith Mountain Lake.

Yet as long as she knew John was seeing other women—publicly he made a point of referring to Haag as his girlfriend—Hannah was not about to end her often-stormy relationship with Browne. Over the years she ricocheted between the two men, leaving John confused and at times heartbroken. "Until she was the only woman in John's life," said Daryl's former assistant, Natalie Cross, "she wasn't about to give Jackson up."

Meanwhile, John was studying for the brutal New York State bar exam in July 1989 when Hannah abruptly picked up and returned to her mercurial rock star boyfriend for the first time. One week later, John failed the bar exam along with 2,187 others.

"I failed the bar exam, too," former New York City mayor Ed Koch wrote John. "It didn't stop me and it won't stop you." Still, John was humiliated by THE HUNK FLUNKS headlines. After all, his sister had aced the bar exam on her first try, was already writing a book on the Bill of Rights, and had to juggle all this with being a full-time mom. (Caroline gave birth to her second child, Tatiana Celia Kennedy Schlossberg, on May 5, 1990.)

John offered no excuses. "Now I have to suck it up," he said, "and give it all I have next time so I won't have to do this again." In the meantime, he was still permitted to earn thirty thousand dollars a year working as one of sixty-four rookie assistant prosecutors under longtime Manhattan district attorney Robert Morgenthau. He would be allowed to prosecute low-level cases once he passed the bar, but for now he was restricted to doing legal research and interviewing defendants.

At this point, John's scofflaw past caught up with him. A quick background check revealed that John had accumulated $2,300 in unpaid parking tickets and that there were several outstanding moving violations, including driving an unregistered vehicle, making an illegal turn, and, of course, speeding.

Once those infractions were quietly cleared away by John's lawyers, he was allowed to report for work at the DA's office on Hogan Place. That day, a mob of reporters blocked his way. Uniformed police escorted him inside and onto the elevator—then asked for his autograph. A tabloid offered one paralegal ten thousand dollars just to surreptitiously take a photo of John at his desk.

JFK Jr. was the only assistant DA permitted to have his own secretary just to handle the mail addressed to him at the office. "There were love letters, invitations to parties, lots of pictures of naked girls," said Jill Konviser, whose office was next to John's. "The other idiots in my office would fight over them."

Another of his colleagues at the DA's office, Owen Carragher Jr., praised John for "fitting in. In ways that are most meaningful, he was just one of us—except with better girlfriends."

With Carragher and the other new arrivals, John was assigned to the complaint room, where the prosecutors meet with defendants twice a week. "It was disgusting, it was filthy," Konviser said, "and it stinks, and people scream at you." Everyone complained—everyone but John.

Still coping with his ADD and a mild form of dyslexia, John took several bar review courses but was "unable to sit still for more than ten minutes at a time," said a fellow lawyer. There was a door off the classroom opening onto a balcony, and, according to his colleague, John jumped up three or four times during the class to open it "for really no reason. He just seemed to have this need to constantly be in motion."

When John failed the bar a second time in early 1990, the headlines were merciless. THE HUNK FLUNKS—AGAIN! blared the front page of the *New York Post*. Confronting the mob of reporters that waited outside the district attorney's office, John struck a hopeful if vaguely defiant tone. "Obviously, I'm very disappointed," he said, pointing out that he had fallen just eleven points short of a passing grade of 660. "Close is only good for horseshoes," he hastened to add, "not for the bar exam. But you know, God willing, I'll go back there in July and I'll pass it then. Or I'll pass it the next time, or I'll pass it when I'm ninety-five. I'm clearly not a major legal genius."

Maybe not, but no one who knew John thought he was dumb. "That whole notion that he was stupid is a myth," Barlow said. "John was very, very intelligent. A little scattered, but *really smart*." John's boss in the DA's office, Michael Cherkasky, agreed. "He was very smart, very committed," Cherkasky said, "and a good lawyer."

Once again, John put a brave face on things. But privately he was, in Barlow's words, "crushed." This failure was so bad, Littell added, "it drove him to drink." John climbed into his newly purchased truck, a blue GMC Typhoon, and checked into a motel in Lake George, some 215 miles north of Manhattan. Alone, he holed up with a bottle of Macallan Scotch.

As upset as John was about the drubbing he was getting in the press, it was no match for Jackie's rage. She concealed her true feelings from the public, as did her son, but privately Jackie railed against the newspaper editors who delighted in portraying John as dim. "They're really having a field day with this," she told Ed Koch. "It's so unfair, and it just makes me so furious."

Failing the bar a second time and the media frenzy it ignited did more than just drive John to drink. It drove him to see a therapist. His entire life, John had been held up to the impossibly high standard set by his father. Now he was forced to take a long, hard look at how he stacked up to the slain president. At twenty-nine—John's age now—his father had already distinguished himself as a war hero, written two bestselling books (one of which won the Pulitzer Prize), and been elected to Congress. Just a few days after John failed the bar exam a second time, a senior prosecutor in his office made a cutting remark about how far JFK had gotten by this age.

"I'm not my father," John fired back.

———

JOHN WOULD CONTINUE to see a therapist on and off for years. For the moment, by merely articulating his feelings of inadequacy to another person, John at least could put things in perspective. "He could drive himself insane trying to compete with the legacy of a legend," Littell observed, "or he could figure out a way to live his own life."

Right now, John had to find a way to pass the bar exam on his third try. If he didn't, he would be forced to give up his job as an assistant DA and—even more important—be derided in the press as a disappointment and a dunce. This time, at Jackie's urging, he hired a tutor for $1,075 to help get him the 660 score he needed to pass.

There were other matters to attend to that summer—starting with the Kennedy Foundation Dinner on June 1, followed by the wedding of his cousin Kerry Kennedy to New York governor Mario Cuomo's son Andrew Cuomo (who would also go on to serve in President Bill Clinton's cabinet and himself be elected governor of New York).

It was during the Kennedy-Cuomo wedding at St. Matthew's Cathedral in Washington that John learned just how much some of his Kennedy cousins resented him. Out of consideration for JFK's family, the bride had placed a round Persian rug over the marble plaque near the altar that marked the spot where the president's coffin was placed during his funeral.

Several young Kennedys had been having a field day with the HUNK FLUNKS headlines, seizing the opportunity to torment their rock star cousin at every turn. One called John over to the center aisle, told him to look down, and then yanked the rug off the marker. John took a step back and gasped. "God," one cousin said, "he doesn't even know where his father's funeral was!"

Another usher at the wedding, James Hairston, was mortified. "Put it back!" he shouted. "Put the rug back!"

When she heard about the incident, Jackie shook her head in disgust. "Now I know I made the right decision," she told Plimpton, "to keep him away from those baboons."

It didn't stop John from getting together with his cousins one more time on July 22, 1990, to celebrate matriarch Rose Kennedy's hundredth birthday. Just two days later, he took the bar exam a third time—only under circumstances that vastly improved his chances of passing. Having established the fact that he suffered from a learning disability, John was given more time to complete the test.

As soon as the test was over, John headed out on a road trip with Billy Noonan. Driving up to Rhode Island, they gave a lift to a teenage couple whose car had broken down on the side of the road. On the way to the young couple's home in Warwick, Rhode Island, John chatted with them but shrugged off any suggestion that he looked "awfully familiar."

Apparently, the teenagers figured it out themselves. A few days later they walked up to John's cousin Patrick Kennedy as he was campaigning for Congress in Rhode Island, and promised they and everyone they knew would vote for him because John had been kind enough to help them out when they were stranded.

Not long after, John faced reporters again—this time after learning he had finally passed the bar exam. "I'm very relieved," he said. "It tastes very sweet at the moment." The next day, family friend Ted Van Dyk called and asked how he liked working in the DA's office.

"It stinks," answered John, who went on to explain that he was going to remain there just long enough to meet his mother's expectations. "Then," he said, "I'm going to do something else."

As it turned out, John spent four years in the prosecutor's office "putting away the bad guys—people who have swindled elderly widows out of their life savings, or who sell drugs to schoolchildren," Michael Cherkasky said. "You're definitely wearing the white hat."

John did not get many opportunities to prosecute cases in court— District Attorney Morgenthau was wary of the circus atmosphere that accompanied John everywhere he went. But John did win the six cases he did manage to prosecute. "He was a natural competitor," Cherkasky said, "and trying a case in court is a one-on-one sport."

John, whose salary as an assistant DA topped out at $41,500, owed some of those convictions to the defendants' desire to unburden themselves to him. "So they tell everything to me, *the prosecutor*, because for some reason they think I'm their friend," John explained. "And then when I send them to jail, they say thanks and it was great meeting you."

"Even though his job was to put me away, I liked the guy," said Venard Garvin, who was sentenced to two to six years in prison for drug possession. In the middle of the trial, Garvin sidled over to John and said, "It's the job. It's not you."

That November, Jackie, relieved that John had silenced his critics in the press by finally passing the bar, rewarded him with a lavish thirtieth-birthday party in one of the largest industrial lofts in the Chelsea section of Manhattan. Although Jackie footed the bill, the official hosts were John and his friend Santina Goodman, another Brown alumnus with a late November birthday.

In keeping with the party's big band theme, John wore a vintage zoot suit and spats, twirling a chain that hung from his pants pocket. He spent much of the evening dancing with his mother, who managed to sneak in undetected through a rear service entrance. Jackie beamed as John blew out the candles on his birthday cake—as always, a homemade chocolate cake prepared by Marta Sgubin. (In keeping with another long-standing family tradition, John later dug into his favorite dessert—floating island—also prepared by Marta.)

Also among the guests that evening was Christina Haag, although it was clear that their five-year affair was over. John had already moved into a bachelor pad in TriBeCa, and the buzz about him and Hannah intensified when she bought an Upper West Side apartment. The fact remained, however, that Hannah still shared a house in California with Jackson Browne. Despite the occasional tryst with John, Daryl still couldn't bring herself to leave the rock star.

John consoled himself with a bevy of beauties, including theatrical director Toni Kotite, models Richardson and Avizienis, and doe-eyed, whispery-voiced Wilhelmina model Julie ("Jules") Baker. "She comes from Pennsylvania," John told Littell, "and she looks just like my mother." John and Jules Baker would date, although not exclusively, for years. When Littell brazenly asked his former roommate what the sex was like with Baker, John replied with an unequivocal "Oh my *God*."

Yet John never gave up on Hannah. After a fight with Browne, she would fly across the country and dive into John's comforting arms.

"He's mean to her," John would say of Browne's tempestuous relationship with Daryl. "They've got a lot of problems."

But so did John and Daryl. It wasn't long before they were walking along a Manhattan street, drawing stares as they quarreled over something innocuous like where to shop or which movie to see. Occasionally, they argued heatedly about politics. "People gave John a lot of room to pontificate," a friend of the couple said. "He was JFK's son, after all. But Daryl grew up around big party donors and politicians as well as movie industry types. She had her own opinions and she let him know."

Hannah was, in fact, well read and witty—all of which ran counter to her windblown, slightly ditzy, sun-kissed California-girl image. "She was smart, *very* smart—nothing like she might seem at first glance," John Perry Barlow said. "She was a great person to be around, but when she was with John they both changed, and not for the better."

Not surprisingly, virtually all of John's male friends liked Hannah. They also realized that she and John were simply too much alike. Daryl was fond of saying that in every successful relationship there had to be a flower and a gardener—one who loved to be tended to and one who loved to do the tending. Unfortunately, Daryl said to John, "We're both flowers."

Everyone laughed off Hannah's remark, but it had the ring of truth. Even while he was trysting with Madonna and the others, John found it impossible to toss aside the torch he carried for Daryl. Hospitalized with an undiagnosed ailment during the filming of *At Play in the Fields of the Lord* in the Brazilian jungle, Hannah was in and out of consciousness for days. Once her fever finally broke, she realized John had filled her room with one thousand long-stemmed American Beauty roses.

————

JOHN'S KENNEDY COUSINS, meanwhile, were once again proving themselves to be something considerably less than gallant. Family loyalty was tested yet again when John's cousin Willie, Jean Kennedy Smith's son and a fourth-year medical student at Georgetown University, was charged with raping twenty-nine-year-old Patricia Bowman on the lawn of the Kennedy estate in Palm Beach. The alleged rape took place in the early-morning hours of March 30, 1991, and followed a wild night of drinking at Palm Beach's Au Bar with Uncle Ted and his son Patrick.

Like much of the nation, Jackie was shocked not only by the charges leveled against Willie Smith, but also by the reports of Ted's loutish behavior. A particularly disturbing image—one that John later said he had a hard time getting out of his mind—was of the Kennedy patriarch, clad only in the top half of his pajamas, behaving lewdly in front of Patrick's date. (John remained ever loyal to his uncle, whom he believed had been built up by the press merely to be torn down again and again. John called this "the Teddy Factor.")

Searching for humor in any situation, John made the sort of cringe-worthy suggestion to Noonan that he wouldn't dare make in public. He suggested placing a sign in the front of the Palm Beach mansion: NO TRESPASSING: VIOLATORS WILL BE VIOLATED.

Willie had always been John's favorite Kennedy cousin, and his mother, Jean, was the closest to Jackie of Jack's sisters. Out of loyalty to their cousin and their aunt, John and Caroline joined the rest of the clan for the annual Labor Day picnic at Hyannis Port. Everyone made themselves available for the inevitable "united we stand" Kennedy family photo op, although Jackie later regretted it.

John spent the next two months primarily in the company of the dazzling, blue-eyed Jackie look-alike Jules Baker. At Charlie's, one of John's favorite hangouts in Cambridge, Massachusetts, they downed cheeseburgers and traded jokes with their friends, ignoring the fact that on the wall above them hung photos of President Kennedy, Jackie, Caroline, and John-John. Later, they went unrecognized at a Harvest Moon Ball in the western suburbs of Boston.

John was happiest, one friend said, "when he was around people who had no idea who he was. His true friends, the ones he could count on who he confided in, weren't famous." A lifelong fan of the blues, he made a secret pilgrimage in October 1991 to the Helena, Arkansas, Bluesfest. Checking into Clarksdale, Mississippi's Riverside Hotel—the hotel where blues legend Bessie Smith died in 1937—he quickly befriended the Riverside's eighty-three-year-old owner, Mrs. Z. L. Hill.

John stayed in one of the Riverside's modest cabins and visited Mrs. Hill's room in the main hotel. "He'd sit on the edge of the bed and they'd talk until dawn," said her son Frank "Rat" Ratcliff. "They talked about the blues, about life."

John returned a few hours later with a breakfast tray for Mrs. Hill, the African-American octogenarian he was now calling "Mother." She, in turn, referred to John as "my son." According to Ratcliff, "That's how she thought of John, as her boy."

Mrs. Hill had recognized John the minute he walked in to register, but she kept his identity secret—even from her own son. "John did not want anybody to know he was here. Nobody. I hate to admit it," Ratcliff said, "but I talked to him every day for four days before I finally realized who he was." Nor did he know the identity of the young woman John had brought him. She remained behind in the cabin, Ratcliff said, and never ventured out with John.

It was clear to Mother Hill and Rat Ratcliff that John was more than just a run-of-the-mill fan of the blues. "He was there to let it all sink in," Ratcliff said. "You could tell he was loving it, just eating it all up. He knew a lot about the blues, but he wanted to learn more." In the end, Ratcliff was impressed that John was "such a regular guy. No putting on airs or anything like that. He'd sit in the lobby and talk with folks for hours."

If there was one Kennedy whose ability to connect with ordinary people seemed effortless, it was John. A few years earlier, his aunt Eunice Shriver had challenged John and his Kennedy cousins to come up with projects directed at helping people with mental disabilities—an obvious next step for the family that had founded the Special Olympics. The cousins voted on the best ideas, and the family foundation doled out fifty thousand dollars to the most innovative proposals.

After months of research, John zeroed in on the inadequate education and low pay of frontline mental-health-care workers. In addition to Reaching Up, which persuaded local officials to fund training programs, he lent the prestige of the family name to the Kennedy Fellows, a group of seventy-five health-care workers selected for a thousand-dollar scholarship each year.

Now John was signing on with the Robin Hood Foundation, a group of influential young New Yorkers who raised money for projects aimed at combating urban decay. John insisted that, unlike other charities, the Robin Hood Foundation and Reaching Up track every dollar being spent. "It's easy to throw money at a problem and walk away," John said. "Your conscience is clear—but is your money getting to the people it's supposed to get to, or is it being wasted? Results," he concluded, sounding more and more like a politician, "that's what really matters."

John followed through, taking the subway to the South Bronx and Harlem to check up on projects funded by the Robin Hood Foundation. He also dropped in unannounced on Kennedy Fellows to ask what courses they were taking, and if there was anything more he could do to help them meet their career goals.

In addition to all of his volunteer work—little of which, by his choice, was known to the public—John appeared as host of *Heart of the City,* a six-part PBS series on the key role volunteers were having in the revitalization of New York. It came as no surprise when offers came pouring in from all the major networks, each seeking to add the name John F. Kennedy Jr. to its roster of on-air talent.

A career in television was certainly worth considering. John's cousin, Maria Shriver, had long been an NBC News star, and "Kissy" Amanpour was burning up the track at CNN. It was also hard to imagine anyone more telegenic or well spoken than JFK Jr. A career in journalism was something John had actively considered for years—but only as a stepping-stone to a life in politics. Becoming "just another talking head on the tube," a friend said, "just didn't interest him."

Career considerations would have to be put aside as John weighed what role, if any, to play in the latest unfolding Kennedy family scandal. Jackie drew the line at attending Willie's sensational, nationally televised rape trial in December, and she asked John and Caroline to stay away as well. Most of the other Kennedys—Eunice, Ethel, Pat, and their children—showed up to lend moral support and proclaim their be-lief in Willie's innocence. Caroline took her mother's advice and stayed away, but John felt an obligation to Willie. He spent five days in the courtroom, allowing television cameras to film him chatting with Wil-lie and placing a reassuring hand on his embattled cousin's shoulder.

Reporters made note of the fact that John was lunching with Willie's high-powered team of lawyers, and asked him if he wasn't worried that standing up for his cousin might tarnish his reputation. "He's helped me out in the past and I was glad to come," John answered. "Willie is my cousin. I grew up with him. I thought I could at least be with him at this difficult time." Smith was eventually acquitted, which John felt all along was the correct verdict. He firmly believed Smith was innocent, although, as Noonan observed, there was "plenty of smoke."

The spotlight was back on John's branch of the family with the re-lease of Oliver Stone's hotly debated conspiracy film *JFK*. John refused to screen the film, much less comment on it—other than to grumble that the hysteria generated by Stone's movie made him feel "depressed." Cornered by one reporter, he conceded that it was getting more and more difficult to avoid what was an inherently disturbing topic for him—namely, who shot his father to death. "Maybe," he said with a sigh, "I'll just have to leave town."

A few weeks later, Hannah was back in town to promote her new film, *Memoirs of an Invisible Man*. Soon they were back to arguing on street corners, only this time their tiff outside his TriBeCa loft was captured by someone with a video camera. "So why did you come back, Daryl?" John yelled. "So why did you come back? So why did you come back?" He repeated the question a half dozen times while Han-nah begged for him to calm down and try to understand her position.

After several painful moments of awkward verbal sparring, she gave John the answer he did not want to hear. "John, I want to make it work with Jackson," she said in a clear voice. "I can't see you anymore."

No matter. In May 1992, John journeyed with his sister to Boston for what would become an annual ritual: the presentation of the John F. Kennedy Profile in Courage Award. Six weeks later, they were together again at the Democratic National Convention in Madison Square Garden for a tribute to their uncle Bobby.

That summer John also found time to flee into the wild—this time as a journalist. The *New York Times* paid John six hundred dollars to write a piece for the Sunday edition's travel section on his kayaking expedition with three friends to the Aland Archipelago, between Finland and Sweden.

John's *Times* story was titled "Four Desk Jockeys in Search of Manageable Danger," but the danger seemed barely manageable when one of his companion's kayaks capsized. The man's legs were so numb that he could neither swim nor walk, leaving John to rescue him from the water, carry him to shore, and wrap him in a sleeping bag.

Not coincidentally, nearly everyone in John's tight circle of friends had a story about some near brush with disaster. Usually the situation was either created or abetted by John, whose own desire to live on the edge often put his friends in jeopardy. There were the documented incidents: when his boat took on water and began to sink, when the Coast Guard had been alerted after he lost his way in the fog and began drifting out into the Atlantic, when he nearly caused an avalanche while helicopter skiing in a restricted area, when he lost control of his bicycle as he tried to outrun a light in midtown Manhattan, when he had to bring his plane down sooner than expected because he suddenly realized he was running dangerously low on fuel. In that last instance, John employed a favorite battle cry to bolster his passengers' spirits: *Coraggio!*

More than once as he paddled his kayak in New York Harbor, John came close to losing a battle of chicken with the Staten Island Ferry. While the captain would frantically blow his horn warning John to get out of the way—in a couple of instances the ferry was brought to a complete stop—JFK Jr. waited until the last minute, waving his arms wildly at the startled passengers. Then there was the Fourth of July when he and a friend kayaked into the middle of New York Harbor to watch the fireworks. Instead of obeying the harbor police and leaving the area, John stayed—and was nearly swamped by dozens of other, considerably larger vessels.

Daredevil John never acknowledged or apologized for scaring his friends—or for exposing them to more danger than perhaps they'd bargained for. When they nearly drowned more than once while exploring the waters off Jamaica in a two-person folding kayak, Christina Haag confronted him. "But John," she said angrily, "we could have *died*."

"Yeah, Chief," he answered, "but what a way to go!"

Expert kayaker Ralph Diaz did not see the humor in his friend's attitude. "John showed an overly casual approach" to the sport, Diaz said. "I was watching him one Saturday taking a kayak into the Hudson—no life jacket, no safety equipment of any kind. It all adds up to a person kind of oblivious to his surroundings. All I kept thinking was, 'This guy is going to get hurt some day.' I was worried that something was going to happen to him."

When it came to Daryl, it was usually John who did the worrying. In September 1992 he got word that Hannah had been hospitalized in Los Angeles once again, for undisclosed reasons. He rushed to her side, packed her up, and brought her back to New York. Soon they were living together in her West Side apartment.

Now that they were back together—Hannah told a none-too-pleased Browne that she was leaving him for JFK Jr.—Daryl and John did nothing to conceal their affair. Paparazzi had a field day photographing them making out on a bench in the park, on a West Side stoop, against a parked car, and on an Amtrak train bound for Providence.

Not every romantic moment was captured on film. One neighbor told the New York *Daily News* that she peered out her kitchen window to see Hannah and John—she wearing a flimsy nightgown, he shirtless—slow-dancing on the roof of her building.

IT'S LOVE, proclaimed the cover of *People*, which described the glamorous pair as having "fame, fortune, fabulous bone structure—and each other." Soon the affair went international, as the lovebirds were spotted vacationing in Switzerland, England, Vietnam, the Philippines, and Hong Kong.

In important ways, John and Daryl were there for each other. He comforted her after the death of her stepfather Jerry Wexler, flying out to Chicago for the glitzy memorial tribute at the Drake Hotel. She, in turn, started behaving like an aunt to John's nieces and to Caroline's third child, John Bouvier Kennedy Schlossberg, born on January 19, 1993. Hannah tagged along when "Grand Jackie," as Rose and Tatiana called her, took everyone to Serendipity's for hamburgers and hot fudge sundaes.

Jackie was smitten with her grandchildren, and could be spotted with them several times a week—pushing Rose and Tatiana on the swings at the East Seventy-ninth Street playground, sharing an ice-cream cone on a park bench with Tatiana, buying cotton candy for Rose. Usually with a little help from one of the nannies, Caroline (John now called her "Old Married Lady") brought the kids to see Grand Jackie at 1040 at least once a week. There Jackie would empty her red wooden treasure chest of its glittering contents—trinkets, scarves, costume jewelry—dress the children up like princesses and pirates, and then lead them on what she called a "fantasy adventure" through the sprawling apartment.

Caroline also loved bringing her kids to Red Gate Farm, where they spent lazy days boating, swimming, and fishing. The grandchildren were also given the run of the house, where Jackie would sit on the floor for hours coloring and playing with them. (Caroline would recall the day neighbor Carly Simon dropped by and helped the irretrievably tone-deaf Grand Jackie teach little Jack Schlossberg to sing "The Itsy-Bitsy Spider.")

"I have never seen my mother so happy," Caroline said, "as when she's around the kids." Despite Hannah's efforts, Jackie was not about to let Daryl into this special world she had created. It wasn't because she didn't like Daryl—she did. Jackie was also suitably impressed by the size of Hannah's fortune—several times larger than the $100 million plus in net assets Tempelsman had helped Jackie accumulate since Ari's death.

Jackie felt that a famously flaky Hollywood sex symbol who had already been photographed squabbling on street corners with her son might not be the best choice for John. Caroline agreed. "She didn't like the position Daryl kept putting her brother in," a friend of Caroline said. "She was always telling John to watch out for himself and not be taken advantage of by any woman."

In the end, she left no doubt as to where she stood on the Hannah issue. "Kiddo, she's nice," Caroline told her little brother. "But she's not the one."

Daryl took another step into Jackie's doghouse on Memorial Day weekend, 1993. With his mother and Maurice vacationing in the south of France, John and Daryl threw a party for friends at Red Gate Farm. When the maid arrived the next morning, she was shocked by what she saw.

"I couldn't believe my eyes," Marian Ronan said. "The house was strewn all over with empty champagne, beer, and wine bottles. The carpets were stained, and there were half-eaten plates of food discarded in every room, and food had even been splashed onto the walls." There were also the remnants of joints and bongs in all the bedrooms and in every bathroom. Feeling even less kindly toward Hannah in the wake of this incident, Jackie restricted the couple to "the Barn," the silo-shaped guest wing that John had occupied from the beginning.

John left the prosecutor's office in July, and spent the rest of the summer with Daryl in New York, Massachusetts, and California. Now that she had apparently dumped Jackson Browne in favor of a serious relationship with John, Hannah was angling for a real commitment. "She was," Daryl's friend Sugar Rautbord said, "*desperate* to marry him."

Hannah came close to doing just that. In late July 1993, she and John took out a marriage license in Santa Monica, and Daryl bought an antique wedding dress at the Rose Bowl Flea Market in Pasadena. After another round of petty quarreling, they decided to put their marriage plans on hold.

By September 1993, Jackie dropped all pretense and began openly shunning Hannah. Whenever John showed up with Daryl at 1040, they sat in the dining room while Jackie stayed in her room eating dinner off a tray. In October, all the Kennedys were set to attend Ted Kennedy Jr.'s wedding in October—until John announced he was bringing Daryl along. Jackie and Caroline canceled at the last minute, leaving John and Daryl alone to dodge the paparazzi. At one point, a visibly frustrated John grasped Hannah's hand, yanking her past the crowd of photographers and into the church.

Not long after Ted Kennedy Jr.'s nuptials, John hastily alerted friends that in two days he and Daryl were going to exchange vows in a top-secret ceremony on Martha's Vineyard. Three hours later, he called them back to say the wedding was off.

———

HANNAH MAY HAVE sensed that another rival for John's affections was already on the horizon. John first encountered Carolyn Bessette while jogging in Central Park in the early fall of 1993. A personal shopper at Calvin Klein, twenty-seven-year-old Bessette counted socialite Blaine Trump, actress Annette Bening, and broadcast journalist Diane Sawyer among her celebrity clients. When John asked her to help him buy a suit for his cousin Teddy's wedding, he wound up with three suits, a half dozen shirts, several ties—and Carolyn's phone number.

Blond, blue-eyed, and sleek at five feet eleven inches tall and 135 pounds, Bessette was not just stunningly beautiful. She was everything the fragile, needy, charmingly flaky Daryl was not—cool, poised, chic, irreverent, and, like Jackie, very much in control. She was also intense. There was, Littell said, "an electricity about her that nearly, though not quite, distracted you from her physical beauty." In these ways, she also resembled her future mother-in-law. "I think," Jamie Auchincloss said, "she may have reminded him more of his mother."

On Veterans Day, John and Carolyn were spotted cuddling and holding hands on a bench in Central Park. Not long after, they sat close to each other on a curb with thousands of others watching the New York City Marathon. The photo of John and his "mystery woman" was published in the *New York Post* and picked up by *People.*

As it turned out, that weekend Bessette was supposed to have been spending time in Connecticut with the family of the man she had been seriously involved with for years, Calvin Klein underwear model Michael Bergin. At the time Bergin, who at twenty-five was nearly a decade younger than John, loomed over Times Square on a billboard advertising Calvin Klein briefs; his looks would later help him win a role on the worldwide hit television series *Baywatch*. As her romance with John blossomed, Bessette clearly did not share the fact that she was pregnant with Bergin's baby and would soon go through with an abortion.

After spotting the photo of Carolyn and John sitting on the curb, Bergin angrily confronted Carolyn. "He's just a friend," she protested disingenuously. "We just chatted. I think he's seeing Daryl Hannah. It's nothing."

"Nothing!" Bergin protested. "Don't act so innocent."

"This is ridiculous!" Carolyn shot back, full of righteous indignation. "I told you already: he doesn't mean anything to me."

At the Manhattan disco Tramps, John confided in John Perry Barlow that he was torn between his loyalty to Hannah and this woman who was having "a major effect on him. He was really struggling," Barlow said. "He just couldn't get his mind off this girl."

Daryl and Carolyn aside, John had more than his share of drama to handle. Tensions were running high for other reasons as well. On November 22, 1993, the thirtieth anniversary of Dallas was marked by prime-time television specials and memorial events scattered across the globe. Dreading the solemn date in history that fell so close to their birthdays, John and Caroline stuck close to home.

Jackie, on the other hand, had made the conscious decision not to live the rest of her life playing the widow. During her brief reign as first lady, Jackie had seized every opportunity to tear through the Virginia countryside on horseback. "Keep her riding," Black Jack Bouvier advised his son-in-law JFK, "and she'll always be in a good mood."

That particular November 22, Jackie ignored the inevitable public relations fallout and spent the day jumping horses at the Piedmont Hunt Club. Midway through the event, the horse that preceded her in the competition knocked some stones off a fence. Jackie's gelding, Clown, sailed over the fence but stumbled on the stones, hurling her to the ground.

Knocked cold, Jackie was rushed to the hospital. She remained unconscious for an alarming thirty minutes, and by the time she came to, doctors discovered a swelling in her abdomen. The consensus at the time was that Jackie had probably suffered a slight groin injury that became infected. That diagnosis seemed to be proven right when, after antibiotics were administered, the swelling went down.

Jackie seemed to have escaped paralysis or worse, but it wasn't her only close call that day. While she was riding in Virginia, an unemployed Indiana man was arrested as he drove through New Jersey asking directions to Jackie's country house in Bernardsville. In his 1982 Dodge pickup, police found a hundred-page manuscript in which the man described himself as a "special agent" in a "paramilitary unit." Concealed beneath a blue pillow they also discovered a .44-caliber handgun and a box of bullets.

John had learned to brush aside such incidents, nearly all of which were never divulged to the public. Nor did he share even with his closest friends the number of times he received phone calls in the middle of the night from someone claiming that his uncle Teddy had been shot, or his mother killed.

His mother's tumble in the Virginia countryside gave him a scare, but otherwise she seemed, as one tabloid breathlessly proclaimed, "64 AND FIT AS FIDDLE. WOW! LOOK AT JACKIE NOW!" Thirty years after Dallas, Jackie had changed remarkably little. To illustrate the point, newspapers ran photos of "Grandma Jackie" running in Central Park, in a sexy two-piece swimsuit on the beach in Martha's Vineyard, outshining everyone in haut couture at a gala in Manhattan. She was, gushed one writer, "the very picture of radiant health."

But one month after her fall, Jackie and Maurice were cruising in the Caribbean aboard his boat the *Relemar* (named after Tempelsman's children Rena, Leon, Marcy) when she suddenly became ill. John's mother was rushed back to New York Hospital–Cornell Medical Center, where a biopsy of swollen lymph nodes in her neck indicated she was suffering from an aggressive form of non-Hodgkin's lymphoma.

The next day, John and his sister arrived at 1040 and took their places on the couch opposite their mother. As she held on tight to Maurice's hand, Jackie told her children the devastating news—and the doctors' unanimous belief that, if she had any chance of making it at all, she would have to begin chemotherapy without delay.

John and Caroline jumped up and embraced their mother. All three wept—a shared moment of sadness that the preternaturally dignified Jackie tolerated just so long. Brushing away her own tears, she reassured her children that she intended to beat the odds.

Still, just a few days after receiving her grim prognosis Jackie instructed her attorneys to draw up a living will that specified no extraordinary measures be taken to prolong her life. The memory of Janet's painful death was still fresh in her mind as Jackie began receiving steroid drugs and chemotherapy. "She was horrified at how much her sister Janet had suffered," Tish Baldrige said, "and she wasn't about to let that happen to her. Jackie always had to be in total control of her own life—that was one thing about her that never changed."

Now she conspired with Maurice and her children to keep her lymphoma a secret. Given the Kennedy family's proven lack of discretion, only Teddy was told that his sister-in-law was battling cancer.

Jackie's first reaction was one of stunned disbelief. "I don't get it," she told Arthur Schlesinger, joking that her disease was "a kind of hubris. I was so proud at being so fit. I did everything right to take care of myself. I swim, and I jog . . . and walk around the reservoir—and now this suddenly happens. Why in the world did I do all those push-ups?"

"She was laughing when she said it," Schlesinger recalled. "She seemed cheery and hopeful, perhaps to keep up the spirits of her friends, and her own."

Incredibly, it was only now that Jackie was finally willing to quit the two-pack-a-day smoking habit she had somehow managed to hide from the public for more than forty years.

After learning that his mother was now in the fight of her life, John no longer seemed willing to put up with Hannah's emotional demands. That January, the couple was walking toward 1040 Fifth—she clutching a bag from the Madison Avenue gourmet store E.A.T., a wrapped package for John's mother tucked under his arm. What happened next would be captured by an enterprising window-shopper with a video camera.

Startling others on the street, John stopped in his tracks and began yelling at Daryl. "Make up your mind!" he shouted. "Where do you want to go?"

Daryl begged him to calm down, but John only grew more aggravated. "So what do you want me to do?" he bellowed, waving his arms in the air. With his thumb, John gestured for Daryl, now crying, to "beat it."

Instead, Daryl, dabbing at her eyes with Kleenex, trailed John as he stomped off in the direction of his mother's apartment. They stayed only a few minutes at 1040, then walked to a nearby restaurant for lunch. John and Hannah emerged forty minutes later, and this time he was angrier than ever. As she moved beseechingly toward him, John kept backing away. Eventually, John hailed a taxi, jumped in, closed the door on Hannah and left her standing, shocked and shivering, on the sidewalk.

None of John's friends were surprised when the JFK Jr.–Daryl Hannah affair imploded. "They were wonderful apart," one said. "But when they walked into a room together, they were just these two huge celebrities competing for the same space. It was exhausting to be around them."

Besides, other things were weighing on John's mind. It soon became apparent that Jackie wouldn't be able to conceal her illness any longer. The side effects of chemotherapy—blotchy skin, hair loss, bloating—could not be effectively hidden under wigs, floppy coats, hats, and scarves. When a photographer tried to take a close-up of Jackie as she left 1040 for a walk in the park, Maurice charged at him. Chastened, the paparazzo backed off.

After the Christmas holidays, rumors that Jackie was suffering from a mysterious ailment proliferated. After consulting John and Caroline, she instructed Nancy Tuckerman to contact Robert D. McFadden of the *New York Times*. On February 11, 1994, Tuckerman confirmed that Jackie was suffering from non-Hodgkin's lymphoma and added that the doctors were "very, very optimistic."

The announcement made front-page headlines around the world, and once again Jackie was in the unfortunate position of having to bear her private pain in public. "Most people think having the world share in your grief lessens your burden," she had once told Teddy White. "It magnifies it."

Even so, Jackie remained resolutely positive. She continued to work, on occasion wearing a turban to the office to cover up her balding pate. "Who knows?" cracked the woman hailed as a fashion avatar. "Maybe I'll start a trend." She also redoubled her efforts to land a blockbuster memoir to top Michael Jackson's 1988 autobiography, *Moonwalk*, Jackie's biggest commercial success.

Toward that end, Jackie telephoned Frank Sinatra, perhaps more out of a desire to hear her friend's voice one last time. Ol' Blue Eyes turned her down, but sent flowers with a note: *You are America's Queen. God bless you, always. Love, Frank.*

"She was so sure, so strong," said her Doubleday colleague Scott Moyers, "and she was carrying on as if this were just a minor nuisance." When another friend from Martha's Vineyard, television journalist Charlayne Hunter-Gault, wrote Jackie a note praising her "style, grace, and beauty," Jackie wrote a warm, "joyful" note in reply. Hunter-Gault sensed nothing of her desperate situation. Jackie's friend ended her letter with "I look forward to seeing you on the Vineyard this summer."

"Definitely," Jackie replied. "This summer."

Recalled Hunter-Gault: "You could just see her smiling."

———

JOHN, MEANWHILE, HAD his own plans to enter the world of publishing. He announced to the family that he and his business partner,

Michael Berman, intended to launch a magazine that would blend celebrity journalism and public affairs.

"Oh, John," Jackie teased, "you're not going to do the *Mad* magazine of politics, are you?" No, he reassured her—more like the *People* magazine of politics.

"Traitor!" was Caroline's only half-in-jest remark. "Why do you want to join the other team?" Jackie acknowledged that there had always been a family connection to the publishing world—from Jackie's work as a photojournalist and book editor to JFK's Pulitzer Prize to Caroline's own status as a bestselling author. But the leap from newspapers and books to a glossy celebrity magazine was too much for a family that had been at war with the paparazzi for decades. "Are you sure," Jackie asked her son, "you want to become one of *them*?" After all, this was the first lady who, when asked what she was going to feed the family's new dog, replied, "Reporters."

At Jackie's urging, Maurice Tempelsman took John aside and warned him that his chances of success in starting up a new magazine were "slim to none." Indeed, even the magazines that eventually proved hugely successful usually went years before finally turning a profit—gobbling up millions in investment dollars in the process.

None of this mattered to John. On a visit to 1040, John kicked around a few title ideas with his mother. "We're thinking of calling it *George*," he told her.

"*George?*" she replied, nonplussed.

"Yeah, you know—*George*, as in the Father of Our Country? *George*."

"John, I think it would be a good idea if you talk to Maurice again," Jackie said. "And this time, listen to what he has to say."

As snowstorms swept across the Northeast that March, Caroline continued to bring her children by 1040 so Grand Jackie could lead them on "fantasy adventures" around her apartment. One weekend when the mercury dipped into the teens, Jackie still ventured into Central Park with all the Schlossbergs to take part in a ferocious snowball fight. Jackie was even strong enough to grab a sled rope and pull Rose and Tatiana across the snow. Jackie seemed happier than she had been in months, and to some extent resigned to the probable outcome of her disease. "Even if I have only five years, so what?" she told Bunny Mellon. "I've had a great run!"

Plummeting temperatures notwithstanding, Jackie insisted on taking her daily walks. Most of the time she was accompanied by Maurice. But every now and then John, who had temporarily moved into a suite at the nearby Surrey Hotel to be closer to his mother, escorted her across Fifth Avenue and into the park.

For these strolls, which sometimes lasted an hour or more if Jackie was up to it, John wore a lucky knit cap and brought one for his mother to wear as well. An admitted aficionado of haberdashery, John boasted a large and varied collection of hats—berets, fedoras, boaters, beanies, camouflage hats, and Irish tweed caps. But the knit hats had special significance. It was a tradition for Jackie and Caroline to give him a new one every year on his birthday. "Each had a special meaning," Sgubin explained. "He became very sentimental about them."

"The only thing John enjoyed during those sad months," said his friend Rob Littell, "was his mother's company." Littell believed that John, seeing how bravely his mother was confronting her future, relied "on *her* strength to carry him through."

John was encouraged by reports he was getting from Jackie's doctors. Despite the fact that she looked and felt terrible, the experts told John that the aggressive chemotherapy treatments had worked; her cancer appeared to be in remission.

When she was feeling strong enough, Jackie and Maurice would catch a movie. *Schindler's List,* Steven Spielberg's Academy Award–winning film about Holocaust survivors, was her last.

In mid-March, Jackie suffered an alarming spell of disorientation. At one point, it was apparent to John and Maurice that she had no idea where—or who—she was. A subsequent MRI showed that while the cancer had vanished from her neck, chest, and abdomen, it had now spread to her spinal cord and brain.

John was crushed. Now there would be more chemotherapy—this time delivered by shunt directly into Jackie's brain through a hole drilled in her skull. Now she would also have to undergo radiation treatments. "It's rough," John told friends, "really rough."

Wearing a pastel pink turban, Jackie spent Easter with John and the Schlossbergs at her New Jersey house. The day was spent dyeing eggs in the kitchen and helping Rose and Tatiana make bonnets for the Bernardsville Easter Parade.

On one of her walks with John, Jackie pointed to fields of tulips and blossoming cherry trees. "Isn't it something?" Jackie said. "One of the most glorious springs I can remember. And after such a terrible winter."

Peter Duchin was one of the friends who paid a call on Jackie around this time. She was, he said, "behaving like you'd expect her to behave— as if she intended to beat this thing." Another friend, author Edna O'Brien, described Jackie as "definitely up, actually quite cheerful."

The singer Carly Simon, one of Jackie's Martha's Vineyard neighbors, was another friend who spent time with her during this period. Yet someone was missing. Over lunch at Simon's, a guest asked Jackie if she saw her sister often. "We've only seen each other once this whole year," Jackie replied. "I never could understand why Lee is so full of animosity."

The following morning, Marta Sgubin called John with the news that Jackie had collapsed at 1040 Fifth. She was rushed to New York Hospital and underwent emergency surgery for a perforated ulcer, one of the many common side effects of chemotherapy. Visiting his mother, John learned that Richard Nixon, who had suffered a stroke, was right down the hall. As coincidences went, this one seemed in a class by itself. JFK's onetime friend turned bitter political rival died eight days after Jackie was admitted, on April 22, 1994.

As soon as she returned home, Jackie broke out her trademark pale blue stationery and began writing notes to her children. She told Marta that it was something she had to do right now—while she could still think clearly.

"The children have been a wonderful gift to me," she wrote to Caroline, "and I'm thankful to have once again seen our world through their eyes. They restore my faith in the family's future. You and Ed have been so wonderful to share them with me so unselfishly."

Her letter to John left no doubt that her expectations for him were great—that she saw him as nothing less than Camelot's standard-bearer. "I understand the pressures you'll forever have to endure as a Kennedy," she wrote, "even though we brought you into this world as an innocent.

"You, especially," Jackie continued, "have a place in history. No matter what course in life you choose, all I can ask is that you and Caroline continue to make me, the Kennedy family, and yourself proud. Stay loyal to those who love you. Especially Maurice. He's a decent man with an abundance of common sense. You will do well to seek his advice."

By early May, the pain was simply unbearable. John told his friend Steven Styles that Jackie phoned her son and sobbed, "I don't think I can take it anymore."

John coped with the stress the best way he knew how—with physical activity. He spent additional hours at the gym, on his bicycle, running through the park. On one of these runs, he took Daryl's dog with him. As John was returning to her co-op on the West Side, he wasn't paying close enough attention and a car struck the dog. Hannah was justifiably upset at John's heedlessness—one of the strains in their complicated relationship—but she had no desire to make him more miserable than he already was.

On May 15—a Sunday—Jackie took Maurice's arm and embarked on one last walk through her beloved Central Park. She wore tan slacks, a long-sleeved pink sweater, a brown wig, and a scarf wound tightly around her neck. Caroline, pushing a stroller with one hand, walked a few steps ahead. Slowly, they made their way toward the 840 acres of winding paths and woods and lawns and lakes that Jackie had known since she was a toddler. But the entire time, Jackie was grimacing in pain; she managed only a few halting steps past the park entrance before having to turn back.

Weak and disoriented, her speech slightly slurred, Jackie was back in New York Hospital the next day. She was diagnosed with pneumonia, but tests also showed that the cancer had spread to her liver, which meant that any further chemotherapy or radiation treatments would be futile. In the short run, however, they urged her to remain in the hospital while they administered antibiotics in an attempt to bring her pneumonia under control.

John knew what his mother would do next. With no interest in prolonging the inevitable, she checked herself out of the hospital. With Maurice holding her hand, she was taken by ambulance to 1040 Fifth, then wheeled into the building on a stretcher. By nightfall, hundreds of camera crews, reporters, photographers, and the just-plain-curious pressed against the blue police barricades set up on the sidewalk in front of Jackie's building.

On May 18, family and friends received the call they had all been dreading. Marta Sgubin told them all to waste no time getting to 1040 Fifth. Jackie's stepbrother, Yusha Auchincloss, got the call at Hammersmith Farm in Newport and drove straight to New York, praying that he would make it on time.

"As you can imagine," Nancy Tuckerman said, "it was a very emotional time for everyone." Caroline was too distraught to function; she sat on a bench in the hallway, gently weeping with Ed Schlossberg at her side. It was left to John to greet visitors as they stepped off the private elevator and into the foyer. That night and throughout the next day, John, Caroline, and Maurice took turns at Jackie's bedside. (Daryl Hannah, on hand to lend John moral support, tried to stay in the background.)

Spelling each other every hour or so, John and his sister read to Jackie from her favorite works of literature—passages from Jean Rhys, Isak Dinesen, and Colette as well as poems by Edna St. Vincent Millay, Robert Frost, and Emily Dickinson. At times they sat with her together in the room, sharing treasured memories in hopes that their mother could hear them. Meanwhile Jackie, her head wrapped in a printed scarf, slipped in and out of consciousness.

John's aunt Lee arrived that evening, followed by Ted Kennedy and his second wife, Victoria Reggie. When she emerged from her sister's room hours later, Lee was weeping. Solemn faced as he left for the night, Ted told reporters: "All the members of the family love her very deeply. We wanted to be with her this evening."

Moments earlier, Jackie came to long enough to see that everyone—John and Caroline in particular—was exhausted. "It's late," she whispered to John. "Go home and get some sleep." They did, but returned two hours later.

It was shortly after noon on Thursday, May 19, when Monsignor Georges Bardes of St. Thomas More Church came to the apartment to administer last rites. When John's uncle Bobby lay dying in Los Angeles twenty-six years earlier, family and friends were allowed to come into his hospital room in groups of two. Once again, they filed in two at a time—Aunt Eunice and Uncle Sargent, Carly Simon and Bunny Mellon, Ted and Victoria, Aunt Pat and Aunt Ethel—to sit by Jackie's bed, hold her hand, or even share bits of gossip.

Waiting their turn to say goodbye, family members and friends stood in the living room murmuring to each other. Periodically, someone would start to weep and John would put a comforting arm around them. Yusha Auchincloss had arrived in time to spend most of the evening there. "But first I had to compose myself," he said. "I told John that I didn't want Jackie to see me upset. I went in and out of her room for short visits over the next few hours—sitting by her bed, holding her hand, whispering some memories of our childhood. Then I kissed her good-bye . . . Jackie had lived life to the fullest, she had no regrets."

That night Jackie lay in her bedroom, bathed in the gentle glow of three antique lamps. Even in her drug-induced sleep, she struggled for breath. Every twenty minutes a doctor came in to check her vital signs and, in accordance with Jackie's wishes, administer enough morphine to ease her into as painless a death as possible.

While Caroline sat in the next room, Maurice and John took turns sitting in a chair next to Jackie's bed. Physically spent and emotionally drained, Maurice left her room for just a few minutes to get some air. When he returned, Jackie had slipped into a final coma.

An hour later, at 10:15 p.m. on May 19, 1994, Jackie's heart stopped beating. It had all happened with such mind-spinning swiftness—it had been only four months since the public learned of her illness—that everyone was struggling to comprehend what had happened. "She just," said Nancy Tuckerman, "sort of slipped away."

———

OUTSIDE, THE WORLD waited for any news concerning Jackie's condition. Initially, Uncle Ted argued that a formal statement should be issued by Nancy Tuckerman. Caroline objected to making any sort of announcement. "We don't owe them anything," she told John.

John, who had always been more media-savvy than his sister, disagreed. He suggested that the best way to break the news was for a family member to speak directly to the press, telling the circumstances of Jackie's death and then asking for time to grieve.

The next morning, John stepped before the scores of photographers and reporters camped outside the building where he had grown up. "Last night, at around 10:15, my mother passed on," he said. "She was surrounded by her friends and family and her books and the people and things that she loved. And she did it in her own way, and we all feel lucky for that, and now she's in God's hands.

"There's been an enormous outpouring of good wishes from everyone in both New York and beyond," he went on. "And I speak for all our family when we say we're extremely grateful. And I hope now that you know, we can just have these next couple of days in relative peace."

Needless to say, that did not happen. True to form, hundreds of onlookers who had gathered in the street strained to catch a glimpse of John, Caroline, and Maurice as they got into a limousine and sped off for the nearby Frank E. Campbell Funeral Chapel. There they picked out Jackie's coffin—"The Presidential" model, dark mahogany with gleaming pewter handles—and discussed funeral arrangements, at least the few they could agree on.

Once back in the apartment, Uncle Ted began quarreling with Jackie's children about the size of the funeral.

Caroline wanted it to be a modest private affair, but the senator insisted that Jackie was simply too important a figure for that. He argued for a funeral at New York's St. Patrick's Cathedral to rival that of Robert Kennedy in 1968.

John remained neutral, focusing instead on hosting the wake that was now taking place in the apartment, and on small details that he felt his mother would have thought were important. John had his mother's coffin placed next to the fireplace in the living room, and then gently arranged her gold-embroidered bedspread over the closed lid. "We need something intimate," he explained, "to dress things up."

The woman who had so meticulously planned JFK's state funeral had given their children substantial latitude in arranging hers; she specified only that she wanted the service to be conducted at St. Ignatius Loyola Church, and that she wished to be interred next to Jack at Arlington National Cemetery.

Showing the gumption she had inherited from her mother, Caroline got her way. There was one small concession: speakers would be set up outside St. Ignatius Loyola so that people gathered on the street would be able to hear the service. John, who had already shown such composure and grace in announcing his mother's death to the world, was now assigned the task of drawing up the guest list. "It's fine," he told Hannah. "I want to keep busy."

As far as Jackie was concerned, Daryl was the last serious woman in her son's life—and the one who, despite Mummy's disapproval, was likely to land him as a husband. That Sunday, she and John, both wearing shorts and T-shirts, caused photographers to scatter as they Rollerbladed up Fifth Avenue on their way to Jackie's hastily arranged wake at 1040.

Many Americans who were having a hard time coping with the

suddenness of Jackie's death were offended by the sight of John skating around town with his star girlfriend. Yet it was all completely in keeping with family tradition. "John felt he was honoring his mother by doing what he loved because he knew that's what *she* would have wanted," Barlow said. Besides, added Larry Newman, "all the Kennedys run out and do something physical at times like these."

More than one hundred people came to the wake, and hundreds more gathered outside on the sidewalk. Guests, most of whom appeared to be in a state of shock, sipped Perrier from wineglasses and absentmindedly nibbled on watercress sandwiches with the crust cut off. John took on the role of official greeter, breaking away periodically to speak for extended periods with his cousin Anthony Radziwill and old friends like Billy Noonan. At one point, John rushed to the aid of an elderly woman—one of Jackie's society friends—who had passed out. "It was incredibly stressful," Tuckerman said. "Everyone was in a daze."

At one point, John took Daryl out to the fourteenth-floor terrace to wave to the throng below—at which point the crowd began singing "The Battle Hymn of the Republic." Joining his friend outside, Noonan told him that Jackie was "more than a First Lady" to the people gathered below. "She was an icon. She was their queen." John smiled and nodded.

On a clear, sunny Monday morning, Jackie returned to St. Ignatius Loyola, the church where she had been baptized and confirmed. To the tune of the hymn "We Gather Together," the heavy casket, covered with a spray of lady's mantle, was carried up the steps of the church by eight pallbearers: seven of Jackie's nephews and John Walsh, the Secret Service agent who had become a father figure to John as well as Caroline.

Lady Bird Johnson and Hillary Rodham Clinton were among the hundreds of politicians, artists, writers, business leaders, social lions, fashion icons, and entertainment figures gathered inside the church. The ceremony was planned around readings from the Scriptures and poems that John hoped would "capture my mother's essence." He explained that three elements in particular had come up again and again: "her love of words, the bonds of home and family, and her spirit of adventure."

The Reverend Walter F. Modrys conducted the Mass, and Jackie's old friend and onetime escort Mike Nichols read a passage from the Bible. Opera diva Jessye Norman sang "Ave Maria," while Caroline read from a book of Edna St. Vincent Millay's poetry that was presented to Jackie when she graduated from Miss Porter's School in Farmington, Connecticut. The slim volume was her prize for winning Miss Porter's literary award.

There was never any doubt that Ted Kennedy would once again be called upon to deliver the eulogy. "No one else looked like her, spoke like her, wrote like her, or was so original in the way she did things," he said. Harking back to Dallas, he pointed out that "she held us together as a family and a country. In large part because of her, we were able to grieve and then go on. She lifted us up, and in the doubt and darkness, she gave her fellow citizens back their pride as Americans."

Jackie's love for John and Caroline was, he continued, "deep and unqualified. She reveled in their accomplishments, she hurt with their sorrows, and she felt sheer joy and delight in spending time with them. At the mere mention of their names, Jackie's eyes would shine and her smile would grow bigger."

From the church, the cortege made its way through Manhattan traffic and on to LaGuardia Airport, where John led the rest of the funeral party onto a chartered plane. President Clinton was on the tarmac at National Airport (later renamed Reagan Airport) to meet the 737 jetliner bearing Jackie's body when it arrived in Washington at 1:30 p.m. From there, the motorcade of minibuses, limousines, and police motorcycles escorted the hearse through the black iron gates of Arlington.

The casket, now covered with ferns and a cross of white lilies of the valley—Jackie's favorite flower—was placed next to Jack's grave. On one side lay John's stillborn sister Arabella. On the other, his infant brother Patrick, whose death only months before Dallas had brought Jackie and Jack closer than they had ever been.

It had been thirty-one years since John and Caroline had watched their mother light the eternal flame here. Now it blazed in the brilliant sunlight as President Clinton spoke. "In the end, she cared most about being a good mother to her children," he said, "and the lives of Caroline and John leave no doubt that she was that, and more. May the flame she lit so long ago burn ever brighter here and always brighter in our hearts."

The children each gave brief readings—first Caroline, then John. Then, as sixty-four bells rang out from Washington's National Cathedral—one for each year of Jackie's life—they knelt down and kissed their mother's coffin. Caroline, her head bowed, stepped back. But John walked the few steps over to the spot where his father lay and, leaning forward, reached out to touch his gravestone.

There was no hiding the depth of Caroline's grief; her face had been tearstained and etched with sorrow for days. But John had revealed nothing of his feelings, never allowing the well-worn Kennedy mask of stoicism to slip. At this moment, it all finally came crashing down on him. It had always been the three of them against the world, and now Mummy was gone. Forever.

With the right hand that had saluted his father more than three decades before, John reached up and brushed a single tear from his cheek.

A person never really becomes a grown-up
until he loses both his parents.
—John

Carolyn is a lot like the woman who
would have been her mother-in-law.
—John Perry Barlow

Carolyn has her own sense of mystery, doesn't she?
—Leticia Baldrige

The press has made my life hell.
Nobody knows what it's like.
—Carolyn Bessette-Kennedy

The next five years should have been
the great years for them.
—Paul Wilmot

11.

"The *Luckiest* Man Alive"

It had been less than two weeks since Jackie was buried at Arlington, and the flag over the Kennedy compound fluttered at half-mast. Yet the mood was festive as Daryl, John, and the Kennedy cousins grunted their way through the family's brutal Memorial Day touch football game.

For the happy couple, now widely believed to be on the verge of announcing their wedding plans, it was just another opportunity for more public displays of affection. At one point during the game, John tackled Daryl and then threw her over his knee and spanked her. "You'll regret this!" she screamed, clearly enjoying every minute of it. "I'll get even!" And with that she jumped up, plowed into him, and then screamed with delight as they rolled around on the lawn.

John, facing a number of other pressing issues, was perfectly happy maintaining the status quo in his relationship with Daryl. Front and center now was the administration of his mother's $150 million estate, the bulk of which was to be divided between her children. Maurice had just begun briefing John and Caroline on the task that lay ahead: finding a way to pay the steep inheritance taxes, which could easily top $30 million.

John and his business partner, Michael Berman, were also fully committed to getting *George* off the ground, and since John had no intention of investing a penny of his own money in the magazine—Maurice and Jackie made him promise that he wouldn't—that meant finding a backer with deep pockets.

No longer willing to wait, Daryl, according to several of her friends, got down on one knee and proposed to John herself—apparently the second time she'd tried this ploy. She was also waxing romantic about her days with Jackson Browne. In fact, during Jackie's wake, jaws dropped as Daryl insisted on telling everyone about her first meeting with Browne—how he picked her out of a concert audience and pulled her up onstage. All of this was in earshot of John, who was still reeling from the loss of his mother only hours earlier.

"Don't push me," John replied to these increasingly desperate pleas. Nor was he particularly moved by her none-too-subtle hints that she might return to Browne. "I don't respond," John said, "to ultimatums."

By July, it was over. After six years, Hannah made the extraordinary decision to return to Browne. John, meanwhile, returned to an old love of his own—Jules Baker, the head-turning model who looked so much like Jackie.

Two months later, Baker was John's date at the wedding of his favorite cousin and closest friend, Tony Radziwill—now an ABC News producer—and Tony's colleague Carole DiFalco. The wedding took place in a white clapboard church in East Hampton, New York, and once again John was best man—a favor Tony would later return. The event was an especially joyous one for John, since only a few years earlier Tony had fought and won a tough battle against testicular cancer. Sadly, the cancer would return with a vengeance within days of Tony and Carole exchanging their wedding vows.

For the moment, John's main concern was once again how to juggle the women in his life. He was still seeing Carolyn Bessette—a close friend of Baker and the bride—although at this point Jules seemed to have the inside track. "Jules looked so much like Jackie it was eerie," one of John's friends remarked. Did being with her provide a way for John to, in a sense, hang on to his mother? "He just wasn't ready to let go, not completely. I'm sure he wasn't consciously aware of it, but there was something of Jackie in all the women he was serious about."

Tony Radziwill's wedding also gave John the opportunity to send a message to his old flame Daryl. Since Aunt Lee's husband Herb Ross, the groom's stepfather, was a friend of Hannah's, she had also been invited. At the reception, John made a beeline for Daryl, greeted her warmly, and gave her a peck on the cheek. Then he walked back to Baker, wrapped her in his arms, and gave her a passionate, lingering kiss.

"I was always there for him," Jules said, "and he was always there for me." But that was the problem. The woman who most intrigued John was the one who, at least for now, played hard to get. While he was squiring Baker to high-profile events all over New York, John was also stealing quiet moments with Carolyn. "She was a very strong one-on-one person," said John's friend Richard Wiese. "John always found her provocative."

On one of those occasions when Carolyn chose to make herself available, John took her on a tour of the waters off Hyannis aboard his powerboat *PT-109*. Facing into the wind like the ship's figurehead that hung from his wall at Brown, John's thong-clad passenger wriggled into a skirt—with a little help from the skipper—and then asked him to carry her ashore so she wouldn't get wet. He happily obliged.

"She knows how to handle men like practically nobody I've ever met," John Perry Barlow said at the time. "She knows where all the levers are, and she is very deft in her operation of them."

In that sense, she was indeed very much like John's mother. "Jackie was a skillful listener," JFK's pal Chuck Spalding observed. "She had this way of focusing on you with those enormous brown eyes and hanging on your every word so the rest of the world just sort of fell away. Men, needless to say, tended to find this irresistible."

Like Jackie, Carolyn had a "genuine appreciation of men," Barlow said, adding that she was "extremely female, and I think it only appropriate there would be a lot of voltage across that gap. She is hardwired to relate to people who are male."

It was impossible to escape the fact that, on the surface, Carolyn bore a strong resemblance to the blond, blue-eyed, Scandinavian-looking Daryl Hannah. Yet there were also striking similarities between Carolyn and Jackie, whom she had never met. Both were slender, tall, and elegant, with broad shoulders, long necks, full lips, patrician profiles—and size-eleven feet that made them both self-conscious. (When he first met Carolyn, John jokingly made note of the fact that her toes were "freakishly long" but gave her style points for using alternating black and white polish on her toenails.)

Jackie and Carolyn also shared an aristocratic bearing that at times bordered on the aloof, a unique sense of style, and a carefully nurtured aura of mystery. In contrast to John, who smoked a single cigarette a day as a point of personal discipline, Carolyn, like Jackie, was a chain smoker. Carolyn made no effort to conceal her near-obsessive need for order and control—another Jackie trait—which served as counterpoint to John's easygoing manner and congenital sloppiness.

Born in the New York City suburb of White Plains, Carolyn was six and her older twin sisters, Lauren and Lisa, eight years old when their parents—public school administrator Ann Marie and kitchen designer William Bessette—split. The following year, Ann Marie married wealthy surgeon Dr. Richard Freeman and moved from the working-class town of Greenburgh, New York, to affluent Greenwich, Connecticut. Carolyn's own father would be largely absent from her life—and that absence, Rob Littell theorized, gave her a certain "wounded" quality. "Her vulnerability, while hidden beneath a tough, funny exterior, made her deeply empathetic to others."

Perhaps, but at St. Mary's Catholic High School, Carolyn broke her share of hearts on the way to being voted "Ultimate Beautiful Person" by her classmates. "She's passionately sexy," said Eugene Carlin, a jock she dated off and on throughout high school. "Beautiful. Sophisticated. Tough. Driven. She can drive you nuts."

Apparently she did just that as an undergraduate at Boston University, where she dated hockey star John Cullen, who went on to play for the Tampa Bay Lightning. Behind Cullen's back, she was reportedly having a torrid affair with his friend and teammate Chris Matchett. Once she'd dumped them both—and posed for a sexy "Girls of BU" calendar—she moved on to Alessandro Benetton, heir to the Benetton fashion empire.

Carolyn graduated from Boston University in 1988 with an education degree but had no interest in pursuing a career in that particular field. Instead, she set her sights on more glamorous pursuits—first as a publicist for nightclubs in the Boston area, then as a model. In 1990, she struck a number of seductive poses in leather, lace, and denim for a series of jeans ads that never ran.

Around the same time, Carolyn's parents cut her off after she maxed out her credit cards, and she went to work as a salesperson in Calvin Klein's Boston store. Tapped by senior management to handle celebrity clients, Bessette moved to New York and promptly befriended the designer, his wife, Kelly, and their daughter Marcie. *Marie Claire* fashion director Sciascia Gambaccini credited Carolyn's wholesome, fresh-scrubbed look with inspiring several of his campaigns. "She's a healthy, beautiful American," she said, "and that's what Calvin likes most." Carolyn "was his muse, definitely."

Not all of Carolyn's habits were healthy. A denizen of New York's nightlife, she often partied until dawn at such fashionable nightspots as the Merc Bar, MK, Au Bar, and Buddha Bar. As a publicist in the fashion industry, she was also invited to snort the occasional line of cocaine.

Carolyn's job at Calvin Klein also meant that she remained in close contact with Michael Bergin; she was instrumental in getting his modeling career off the ground, and the torch Bergin once carried for her still smoldered. Understandably perturbed by John's dalliances with other women as well as his irritating habit of showing up for their dates late or not at all, Carolyn was not above using her hunky friend to make him jealous.

Unlike so many of the other women he encountered, Carolyn clearly was no pushover. She had been hired by Calvin Klein to handle celebrity clients because she didn't appear to be intimidated by anyone—and John was no exception. Carole Radziwill remembered a favorite phrase of Carolyn's when she thought something was absurd—"I don't think we'll be doing *that*"—and how, like John, Bessette stabbed at the air with her hands to make a point.

"Most women sort of became tongue-tied around John," his college buddy Richard Wiese said. "But that wasn't Carolyn's problem. She was very strong-minded and knew what she wanted and had absolutely no difficulty speaking her mind."

As besotted and bewildered as he was by Carolyn, John had other pressing matters to attend to—not the least of which was the disposition of Mummy's estate. Jackie had named Maurice and her lawyer, Alexander Folger, as executors, but ultimately it was up to John and Caroline to see that her final wishes were carried out.

It was no surprise that the bulk of their mother's fortune was divided equally between Caroline and John. In a final snub, she made no provision for her envious sister, Lee, "because I have already done so during my lifetime." However, she left $500,000 in trust to each of Lee's children, Tony and Tina. Jackie also bequeathed $250,000 to Nancy Tuckerman and $50,000 to her longtime maid Provi Paredes, while $100,000 went to another niece, Janet Auchincloss Rutherfurd's daughter Alexandra.

Even in death, Jackie did what she could to ensure that her children were safe. She had asked that her chief bodyguard, former Secret Service agent John Viggiano, prepare a list of security risks to John and Caroline. His chilling report, attached as an addendum to Jackie's will, named several stalkers, including a Brooklyn man who was convinced that he, not Ed Schlossberg, should be married to Caroline, a convicted wife-beater who was convinced he had been married to Jackie and was the real father of her children, and—most terrifying of all—the double murderer who appeared at the front door of 1040 to declare his love for Jackie and the children. "The mental instability of many of the individuals involved," Viggiano concluded, "and the harassing nature of their communications, represent a significant threat to the personal security of Mrs. Onassis's descendants."

Neither John nor Caroline thought there was much they could do about the threats, other than to try to keep their precise addresses out of the newspapers. "If some nut out there wants to do something," John said, echoing his father's prophetic words, "there's nothing I can do about it. I'm not going to live my life worrying about things I can't control."

If anything, John was moved by the outpouring of affection from his fellow New Yorkers in the wake of his mother's death. The city moved swiftly to rename the former High School of Performing Arts on Forty-sixth Street—the inspiration for the 1980 movie *Fame* and the television series that followed—as Jacqueline Kennedy Onassis High School. Even more gratifying to John was the city's decision to name the Central Park Reservoir after her. "She was as much a part of this park," said one park worker who had watched her take her runs along the 1.57-mile jogging path, "as this body of water."

Then there was 1040. Since Caroline's family was firmly rooted in their apartment on Park Avenue, it seemed logical for John to move into the stunning Fifth Avenue apartment he once called home.

But he couldn't. "Too many memories," he said. "Can't handle it." Instead, John set up housekeeping far away from the Upper East Side, in a $700,000, 2,600-square-foot tenth-floor penthouse co-op at 20 North Moore Street in TriBeCa.

Since neither John nor Caroline had any intention of using 1040, Maurice urged them to sell it. In January 1995, billionaire David Koch bought Jackie's apartment for $9.5 million—all of which went to pay estate taxes. (By 2014 David Koch would be the fourth-richest man in the United States and New York's wealthiest citizen. He and his older brother Charles would be best known for bankrolling conservative causes.)

Caroline could not bring herself to watch movers empty the apartment of her mother's belongings, but John sat alone on the curb across the street and watched the transition without saying a word. "That's the kind of thing you'd expect John to do," John Perry Barlow said. "John was a very sentimental guy."

A few days later, John suffered another loss when his grandmother Rose died at the age of 104. In reality, John had never been especially close to the Kennedy matriarch. "Jackie kept John, in particular, away from Rose," said Rose Kennedy's secretary, Barbara Gibson. "Jackie didn't want the children to be 'too Kennedy.' I noticed that she felt most strongly about John not being too close to his grandmother. Jackie seemed to want to keep him really close to her. In the end, it worked, because although Caroline and Rose were close—writing to each other regularly—Rose hardly had much to do with John at all."

On January 25, 1995, John and Caroline were among the hundreds of mourners who attended Rose's funeral at St. Stephen's Church in Boston. The eldest daughter of legendary Boston mayor John Francis "Honey Fitz" Fitzgerald and the wife of one of America's wealthiest men, Rose attended Mass at Stephen's every Sunday and always placed a single dollar bill in the collection plate.

Over the previous six months, Random Venture cofounders John and Michael Berman had also been passing the collection plate, trying to raise start-up capital for *George*. Finally, in March 1995, Hachette Filipacchi, publishers of twenty-two magazines ranging from *Women's Day* and *Elle* to *Road & Track*, agreed to bankroll *George* to the tune of $20 million over five years or until it turned a profit—whichever came first.

Caroline was still wary of *George,* seeing it mainly as just another way for someone else to trade on the family name. About this, John had no illusions. Despite his frequent protestations that "*George* isn't about me," of course it was and he knew it. "Having John Kennedy as editor in chief," said Hachette's bottom-line-driven U.S. chief, David Pecker, "is going to be a big benefit to the magazine. He has access to almost everyone."

John's unsurpassed celebrity status certainly gave him an upper hand in journalism's game of the "get." It was difficult to imagine the movie star or politician who wouldn't at least take a call from JFK Jr. Even more important was JFK Jr.'s value as a frontman for the magazine, as well as a magnet for subscribers and advertisers. In the end,

Pecker and Hachette would wind up reportedly sinking millions more than the originally promised $20 million into *George*—"that," said one Hachette executive, "is how charming John could be."

As eager as John was to try his hand at journalism—and on his own terms—*George* served another important purpose. For years John had been pressured by party operatives in Massachusetts and New York to run for office, and for years he had skirted the issue. "You'd better be damned sure it's what you want to do," he said, "and that the rest of your life is set up to accommodate that. It takes a certain toll on your personality and on your family life. I've seen it personally. So if I were to do it, I would make sure it was what I wanted to do and that I didn't do it because people thought I should."

George was a tentative first step toward a life in politics. "I didn't understand why movie actors were the only ones who could sell magazines and why people in entertainment were the only heroes of popular culture," John said. "I thought if I could parachute behind enemy lines, in a way, and join the journalistic profession, that I could begin to let my perspective about politics seep in and maybe influence the presentation of politics."

John hastened to remind his critics that his father had covered the founding of the United Nations in 1945 as a working reporter for the Hearst newspaper chain. "For me," John explained, "the marriage of publishing and politics simply weaves together the two family businesses."

One month after Hachette inked its deal with Random Ventures, Carolyn moved in with John. She had her work cut out for her. John's TriBeCa loft was an industrial space when he bought it, and he paid an architect over $300,000 to transform it into a stylish bachelor pad. What he ended up getting was an industrial space with a kitchen, one bedroom, one office, two basic bathrooms, and two small closets. It was badly lit, and furnished with pieces from 1040 that didn't match. Carolyn called the place "the Warehouse" or, alternately, "Home Depot."

While the new woman of the house thought of ways to make it more livable, John was putting in fifteen-hour days on the launch of *George*.

As the September deadline approached, he was looking pale and drawn. In the span of three weeks, he dropped fifteen pounds. During a run with his friend Gary Ginsberg, who had come aboard as an editor at *George,* the normally indefatigable John nearly collapsed; at one point, Ginsberg looked back to see his friend gasping for air, slumped against a tree.

Carolyn and Caroline were worried. In view of his father's history of Addison's disease—a potentially fatal autoimmune disorder—and Jackie's lymphoma, the women in John's life urged him to see a doctor.

John checked into New York Hospital, and after undergoing a series of tests phoned Caroline with the news. According to noted New York endocrinologist James Hurley, John was suffering from Grave's disease, an incurable hyperthyroid condition. John quickly brought the disease under control with drugs that, he was told by his doctors, he would have to take for the rest of his life.

That wasn't the only thing, apparently, that was hyperactive about John in the summer of 1995. He told a business colleague that, before her marriage to Antonio Banderas, actress Melanie Griffith was persistent in her attempts to start up a relationship. "I had to bolt the door," he joked.

In late July, Carolyn and John accepted an invitation to dine with Sharon Stone at Tashmoo Farm, the waterfront Martha's Vineyard estate the actress was leasing for the season. A week later, John returned to Martha's Vineyard and Stone, only this time alone.

Carolyn only learned of John's solo rendezvous with the alluring *Basic Instinct* star in late August, when the *National Enquirer* trumpeted news of a "sizzling secret romance" between JFK Jr. and Stone on its front page. Carolyn was unable to dig up evidence of a romance, sizzling or otherwise. But she did confirm that John had gone to the Vineyard to spend time with Stone, and that was enough. After an angry confrontation—one of the many that punctuated their relationship—Carolyn threatened to move out.

As they always did, Carolyn and John made up within hours. On September 1, John reached into his pocket and pulled out a small box. Dropping to one knee, he opened the box to reveal a sapphire-and-diamond band. This was a copy of Jackie's favorite everyday piece of jewelry, designed for her by Maurice Tempelsman. Since she wore it everywhere—even in the water—Jackie called it her "Swimming Ring."

"Will you marry me?" he asked.

Carolyn was speechless. She later told Carole Radziwill that she was taken by surprise, even though by this point she knew a proposal was inevitable. She also felt at the time that, while the ring was nice and she appreciated its sentimental value, it certainly wasn't the engagement ring she would have picked out.

John expected to hear an immediate and resounding "Yes!" But he didn't. Instead, Carolyn equivocated. "I'll think about it," she replied, only half in jest.

"She loves him," Radziwill said after Carolyn confided in her just a few days after the proposal. "But she isn't in a hurry to be his wife." Perhaps she dreaded the prospect of forever being pursued by the paparazzi, or having to second-guess her every move as the wife of a future politician. Maybe she was reluctant to submerge so much of her own identity, to exist as a mere appendage to one of the nation's most celebrated—even beloved—figures. For the time being, their quasi-engagement was top secret. Observed Radziwill: "She would like to stay secretly engaged forever, I think."

If he was hurt by Carolyn's reluctance to say yes—tabloids were reporting the rumor that she was "stringing him along"—John gave no indication of it. When Carolyn dropped into the *George* offices, magazine staffer Richard Blow recalled, John was "ecstatic . . . He would gaze upon her as if he couldn't believe what his eyes were taking in. He could not stop touching her, running his fingers through her hair, stroking her arms." Carolyn seldom responded in kind.

Carolyn's puzzling reluctance to commit and his Graves disease aside, John looked confident and fit as he waited to step before more than two hundred reporters on the morning of September 8, 1995, to announce the birth of *George*. The setting—New York's neoclassical

Federal Hall—was chosen by John for its historic significance: It was here that George Washington was first sworn in as president in 1789.

Carolyn helped him pick out the dark blue suit he wore for this occasion, but one sartorial touch—a pocket square—was distinctly his; John wore a pocket square for luck when he considered an event particularly important.

Worried that reporters would simply bombard him with questions about his private life, John had already tapped Clinton spinmeisters Paul Begala and Michael Sheehan for advice. By way of rehearsal, they staged a mock press conference, peppering John with potentially embarrassing questions:

"You failed the bar exam two times. Are you lazy or just stupid?" "Who is your new girlfriend?" "Do you wear boxers or briefs?"

At the unveiling, Michael Berman spoke first. "I feel a little bit like Barry Manilow right before introducing Bruce Springsteen," he quipped. "Being John Kennedy's partner," Berman continued, "is a lot like being Dolly Parton's feet. It's nice, but you tend to get overshadowed."

John then walked to the podium and looked out at the crowd. "Ladies and gentlemen," he said, "meet *George*." Out swung a mounted display of the cover: supermodel Cindy Crawford as a bare-midriffed, bewigged George Washington. In a seldom-seen gesture, reporters burst into applause.

"I don't think I've seen as many of you in one place," John began, "since they announced the results of my first bar exam." After conceding that he hoped to wind up as president "of a very successful publishing venture," John volunteered answers to a series of personal questions before anyone could ask them: "Yes. No. We're merely good friends. None of your business. Honest, she's my cousin from Rhode Island. I've worn both. Maybe someday, but not in New Jersey."

Now that his audience had been won over by his disarming self-deprecation and easy grace, John explained what he hoped to accomplish with *George*. "Politics isn't dull—why should a magazine covering it be? Politics is about triumph and loss. Politics is about the pursuit of power and the price of ambition." As for John's insistence that *George* would be nonpartisan: "Uncle Ted said, 'John, if I'm still talking to you by Thanksgiving, you're not doing your job.' "

"How do you feel about joining the media," one reporter blurted out, "that has made your life hell?"

John cocked his head and smiled. "You didn't make my life hell," he replied.

"What would your mother say if she could see *George*?" someone else called out.

The room fell suddenly silent. John took a moment, and then admitted that he was glad she wasn't at the press conference—that it would have made him nervous. But, he added, "My mother would be mildly amused to see me up here, and very proud."

In addition to being the face of the magazine, John agreed to contribute an interview to every issue—a regular feature that, given his ability to woo practically anyone, was a cornerstone of *George*'s editorial content. The first issue contained John's interview with wheelchair-bound George Wallace, the firebrand former governor of Alabama who had been shot and paralyzed in an assassination attempt in 1972. There was also a piece by John's old flame Madonna, titled "What Would I Do If I Were President?"

Keeping up his end of the bargain, John produced newsmaking interviews with the divergent likes of Fidel Castro, Garth Brooks, Louis Farrakhan, and two of his personal heroes: Muhammad Ali and Billy Graham. Taking a hands-on approach, John also came up with story ideas, wrote the editor's note, edited copy, crafted headlines, and oversaw the layout of the magazine. He also picked up the phone to charm established writers into contributing to the magazine and the biggest names in entertainment, politics, business, fashion, music, sports, and foreign affairs into being profiled in its pages.

John clearly reveled in the fact that he was doing something wholly unexpected—something the die-hard "Kennedyphiles," as he called them, might find unsettling. "I have a slightly contrarian impulse I can't seem to shake," he admitted. "It's kind of drenched in irony, right? Me in a media conglomerate."

George racked up an unheard-of 175 ad pages and sold out its first printing of a half million copies in days. A second printing of 100,000 copies was rushed out and vanished just as quickly. By any measure, the magazine appeared to be a massive hit.

Curiosity was the major selling factor—that, and the simple fact that John was willing to do whatever it took to sell *George* to the American public. While he would never put himself on the cover, other magazines jumped at the chance. The week *George* went on sale, John graced the cover of *New York, Esquire,* and *Newsweek.* To hype his creation, John, who had never agreed to do a lengthy TV interview before, sat down before the cameras with Rosie O'Donnell, Oprah Winfrey, and Barbara Walters—to name a few. "Sometimes the weight of expectations, of doing anything," he confessed to the *Washington Post,* "can be a little heavy . . ."

Determined to have some fun along the way, John seized the opportunity to make his TV acting debut on the hit prime-time sitcom *Murphy Brown.* The ninety-second cameo had John offering Brown, played by Candice Bergen, a copy of *George* with her face on the cover. When John tells her he plans to give her a subscription as a wedding gift, Brown laughs it off. "Don't come crying to me," John tells her as he leaves in a huff, "when you have to pay full newsstand price."

As he did everything he could to keep his magazine front and center, John seemed more and more confident that he had made the right choice. "It's pretty cool," he said of his now all-consuming mission. "I think everyone needs to feel that they've created something that was their own, on their own terms."

Rather than join the Kennedy clan, Carolyn and John spent Thanksgiving 1995 at a secluded resort in Guanaja, Honduras. Writer Peter Alson, who was among the dozen or so friends who went along on the trip, casually asked John where he would normally be spending the Thanksgiving holiday. When John suddenly became emotional, Alson realized that the day was November 22, the thirty-second anniversary of Dallas, and this was only the second Thanksgiving since Jackie passed away. Alson felt "moved" that his friend "could even for a moment be so vulnerable."

Increasingly, John was able to lose himself in his work, leaving Carolyn alone for longer and longer stretches of time. Unable to venture outside without being set upon by photographers, she spent hours at home with their black-and-white Canaan puppy, Friday. As smitten as she was with the dog ("They were both insanely in love with Friday—he was more like their rambunctious child," a friend said), Carolyn felt trapped.

Overnight, Barlow explained, Carolyn had become "a *thing* in the eyes of the public, and she was treated accordingly. She had no concept of what it was going to be like—people camped out on your doorstep day and night. She felt like a refugee." Or, as Carolyn herself put it, like "a hunted animal."

It didn't help that John, in addition to being absent much of the time, could also be massively inconsiderate. It was not uncommon for him to forget that they had plans for the evening and go straight from the office to the gym instead, leaving Carolyn to cool her heels for hours. Other times he might show up at home with dinner guests he had never bothered to tell her about, leaving Carolyn to scramble for something to serve. "It wasn't that he was mean," one of their friends said. "John was just like a little kid, and she was the grown-up."

By early 1996, friends were noticing a distinct change in Carolyn's behavior. "She was still warm and friendly and drop-dead gorgeous," one said, "but now there were mood swings and periods of depression. She was upset, distracted." Everyone chalked it up to the pressures of being JFK Jr.'s fiancée. What they didn't know—and what she hadn't told John—was that she was pregnant.

Had he known, John would have been thrilled. He had been telling his closest friends for months that he was ready to become a father, and that he had even picked out a name that would work for both a boy and a girl: Flynn.

Trouble was, Carolyn was not sure she was ready for motherhood.

Moreover, she worried about subjecting a child to the media onslaught she now struggled with. Carolyn, who had never told John that she had already had two abortions, knew he would never allow her to have a third.

Their next big blowup would have nothing to do with the baby issue, although the secret she was keeping from John must have contributed to Carolyn's precarious mental state. On February 25, 1996, as they took a Sunday-morning stroll with their dog, Friday, through New York's Washington Square Park, they both snapped. Without warning, John grabbed Carolyn's hand and tore Jackie's "Swimming Ring"—their engagement ring—off her finger. "What's your problem?" Carolyn hollered at him. Then, as several bystanders looked on, John took the leash from her hand and stormed off with Friday.

Screaming through her sobs, Carolyn chased after John and grabbed him by the throat. The skirmish continued as they left the park, and eventually John, defeated, sat on the curb and cried. Carolyn walked up to him and demanded the ring. "Give it to me!" she shouted. John did, and she knelt down next to him.

They were both sobbing now, and for one tender moment it looked as if they had reconciled—until John pushed her away, reigniting the conflict. Carolyn grappled for the leash. "You've got your ring!" he yelled. "You're not getting my dog!"

"It's *our* dog!" she fired back before marching off with Friday. Later, Carolyn returned and led John to a bench for a quiet talk. Through their tears, they made up with a passionate embrace.

An enterprising paparazzo had captured the entire incident on videotape, and what quickly became known as "the Brawl in the Park" was being talked about everywhere. Still trying to establish his credentials a serious publishing executive, John was humiliated. "It was very undignified," Barlow said, "and so unlike John." Just days after the tape was aired on national television, John appeared on Howard Stern's syndicated radio show. Had he seen the tape? the shock jock asked.

"I didn't have to see it," John replied coolly. "I was in it."

SEVERAL WEEKS AFTER their celebrated brawl, Carolyn miscarried. Although she had lived with John on North Moore Street, she had never given up her own one-bedroom in Greenwich Village. Instead of telling John about her pregnancy and miscarriage, she invited her ex-lover, Michael Bergin, to the apartment and told him everything. Then they made love and fell asleep in each other's arms.

Early the next morning, a friend pounded on Carolyn's door, warning her that John was worried that she hadn't returned home, and was on his way over. Bergin, half dressed, fled Carolyn's apartment in a panic. "I knew it was wrong, and she knew it was wrong," Bergin later reflected, "but we both found ways to justify our behavior . . . What did that say about their relationship? And what did it say about ours?"

Caroline also had her doubts, fueled by the tabloid rumors, the controversial "Brawl in the Park" videotape, and the obvious hold Carolyn had over her brother. When friends asked if a wedding was imminent, Ed Schlossberg shot down the idea. "Caroline," he sniffed, "doesn't *know* her."

Yet one week after Carolyn's tryst with Bergin, she and John looked very much like a couple in love as they walked arm in arm along Paris's Left Bank. He had wanted to be at least an ocean away when some 1,195 lots from the estate of Jacqueline Kennedy Onassis went under the gavel at Sotheby's in New York—the most-ballyhooed estate sale in memory.

The historic auction, which had Jackie's blessing, raised an astonishing $34,461,495—enough to pay off the taxes on the estate. Only $200,000 remained for John and Caroline from the sale—"After all that? A lousy $100,000 each?" John complained—yet they still wound up splitting an after-tax estate of more than $100 million.

In the months before Sotheby's cataloged Jackie's possessions, John and Caroline faced the arduous and often emotional task of culling through their mother's things—separating what they might want to keep for sentimental reasons from what they might donate to the Kennedy Library. Ultimately, they donated two hundreds works of art and artifacts—including the wedding dress Jackie wore when she married JFK—as well as 4,500 photographs and 38,000 pages of documents to the library.

Inevitably, there were those who questioned whether selling JFK's rocking chair, golf clubs, and humidor—not to mention Jackie's clothes and jewelry and John-John's high chair—was in the best of taste. What would Jackie have thought of this record-smashing fire sale of her personal belongings? "Are you kidding?" said her friend Dina Merrill, the actress who was also heir to the Post cereal fortune. "I'm sure Jackie would have been *thrilled*."

"Thrilled" is probably not the word to describe what Jackie would have thought about *George*—at least not the September 1996 cover, for which Drew Barrymore reenacted Marilyn Monroe's infamous "Happy Birthday, Mr. *Pres-i-dent*" song to JFK.

"It's reprising a song sung to my father in 1962," John said with a shrug. "I don't see what possible taste questions could be involved. If I don't find it tasteless, I don't know why anyone would." He went on to describe it as "part of the iconography of American politics—an enduring image." That "enduring image" had the desired effect, stirring up controversy and newsstand sales.

John was willing to take his button-pushing even further. When Hillary Clinton refused to pose for the cover, he came up with the idea of dressing up his former lover Madonna as his mother. "Wouldn't that be a riot?" he asked his dumbfounded assistant, RoseMarie Terenzio. "We'll have her in a pillbox hat, sitting on a stack of books."

John dashed off a note describing his idea, but she said no. "Dear Johnny Boy," Madonna answered in her distinctive, loopy handwriting.

Thanks for asking me to be your mother but I'm afraid I could never do her justice. My eyebrows aren't thick enough, for one. When you want me to portray Eva Braun or Pamela Harriman I might say yes! Hope you're well.

Love, Madonna

It seemed unimaginable, but John and Carolyn had been married two full days before the press reported the story. To John's credit, their September 21, 1996, wedding was pulled off with all the precision and stealth of a commando raid. "It required the skill of a James Bond and the whole CIA," Tish Baldrige said. "Jackie must be smiling in heaven."

Three days earlier, some forty guests—mostly family—started arriving by private plane and boat on tiny Cumberland Island (population 21), just off the Georgia coast. Everyone checked into the island's only hotel, the Greyfield Inn, which had once been the winter retreat of the Carnegie family.

According to the caterer, Jodee Sadowsky, guests were "forced to really rough it. The inn only has bathtubs. There's only one shower, and it's outdoors. So every morning everyone stood in line. Maria Shriver was right behind me in her fuzzy slippers."

That night at the rehearsal dinner, John stood up to toast his bride. With a nod to the *People* magazine cover that launched him as a sex symbol, John declared himself to be "the *luckiest* man alive."

The next evening, John and Carolyn exchanged vows during a candlelight ceremony in the Brack Chapel of the First African Baptist Church, an unadorned white clapboard structure that had been built in 1893 by former slaves.

The bride wore a $40,000 pearl-colored Narciso Rodriguez silk crepe floor-length gown, long gloves, and a veil of silk tulle. Her platinum hair was pulled back in a chignon, held in place with a comb that had belonged to Jackie—a gift to Carolyn from her new sister-in-law. She walked in, John Perry Barlow said, "looking like a beautiful ghost."

John, meanwhile, made several sartorial nods to his dad. He wore a midnight-blue wool suit and white vest, one of his father's white shirts, and his father's watch. All the men in the wedding party also wore a blue cornflower—JFK's favorite—as a boutonniere.

It was very much a family affair. Carolyn's sister Lisa, her stepfather, and her mother were there. So was the last love of Jackie's life, Maurice, as well as Uncle Ted, Aunt Lee, and John's surrogate mom, Marta Sgubin. Caroline, so instrumental in planning the clandestine nuptials, was also matron of honor. Her son Jack Schlossberg was the ring bearer, while John's nieces, Rose and Tatiana, were flower girls. Caroline and Sgubin became emotional when they realized Carolyn was holding a bouquet of lilies of the valley, Jackie's favorite flower.

John's cousin and best friend, Tony Radziwill, was best man. Tony's ongoing battle with cancer would be a heavy burden for John to bear, but for now he was holding his own.

"I shed tears of absolute joy as John and his bride exchanged vows," Marta said. "He has always been a very, very sensitive boy, and as I watched him I could read in his eyes how much he wished his mother could have been there to see him married."

At the wedding dinner, Ted once again invoked Camelot to reduce half the guests to tears. "I know that Jack and Jackie would be very proud of them," he said, "and so full of love for them as they begin their future together."

Carolyn never stopped agonizing about the kind of life that lay ahead—the expectations, the loss of privacy, how it all would affect any children they might have.

Maintaining her own identity was another pressing issue for John's bride. While she and John were filling out the necessary paperwork and getting blood tests, Camden County Court Clerk Shirley Wise asked if Carolyn was taking John's surname.

"I still want to be known as Bessette—Bessette-Kennedy," she said. "I want the name with a hyphen."

Wise was taken aback. "You could have knocked me over with a feather," she said. "After all this, she didn't want to take the world's most famous name!"

Before the world knew of the wedding—and Carolyn was crowned "the New Queen of Camelot" by a hyperventilating press—they had embarked on their honeymoon: three days in Turkey, followed by a ten-day cruise of the Aegean aboard the 123-foot double-masted schooner *Althea*.

Once they were back in New York, John and Carolyn stepped outside their North Moore Street building for the first time as man and wife. Polite to a fault, John gently pleaded with his fellow journalists as solemn-faced Carolyn looked on.

"This is a big change for anyone, and for a private citizen even more so," John said. "I ask that you give Carolyn all the privacy and room you can."

Not likely. As she tried to make her way into Caroline's Park Avenue building for a post-wedding party, Carolyn was blinded by photographer's flashbulbs. "Please!" she yelled as she shielded her eyes. "I can't see!"

It was clear from the outset that the photographers and reporters who were so charmed by John felt the opposite way about her. "John was a real gentleman," photographer David McGough said. "He was very polite to photographers at events, and would stop and smile for them. He knew how to give—but she never did. She could be cold as ice."

The grudge match between Carolyn and the press had been going on for some time. At first, she said, she had viewed the paparazzi as "a kind of a joke. But then it just got bizarre. I realized that a lot of the photographers really didn't like me. They wanted me to do something wrong, so they could photograph it."

She had a point. When she fell down the stairs outside 20 North Moore, photographers swung into action, but no one came to Carolyn's aid. "They just went crazy," said Carolyn, who pulled herself together and gathered her belongings. "Nobody helped me up. They just kept snapping."

Now that she was Mrs. Bessette-Kennedy, Carolyn had to put up with photographers shouting "whore," "bitch," and even more graphic expletives at her in an attempt to elicit an angry response.

Jackie would have been sympathetic. She had fought for years to keep the press at bay, ultimately realizing that it was an unwinnable war. Rather than defeat the press, she had learned, at least to some extent, to manipulate it.

Yet John understood that the ground rules had changed considerably since the days when, as the wife of a young senator bound for the White House, Jackie was first thrust into the limelight. Now photographers were willing to do whatever it took to snare that dramatic photo that might fetch six figures from a tabloid.

"My wife went from being a private citizen to a public one overnight . . . It was taxing," John later said, not willing to publicly concede that she was cracking under the pressure. "I have a thick skin about it, but I think people sort of forget how hard that can be. Carolyn is a very private woman. It's like you go from having a life you've built on your own terms and all of a sudden it's being snatched away from you. It's hard."

In the end, Carolyn had no interest in playing the game the way John and Jackie did. Instead, she and her husband found refuge in places like Socrates on Hudson Street, where waitress Bia Ayiotis served John breakfast three or four times a week.

She was taken aback when John first ordered in Greek. "My stepfather," he explained, "was Greek."

"He'd sit at the counter or in a booth with his baseball cap on and read his paper in peace," Ayiotis said. "For his power and his money, he was a very plain person. He was a sweetheart."

The inevitable stares and whispers didn't bother John; like his mother, who often grabbed a sandwich at the counter or ate a hot dog she had purchased from a vendor on the street, he was able to screen out the distractions. It was a skill Carolyn had yet to master. Even at out-of-the-way places like Socrates and Bubby's, she was uneasy. "She would have to hide out in here," Bubby's co-owner, Seth Price, recalled. "She'd go out the back door to get out. It was just horrible. She just wanted to spend time with her husband."

"This is ridiculous," Carolyn complained to RoseMarie Terenzio. "They chase me down the street." John's assistant knew what Carolyn knew—that the paparazzi had reached "new levels of viciousness" and were "patiently waiting for her to mess up, act out, or go crazy." Terenzio "pitied her. The girl was a sitting duck."

Given enough time, Carolyn might have learned how to hide in plain sight from the master. "John was a magician. He could just flat-out disappear," Barlow said, recalling the time photographers tried to corner the two friends as they left a Bruce Springsteen concert at Madison Square Garden. Barlow turned to talk to John "and he had vanished." While the paparazzi scattered to find him, Barlow heard someone whispering. "Psst. Psst, over here," John called before materializing from behind a concrete column. "He'd been standing there, right in the middle of everything the whole time," Barlow said. "John knew how not to be seen if he didn't want to be seen, and he did it often."

Knowing, as Jackie did, that the press ramped up its coverage considerably whenever November 22 rolled around, John spirited Carolyn out of town on the thirty-third anniversary of his father's murder. This time they sneaked off to Argos, Indiana, to visit Lloyd Howard, design engineer for Buckeye Industries. The year before, John purchased his first ultralight Buckeye powered parachute, and since then he and Howard had become friends.

"My mother was always afraid for me," John admitted to Howard. "She didn't want me flying." Howard believed John was "more cautious than most people *because* of his mother—that was ingrained in him. He still heard her voice whispering in his ear, you know: 'Please be careful.'"

Despite Howard's conviction that John was a cautious flyer, he actually had several close calls piloting his ultralight. In Hyannis Port, police rushed to the Kennedy compound when locals dialed 911, claiming that a man flying a flimsy-looking contraption was being blown out over the Atlantic. Struggling with the controls, John finally guided the ultalight Buckeye back to land. "You could have been killed," one police officer told him.

"I wasn't worried," John replied confidently.

During the Kennedys' visit to Indiana, John also told Howard that he had every intention of running for office—although not right now. "My mom sort of pressured me to get into politics," he told Howard. "She expected me to follow in my father's footsteps, and of course I will. But I don't think the time is right just yet."

As for Carolyn, Howard echoed the sentiment expressed by most people who got to know her. Having seen photographs of John's cool blond spouse in the newspapers, Howard expected Carolyn to be aloof. Instead, when they met, she gave Howard a "big bear hug. Carolyn was even more outgoing than John was. She was very open, very warm, very friendly."

Carolyn also exhibited a motherly concern for John's welfare that Jackie would have appreciated. "She babied John; she treated him like her child—always asking how he felt, reminding him to wear a scarf, that sort of thing," Howard said. "I'd heard all the rumors about trouble in their marriage, but they said it wasn't true. They seemed to me to be about as in love with each other as two people could get."

They now had new nicknames for each other. He called her "Kitty Cat," and she called him "Mouse." Yet for all the outward signs of marital bliss, the constant drumbeat of unsavory speculation continued. Carolyn was now said to be abusing drugs (specifically antidepressants and cocaine), to have suffered a miscarriage (which turned out to be true), and to be seeking treatment for infertility.

It was all clearly taking its toll. At one point, John jumped onto the hood of a Jeep being driven by celebrity photographer Angie Coqueran and banged on the window. Coqueran, he believed, had been responsible for the "Brawl in the Park" video. After screaming threats at Coqueran—"I know who you are, and I'm going to get you!"—John grabbed her by the collar. Then he went after Coqueran's male partner, screaming, "Leave us the hell alone!"

This time Carolyn tried to stop her husband, but he would have none of it. Now furious at Carolyn as well as the paparazzi, John took off alone, leaving his wife sobbing on the sidewalk. "I didn't blame him one bit for getting angry," said Coqueran, who described John as being "gentle as a bunny with us—even when he was pissed off. He tried to strangle me and I *still* love the guy—that's how great he was."

John was not unaware of the effect he had on people, and now that *George* was well into its second year, John began to seriously consider a run for office. When New York's longtime Democratic senator Daniel Patrick Moynihan announced in 2000 that he would not seek reelection, Democratic leaders approached John. In January 1997, before

Hillary Clinton expressed interest in the seat, John told New York State Democratic chairwoman Judith Hope that he wanted to run. He had good reason to believe now was the time: a straw poll done at the time showed that, out of all the probable Democratic candidates—including Hillary—John would win handily.

While John now resolved to run for office, he also worked on keeping *George* afloat in the face of declining circulation and ad revenues. Carolyn, meanwhile, flew to Milan in July 1997 to attend the funeral of her friend, fashion designer Gianni Versace, who had been senselessly gunned down in front of his Miami Beach mansion.

At the funeral, Carolyn just happened to be seated directly behind Princess Diana. Not long before, Diana had praised Jackie for the way she raised her children, and said she hoped her sons, William and Harry, would be able to handle the media as gracefully as John had. Even before her generous comments, John had been won over by the People's Princess. "Diana had the most unusual upwards glance," he told a friend, "really seductive . . . the most unusual blue eyes."

Five weeks after Carolyn spoke briefly with Diana in Milan, the princess was killed in a crash after a high-speed chase through the streets of Paris. Like many, Carolyn blamed the paparazzi. "I'm not sure what I'm going to do about Carolyn," John told Billy Noonan. "She's really spooked now."

Diana's death only served to harden Carolyn's resolve not to have children anytime soon. "How can I bring JFK III into his world?" she asked. "They'll never leave me alone." Having a child would be "just too cruel," she added. "Just another form of child abuse."

These are not the words Jackie would have wanted to hear. As first lady and the widow of an assassinated president, she faced unimaginable hardships yet still succeeded in raising two happy, well-adjusted children.

Jackie had accomplished this, of course, by shielding John and Caroline from their problematic Kennedy cousins, who seemed to be getting into more trouble than ever. Michael Kennedy, the sixth of Bobby and Ethel's eleven children, now stood accused of sleeping with his family's underage babysitter. Michael's older brother Joe, meanwhile, was under fire for engineering the annulment of his twelve-year marriage to Sheila Rauch—an unfolding scandal that would cause Joe to drop out of the race for Massachusetts governor.

What John did next would have horrified Jackie, who, if not always enthusiastic about supporting her Kennedy in-laws, never publicly criticized them. In an effort to generate controversy and give newsstand sales a much-needed shot in the arm, John used the editorial page of *George* to pillory his cousins as "poster boys for bad behavior."

To ensure that his piece would garner maximum attention, John struck a nude pose—albeit discreetly obscured by a shadow—for the accompanying photograph. Under the headline "Don't Sit Under the Apple Tree," John was shown sitting on the ground, his gaze directed upward at the forbidden fruit.

Joe's retort was brief and stinging. "Ask not what you can do for your cousin," he sneered, "but what you can do for his magazine."

John tried, somewhat disingenuously, to explain to his cousins that his *George* commentary was intended to be ironic—that it was designed to show that the press was unfairly piling on Joe and Michael merely because they were Kennedys. "If they're too stupid to understand," he finally said, throwing up his hands, "then screw it."

As the 1997 holidays approached, there were more heated confrontations with the press. One afternoon, John turned a video camera on the paparazzi and threatened to use it as Exhibit A in a lawsuit against them. Carolyn grew so fed up at one point that she chased down a female photographer, grabbed her by the shoulders, and spit in her face.

Confronted with tensions at the office, the ever-insatiable tabloid press, and mounting strain in his marriage, John sought avenues of escape. In December, he secretly began taking flying lessons at the Flight Safety Academy in Vero Beach, Florida.

———

CAROLYN SHARED JACKIE'S concerns about the notoriously unfocused John piloting a plane. "I mean it, John, I have a bad feeling about this," she was overheard telling him the day after Christmas 1997. "I don't want you taking flying lessons." With some additional prodding from Uncle Teddy, John promised to give up his dream of piloting his own plane. For the time being, he claimed, he was willing to settle for flying the Buckeye ultralight (his aptly nicknamed "flying lawn mower"), which did not require a pilot's license.

Not all risks required leaving the ground. The family "curse" reared its head yet again on New Year's Eve, when Michael Kennedy, vacationing with his family in Aspen, slammed headlong into a tree while playing a typically reckless Kennedy game of night football on skis. John's cousin Rory desperately tried to revive her brother with mouth-to-mouth resuscitation. When that failed, she cradled Michael's bleeding head as his children knelt in the snow, crying.

At Michael's funeral on Cape Cod, John appeared far more distraught than he had been at any of the previous funerals he had attended—even his mother's. After the service, John, weeping openly, threw his arms around Douglas Kennedy, one of Michael's brothers. Eldest brother Joe, clearly unimpressed, ignored his Kennedy-Bouvier cousin.

Michael's death only made those who loved John more aware than ever that he was tempting fate by taking to the skies, even in the ultralight that didn't require a pilot's license. Carolyn never stopped hinting at her concern. At her thirty-second birthday party, Carolyn paused before blowing out candles on her cake. "What's your wish?" he asked. "To know," she said, "that you'll always be around."

A month later, they were among the guests invited to attend a state dinner for British prime minister Tony Blair at the White House. Did John remember living here? someone asked. "Only vaguely," he said. Did he want to again? "Only vaguely." John smiled.

That final year, John and Carolyn seemed, on balance, to be happier than they had ever been. At the White House Correspondents Association dinner that spring, she plopped in John's lap and they cuddled and giggled for the cameras. "They laughed a lot together," Paul Wilmot said. "They were a very warm, happy couple. He had probably found his true soul mate in her."

The reason for Carolyn's positive new attitude, she told the New York *Daily News,* was that she simply stopped reading what was written about her in the newspapers. Unlike Jackie, who eagerly lapped up every syllable, Carolyn claimed she was "a happier person, and maybe a better person, for not knowing."

That, and the fact that Carolyn was now taking antidepressants (recreational drugs were no longer in the picture) and undergoing intense psychotherapy five days a week. Even with all the pharmaceutical and psychiatric help, it was difficult to hear what John had to tell her that April: Not only had he reneged on his promise to give up his flying lessons, but John had already secretly earned his pilot's license.

John's sister told a friend that she felt like crying when she heard the news. "You know Mummy didn't want you to fly," she told John. "I think you know how angry she'd be with you right now—and how worried she'd be . . ."

Although there had always been tension between Carolyn and Caroline, this was one subject on which they agreed. After a time, however, it became clear there was nothing either could do or say to change his mind. The only person who would have succeeded in doing that was Jackie.

Not that any friend or fellow Kennedy was particularly eager to fly with the novice aviator, no matter how hard he tried to convince them that it was perfectly safe. "John may have pushed his limitations getting his pilot's license," Willie Smith said half in jest, "but he hasn't overcome them yet. He's yet to persuade any of his relatives to fly with him."

In 1998, John took to the skies alone in his new Cessna with N529JFK on the fuselage. In time, he was able to persuade a handful of acquaintances to join him. All summer long, John buzzed Red Gate Farm, recalled his Martha's Vineyard neighbor Tony DiLorenzo. "Not only that, John would buzz it, go up, dive down, and show all his friends where his house was." By the summer of 1999, John was back in the skies over his mother's house, swooping down and pulling up at the last minute—only now in his more powerful, souped-up Piper Saratoga. "A great guy," DiLorenzo said, "but sadly, he was a showboater."

In this, he was nothing at all like his mother, who rarely ventured from her secluded Shangri-la when she was on the Vineyard. While Jackie contented herself running along her 4,620 feet of private beach, swimming in the Atlantic, or paddling her canoe on Squibnocket Pond, John made a point of getting out and mingling with tourists as well as the locals.

On most weekends during the summer months, John could be seen pulling up to the Harbor House in Edgartown in his vintage black GTO convertible, standing with his bike on the tiny ferry that linked Edgartown to Chappaquiddick, Rollerblading toward Menemsha, or downing margaritas with Carolyn at an Oak Bluffs dive called the Lampost.

The couple would rendezvous at Red Gate Farm nearly every weekend that summer. Carolyn flew up with him in the Piper Saratoga a few times—but only when an instructor tagged along or, if John was flying without a copilot, strictly during daylight hours. She preferred, however, to take a scheduled flight from New York's LaGuardia Airport or the ferry from Hyannis.

———

THAT SUMMER OF 1999, Carolyn and John hosted two very special guests on the Vineyard. Tony Radziwill had been battling cancer for more than a decade, but now the outcome was clear. "Tony's illness was really tearing John up," Barlow said. "He did everything he could for Tony, but he knew he was dying . . ." At John's insistence, Tony Radziwill was spending his final few weeks with his wife, Carole, at Red Gate Farm. "It's what Mummy would have wanted," John told Carolyn. "She loved Tony like a son."

The imminent loss of his surrogate brother was not the only cross John had to bear that summer. In addition to the nonstop round of galas, openings, and fund-raisers in New York, Boston, and Washington, John was in the process of buying out his sister's share in Red Gate Farm. Now he and Caroline were reportedly squabbling over certain items of furniture that were left to them by their mother. John confided in his cousin Bobby Kennedy Jr. that he was "hurt" by his sister

Caroline's actions, while Carolyn told Bobby's wife, Mary, that the bitter feud with his sister over Jackie's belongings had left John "so depressed" he was finding it hard to function. "He's under a lot of stress, you know," Carolyn explained, "and it's killing him."

One of the biggest challenges facing John was finding a way to save *George* from extinction. After a wildly successful beginning—fueled almost entirely by John's celebrity and personal charisma—the magazine, which never found its footing with advertisers, was drowning in a sea of red ink. Now Hachette was ready to pull the plug, forcing John to scramble for investors to keep *George* alive. "He loves his staff," Carolyn told one of her fashion world friends. "He'll feel terrible if they lose their jobs. He'll feel responsible."

By mid-July, however, John realized he was fighting a losing battle. He was ready to shut the magazine down and finally make the big leap into politics. Only months before, Barlow and former Republican senator from New York Alphonse D'Amato teamed up to convince John to run for mayor of New York—as a Republican. "John was really thinking it over," Barlow said. "In many ways, John was quite conservative. Socially, I think he was more of a Republican than a Democrat. He would have made a great mayor. He really understood New York and he loved it deeply."

In the end, John was still convinced his best shot was at running for Moynihan's Senate seat. Hillary Clinton had hesitated to enter the race largely because she feared John, who was being touted behind the scenes as her principal rival for the nomination, would be a formidable foe. John was both heir to the Kennedy magic and *People*'s "Sexiest Man Alive," as well as the consummate New Yorker, a resident of the city since the age of three. Although New York had no residency requirements, Hillary, who had never spent more than a few days at a time in New York, would almost certainly be branded a carpetbagger.

There were other, more personal reasons for Hillary's initial reluctance to battle John for the nomination. She and Bill had forged a close friendship with Jackie, and Hillary felt a special attachment to her children; Caroline, in fact, had become a close confidante of daughter Chelsea Clinton. "She was really torn," said one of Hillary's supporters in New York. "She liked John and hated the idea of running against him, and she also felt he would be impossible to beat on his home turf." This had been Bobby Kennedy's seat, Hillary pointed out, and she felt "if John wanted it, he should have it."

As late as the summer of 1999, Hillary actively worried about JFK Jr. and sought assurances from state party officials that he would not be a last-minute entry into the race. "People love John," she conceded, "more than they love me." Ed Koch agreed. "I love Hillary," he said, "but if John Kennedy had been in the race, there is no way she could have won the nomination. He had the Kennedy name, and a charisma all his own. The Senate seat was his for the asking."

In early July, Hillary finally made her move and formally announced her candidacy. But she was still concerned about the possibility that John might decide to toss his hat into the ring. As it turned out, she was right. John was now more confident than ever that he could easily beat her at the polls. He believed Hillary was vulnerable not only because of the Monica Lewinsky affair, her husband's subsequent impeachment, and a slew of brewing scandals in the Clinton White House, but mainly because she simply had no connection to the state he loved.

As Hillary had feared, young Kennedy planned on making much of Hillary's carpetbagger status. "Wait until she gets here," John told his friend Billy Noonan. "She's gonna get her head handed to her." He was going to fill Noonan in on the details of his upcoming campaign for the U.S. Senate—how and when he intended to make the announcement, what advice he was getting from Uncle Teddy, the endorsements and backing he was already lining up—when they all got together on Nantucket to celebrate Noonan's fifth wedding anniversary on July 16. Then they'd be off to attend his cousin Rory's wedding in Hyannis Port.

If, of course, all went according to plan.

———

EXCEPT FOR THOSE few close friends who expected John—their seemingly indestructible "Master of Disaster"—to survive any tight situation, the world held its breath and prepared for the worst. The plane had been missing only a matter of hours when the first bits of debris—Lauren Bessette's black overnight bag, a square aqua duffel bag, a plane wheel—began washing up on Philbin Beach, virtually at the doorstep of Red Gate Farm. Then, after a four-day search by the Navy and Coast Guard—the most expensive for a private aircraft in U.S. history—John's plane was finally found lying upside down at a depth of 116 feet some seven and a half miles southwest of Martha's Vineyard.

Unaware that the spot where John's plane went down was within sight of where he was standing, Tony had been the first to call Caroline on vacation in Idaho and tell her John's plane was missing. Now, after four days during which the nation had held its breath but not its tears, it was left to Caroline to decide how best to say goodbye.

An emotional Bill Clinton, who at sixteen had shaken hands with JFK in the White House Rose Garden, solemnly offered words of support on the behalf of the nation. "For more than forty years now," he said, "the Kennedy family has inspired Americans . . . Through it all, they have suffered much and given more."

Once the bodies were found, it fell to Uncle Teddy to speak for the family. "We are all filled with unspeakable grief and sadness," the senator's statement read. "John was a shining light in all our lives, and in the lives of the nation and the world that came to know him as a little boy."

———

NOW CAROLINE STOOD alone, insisting on a relatively modest family service in the church that had meant so much to their little family of three—St. Thomas More, the modest neo-Gothic stone church just a few blocks from 1040 Fifth Avenue where Jackie took her children to Mass every Sunday and where Caroline still worshipped. A Mass was said at St. Thomas More for John's mother and father on their birthdays. Now, it occurred to Caroline, one would be said there for John on his birthday, as well.

Caroline, known among the Kennedys for her will of steel, prevailed.

Addressing 315 mourners—including the first family—Uncle Teddy at first tried to lighten the mood. "Once," he began, "they asked John what he would do if he went into politics and was elected president, he said, 'I guess the first thing is call up Uncle Teddy and gloat.' I loved that. It was so like his father."

Teddy delivered the rest of his touching eulogy in a quavering voice, against a backdrop of muffled sobs. John was "one of Jackie's two miracles," the senator said, and would "live forever in our beguiled and broken hearts."

Yet even before Uncle Teddy could say goodbye, Caroline had to decide where her brother's cremated remains would be interred. It was widely assumed that John would be buried alongside his parents and his siblings at Arlington, and President Clinton personally approved plans to lay John to rest next to the Eternal Flame. But when it became clear that Carolyn would not be permitted to join him, her mother, Ann Freeman, objected.

There was another possibility—that John and Carolyn be buried at the Brookline cemetery that was the resting place of a number of Kennedy family members, including Joe and Rose. The Bessettes nixed this idea as well, on the grounds that Carolyn's family had no ties to Massachusetts.

Searching for a solution—she was keenly aware that Ann Freeman had lost two children in a plane piloted by John—Caroline remembered that her brother had once said in passing that he wanted to be buried at sea. He may have given it thought, or it may have been an idle musing—either way, it seemed right to Caroline.

On Thursday, July 22, 1999 at 9 a.m., seventeen of John's and Carolyn's relatives boarded the cutter *Sanibel* and were taken to the Navy destroyer USS *Briscoe*. With an escort of three additional cutters, the *Briscoe* headed out to sea. Their red and swollen eyes concealed behind dark glasses, mourners sat in folding chairs until the ship stopped not far from where John's plane went down.

Moving to the stern, everyone stood while Father Charles O'Byrne, the priest who married John and Carolyn, and two Navy chaplains brought out three Tiffany blue cardboard boxes and set them down on a small table. Father O'Byrne then said a brief Mass, but no one seemed to hear what he was saying—the mourners simply stared, uncomprehending, at the boxes in front of them.

A brass quintet from the Newport Navy Band played "Abide with Me" as Caroline, Uncle Teddy, and other family members climbed down a ladder to a platform just above the waterline. Then, as the quintet played the Navy hymn "Eternal Father," Caroline took the Tiffany blue box marked JOHN F. KENNEDY JR. and scattered her brother's ashes over the waves.

————

IF JFK'S BRUTAL murder at age forty-six was tragic, than John's senseless death at thirty-eight seemed incomprehensibly so. Caroline, understandably, was "crushed—shattered," Marta Sgubin said of the weeks and months that followed John's funeral. "She was weeping constantly." Now, John's big sister was the keeper of the flame—sole heir to a legacy of power, wealth, dreams both realized and unfulfilled, and unfathomable anguish.

As close as they were in so many ways, John and Caroline, who would go on to make her own mark in public service as United States ambassador to Japan, were also worlds apart temperamentally. She was grounded, guarded, cautious. He was free-spirited, charismatic, and fearless—often to the point of recklessness. Jackie and Caroline were pillars of support for John, and in their mother's final months they were both there for her. It was John, however, who stepped before the cameras to graciously, almost poetically, announce Jackie's death to the world. It was John who helped guide his sister through the crush of reporters gathered outside 1040 Fifth, it was John who supported his sister at Jackie's funeral, and it was John who knelt down to plant a final kiss on their mother's coffin at Arlington National Cemetery.

For all of his thirty-eight years, John had struggled to reconcile his own dreams and desires with what the rest of the world—not least of all his powerfully persuasive mother—expected of him. Charismatic, witty, poised, even better-looking than his famously handsome father, John was more than equipped to handle the task. Forced to confront and overcome soul-crushing personal losses from an early age, he also exhibited a streak of compassion uncommon among his peers—an ability to connect with others in a way that set him apart from the back-slapping bravado of his fellow Kennedys.

There seemed little doubt in the minds of those who knew him that John was on the brink of a bright political future. "He was probably a more natural politician than any of the other Kennedys," David Halberstam said, "and that includes his father. John had all the makings of a political superstar—once he decided that's what he wanted."

From those days peeking out from beneath his father's Oval Office desk to that final flight into the void, John strove to be one thing above all else: utterly, even defiantly, normal.

It was in the abiding belief that he was much like a member of our own family—a son or brother, or perhaps a nephew, a grandson—that we felt we knew him, and watched with no small degree of fascination and pride as he grew into manhood.

Torn between living out the mythic dreams of Camelot and living life on his own terms, John—like good sons everywhere—did the only thing he could do: his best.

Acknowledgments

When television news anchors first breathlessly reported that John F. Kennedy Jr.'s plane was missing off Martha's Vineyard on July 16, 1999, I had no illusions about the outcome. In the process of writing *The Day Diana Died* and two previous books about the Kennedys (*Jack and Jackie* and *Jackie After Jack*), I had already immersed myself in the lives of public figures cut down at the height of their fame—people who, though admired and even adored during their brief lifetimes, achieved a mythic status in death. That Camelot's cherished Crown Prince should die so senselessly and so young seemed unimaginable, and at the same time completely predictable.

From history's most famous salute to the plane crash that took place within sight of his mother's beachfront estate, John's story was a bittersweet saga of family, fate, and promise unfulfilled. It is also the story of a remarkable young widow whose inherent sense of dignity held a nation together during one of its darkest hours, and the son she dreamed might someday take his place in history.

A daunting amount of research is essential for any exhaustive biography, and this was particularly true of *The Good Son*. In a sense, I have been working on this book for more than two decades, interviewing hundreds of family members, friends, lovers, classmates, teachers, staffers, servants, neighbors, and colleagues as well as the reporters and photographers who covered Jackie and John over the years. Given Jackie's penchant for privacy, a few sources—but only a few—preferred to remain anonymous.

As with my last book on the Kennedys, the 2013 bestseller *These Few Precious Days: The Final Year of Jack with Jackie,* I went back to the tapes and notes of my interviews with many key figures from the Kennedy Era who had asked that I keep certain pieces of information confidential. I honored that wish during their lifetimes. However, many of these sources have now passed away, releasing me from that obligation. What remains is a trove of fresh details and insights that shed new light on the mother and son known to millions simply as Jackie and John.

Once again I've been given the opportunity to work with some of the most talented people in the publishing industry. I am particularly grateful to my editor, Mitchell Ivers—great friend, total pro. I'm also indebted to the rest of the Gallery/Simon & Schuster team, especially Carolyn Reidy, Louise Burke, Jen Bergstrom, Jennifer Robinson, Natasha Simons, Paul O'Halloran, Kelly Roberts, Lisa Rivlin, Eric Rayman, Felice Javit, Tom Pitoniak, Carly Sommerstein, Ruth Lee-Mui, and Janet Perr.

Ellen Levine, my literary agent and pal for over thirty years, has heard me thank her countless times for her wise counsel, her fearless advocacy, and—most important of all—her friendship. I can only say that I mean it now more than ever. Over these many years, it's also been a pleasure to work with Ellen's extraordinarily talented team at Trident Media Group—Claire Roberts, Alexa Stark, Meredith Miller, and Alexander Slater.

After forty-two years, I don't have to tell my wife, Valerie, that she is witty, vibrant, headstrong, brilliant, totally outrageous—and utterly indispensable to the many people who love her. Our gorgeous and brainy daughters, Kate and Kelly, never cease to amaze. Kate, already a well-respected Washington journalist, has embarked on a book-writing career of her own. She and her husband, Brooke Brower, another highly regarded member of the Washington press corps, have also given us two absurdly attractive grandchildren: Graham Andersen Brower and Charlotte Beatrice Brower—the "Charlie" to whom this book is dedicated. Our youngest daughter, Kelly, meanwhile, boasts a wealth of knowledge covering a wide range of subjects and stands at the threshold of her own promising career in whatever field she chooses.

Additional thanks to Theodore Sorensen, David Halberstam, George Plimpton, Letitia Baldrige, John Perry Barlow, Pierre Salinger, Marta Sgubin, Kyle Bailey, Charles "Chuck" Spalding, Keith Stein, Peter Duchin, Cecil Stoughton, Arthur Marx, Kitty Carlisle Hart, Arthur Schlesinger Jr., Paul "Red" Fay, Michael Cherkasky, Evelyn Lincoln, John Kenneth Galbraith, Robert MacNeil, David Rockefeller, Angie Coqueran, Jack Anderson, Lloyd Howard, Roswell Gilpatric, Charles Addams, Sister Joanne Frey, Hugh "Yusha" Auchincloss, Julie Baker, Jamie Auchincloss, George Smathers, John Davis, Martha Bartlett, Clare Boothe Luce, Lois Cappelen, Jacques Lowe, David McGough, John Husted, Laurence Leamer, Larry Lorenzo, Daniel Patrick Moynihan, Jack Valenti, Rick Guy, Ed Koch, Rick Lazio, Tom Freeman, Frank Ratcliff, Michael Berman, Oleg Cassini, John Marion, Larry Newman, Priscilla McMillan, Dorothy Oliger, Henry Grunwald, Wendy Leigh, Michael Gross, Anne Vanderhoop, Mesfin Gebreegziabher, James Hill, Charles Bartlett, Paul Adao, Helen Thomas, Bia Ayiotis, Roy Cohn, Jesse Birnbaum, Joseph Pullia, Judith Hope, Ralph Diaz, Paula Dranov, Dudley Freeman, Jerry Wiener, Angier Biddle Duke, Rosemary McClure, Anthony Comenale, Tobias Markowitz, Jeanette Peterson, James E. O'Neill, Godfrey McHugh, Jean Chapin, Alfred Eisenstaedt, Nancy Dickerson Whitehead, Lawrence R. Mulligan, Robert Drew, Alex Gotfryd, Sandy Richardson, Aileen Mehle, Doris Lilly, Perry Peltz, Dr. Janet Travell, Ray Robinson, Ricardo Richards, Betty Beale, Charles Collingwood, Theodore White, Shirley Clurman, Cora Isabelle Peterson, Charles Furneaux, Robert Pierce, Valerie Wimmer, Maryrose Grossman, Brad Darrach, Patricia Lawford Stewart, Vincent Russo, Betsy Loth, Earl Blackwell, Ham Brown, Molly Fosburgh, Dorothy Schoenbrun, Cranston Jones, Maura Porter, Joe Duran, Jean Chapin, Fred Friendly, Jeanette Walls, Gary Gunderson, Richard Schaffer,

Farris L. Rookstool III, Janet Lizop, Michelle Lapautre, the Countess of Romanones, Wickham Boyle, Yvette Reyes, Michael Shulman, Fred Williams, Megan Desnoyers, Holly Owen, Drew Middleton, Betty Kelly, Mary Beth Whelan, Theresa Dellegrazie, Laura Watts, Kendra Kabasele, Matthew Lutts, Denis Reggie, Norman Currie, Bob Cosenza, Richard B. Stolley, William Johnson, Zoe Andersen, Barry Schenck, Debbie Goodsite, Ray Whelan Jr., and the John F. Kennedy Presidential Library and Museum, Phillips Academy, the National Transportation Safety Board, the Rockefeller Library at Brown University, Columbia University Oral History Project, Sotheby's, the Robin Hood Foundation, Reaching Up, the United States Secret Service, the Federal Bureau of Investigation, the New York Public Library, the Butler Library at Columbia University and Columbia University's Rare Book and Manuscript Library, the Lyndon Baines Johnson Library, the Redwood Library and Atheneum of Newport, the Barnstable Public Library, the Georgetown University Library, the Gunn Memorial Library, the Archdiocese of Boston, the Archdiocese of New York, St. Thomas More Church, the Hotel Carlyle, Essex County Airport, Martha's Vineyard Airport, the Silas Bronson Library, the Southbury Library, the Brookfield Library, the Bancroft Library at the University of California–Berkeley, the New Milford Library, the New York University Law Library, Corbis, Rex USA, the Coqueran Group, Planned Television Arts, Barraclough Carey Productions, *The Folding Kayak,* the United States Coast Guard, St. David's School, Collegiate, the *Cape Cod Times,* the Litchfield Business Center, the Edgartown Library, Reuters, Globe Photos, the Associated Press.

Sources and Chapter Notes

These chapter notes have been assembled to present an overview of the sources drawn upon in preparing *The Good Son,* but they are by no means all-inclusive. The author has respected the wishes of several interview subjects to remain anonymous and therefore has not listed them either here or elsewhere in the text. The archives, oral history, and audiovisual collections of the John Fitzgerald Kennedy Presidential Library and Museum, the Lyndon Baines Johnson Library, the Houghton Library at Harvard, and the libraries of Brown, Princeton, Columbia, and Yale universities provided a wealth of historical detail. There was also the release, between 1993 and 2012, of more than 260 hours of taped conversations that took place in the Oval Office and in the Cabinet Room of the White House as well as the release in 2011 of seven taped conversations Jackie had with Arthur Schlesinger Jr. in 1964. In addition, the countless press reports and news articles written about the Kennedy family over the past six decades have been a valuable resource in the attempt to accurately portray not only the unique relationship that existed between Jacqueline Kennedy Onassis and John Fitzgerald Kennedy Jr., but John's life post-Jackie as well. These accounts have been published in a wide range of publications, including the *New York Times, Wall Street Journal, Washington Post,* New York *Daily News, Chicago Tribune, New York Post, Boston Globe, Los*

Angeles Times, USA Today, Chicago Sun-Times, Time, Newsweek, Life, New Yorker, Times of London, *Paris-Match, New York, New York Observer, Look, Saturday Evening Post, Economist,* and *Vanity Fair* in addition to reports carried on the Associated Press, United Press International, Knight-Ridder, Gannett, and Reuters wires.

CHAPTERS 1 AND 2

These chapters were based in part on author interviews and conversations with Dr. Bob Arnot, Kyle Bailey, Arthur Marx, John Perry Barlow, Keith Stein, Julie Baker, George Smathers, Letitia Baldrige, Lloyd Howard, Pierre Salinger, Arthur Schlesinger Jr., Evelyn Lincoln, Theodore Sorensen, Jack Tabibian, Cecil Stoughton, Gore Vidal, Godfrey McHugh, Angier Biddle Duke, Mary Gallagher, Chuck Spalding, Mesfin Gebreegziabher, Larry Lorenzo, Jacques Lowe, Jerry Wiener, Ralph Diaz, Anne Vanderhoop, Anthony Comenale, Nancy Dickerson Whitehead, Lois Capellen, and Dr. Janet Travell.

The author also drew on numerous oral histories, including those given by Robert F. Kennedy, Rose Fitzgerald Kennedy, Richard Cardinal Cushing, Nancy Tuckerman, Eunice Kennedy Shriver, Maud Shaw, Janet Lee Bouvier Auchincloss, Pope Paul VI, Robert McNamara, Dave Powers, Dean Rusk, Betty Thomas, J. B. West, Admiral George Burkley, Paul "Red" Fay, Pamela Turnure, Walt Rostow, Peter Lawford, Father John C. Cavanaugh, Arthur Krock, Stanley Tretick, Douglas Dillon, William Walton, and Leonard Bernstein. Jacqueline Kennedy Onassis's oral history was done by Terry L. Birdwhistell in New York on May 13, 1981, as part of the John Sherman Cooper Oral History Project of the University of Kentucky Library.

Federal Bureau of Investigation, Secret Service, and National Security Agency files, newly released through the Freedom of Information Act, were of considerable value—as were White House staff files and the papers of JFK, Jacqueline Kennedy Onassis, Robert Kennedy, Rose Kennedy, Kenneth O'Donnell, Dave Powers, Kirk LeMoyne "Lem" Billings, Lawrence O'Brien, William vanden Heuvel, and Sir Alec Douglas-Home. Published sources included Angie Cannon and Peter

Cary, "The Final Hours," *U.S. News & World Report*, August 2, 1999; "He Was America's Prince," *Time*, July 26, 1999; "Tragic Echoes," *Newsweek*, July 26, 1999; Sally Bedell Smith, *Grace and Power* (New York: Random House, 2004); "Charmed Life, Tragic Death," *People*, August 2, 1999; Dr. Robert Arnot, "FAA False Visibility Reports: Lost in the Darkness and the Haze," *2000 Eve's Magazine*, March 2000; "The Preliminary Report of the National Transportation Safety Board, NTSB Identification NYC99MA178," http:/www.ntsb.gov/Aviation/NYC/99A178.htm; Peter Collier, "A Kennedy Apart: JFK Jr. Was His Own Man," *National Review*, August 9, 1999; "Charity Group Recalls John Kennedy Jr.," *New York Times*, December 8, 1999; Ed Vulliamy, "Why Kennedy Aircraft's Reputation Called Good," Associated Press, July 18, 1999; Ed Vulliamy, "Why Kennedy Crashed," *New York Observer*, July 24, 1999; "Sad Vigil," New York *Daily News*, July 19, 1999; Mary Barrelli Gallagher, *My Life with Jacqueline Kennedy* (New York: David McKay, 1969); Maud Shaw, *White House Nannie: My Years with Caroline and John Kennedy, Jr.* (New York: New American Library, 1965); Ted Widmer, *Listening In: The Secret White House Recordings of John F. Kennedy* (New York: Hyperion, 2012); "More Tears: JFK JR., Wife and Her Sister Presumed Dead in Plane Crash," *New York Post*, July 18, 1999; *Jacqueline Kennedy: Historic Conversations on Life with John F. Kennedy* (New York: Hyperion, 2011); Kitty Kelley, *Capturing Camelot* (New York: A Thomas Dunne Book/St. Martin's Press, 2012); "Tragic Echoes," *Newsweek*, July 26, 1999.

CHAPTERS 3–5

For this chapter, the author drew on conversations with George Plimpton, John Kenneth Galbraith, John Sargent, David Halberstam, Charles Addams, Kitty Carlisle Hart, Arthur Schlesinger Jr., Theodore H. White, Letitia Baldrige, Gore Vidal, George Smathers, Evelyn Lincoln, Joe Fox, Chuck Spalding, Yusha Auchincloss, Doris Lilly, Theodore Sorensen, Jamie Auchincloss, Ham Brown, Sister Joanne Frey, Truman Capote, Jacques Lowe, Oleg Cassini, Patricia Lawford Stewart, the Countess of Romanones, Priscilla McMillan, Willard K. Rice, Clare

Boothe Luce, Dr. Janet Travell, Betty Beale, Angier Biddle Duke, Alfred Eisenstaedt, Charles Furneaux, Larry Newman.

Among the published sources consulted: William Manchester, *The Death of a President* (New York: Harper & Row, 1967); Janny Scott, "In Tapes, Candid Talk by a Young Widow," *New York Times*, September 11, 2011; Robert Sam Anson, *"They've Killed the President!" The Search for the Murderers of John F. Kennedy* (New York: Bantam, 1975); *The Warren Commission Report* (Washington, D.C.: U.S. Government Printing Office), 1964; Arthur Schlesinger Jr., *A Thousand Days*, (Boston: Houghton Mifflin, 1965); Ben Bradlee, *A Good Life* (New York: Simon & Schuster, 1995); Jack Anderson, *Washington Exposé* (Washington, D.C.: Public Affairs Press, 1967); Kenneth P. O'Donnell and David F. Powers with Joe McCarthy, *Johnny, We Hardly Knew Ye* (Boston: Little, Brown, 1970); Lady Bird Johnson, *A White House Diary* (New York: Holt, Rinehart & Winston, 1970); Jim Bishop, *The Day Kennedy Was Shot* (New York: Funk & Wagnall, 1968); Theodore Sorensen, *Kennedy* (New York: Harper & Row, 1965); George Vecsey, "And There Were Jackie, John and Caroline," *New York Times*, September 1969; Christopher Hitchens, "Widow of Opportunity," *Vanity Fair*, December 2011.

CHAPTERS 6–8

Information for these chapters was based in part on conversations with Roswell Gilpatric, Jack Anderson, George Plimpton, Peter Duchin, Yusha Auchincloss, Kitty Carlisle Hart, Aileen Mehle, Louis Auchincloss, Sandy Richardson, Chuck Spalding, Jamie Auchincloss, Pierre Salinger, Larry Newman, Ham Brown, Patricia Lawford Stewart, Marta Sgubin, Arthur Schlesinger Jr., Ron Gallela, Shana Alexander, Thomas Hoving, George Smathers, Marvin Mitchelson, John Davis, David Rockefeller, John Kenneth Galbraith, David Halberstam, Roy Cohn, Halston, Doris Lilly, Mollie Fosburgh, Brad Darrach, Billy Baldwin, Joe Baum, Louis Nizer, Lady Elsa Bowker, William S. Paley, Helen Thomas, Steve Rubell, Edward Francis, Earl Blackwell, David McGough, John Marion.

Articles and other published sources for this period included Peter

Strafford, "U.S. Acts to Protect the Kennedy Children," *Times,* London, May 4, 1972; William Manchester, *Controversy and Other Essays in Journalism: 1950–1975* (Boston: Little, Brown, 1976); Enid Nemy, "Here John Kennedy Jr. Will Be 'Just Another Boy,' " *New York Times,* August 22, 1968; Nancy Moran, "John Kennedy Got into Collegiate School for Boys—Could *Your* Son?," *McCall's,* March 1969; Wendy Leigh, *Prince Charming* (New York: Signet, 1994); "John-John, Caroline Revisit White House," United Press International, February 5, 1971; "Mrs. Kennedy Knew It Was Illegal, Says Vatican," *Times,* London, October 22, 1968; Peter Evans, *Ari: The Life and Times of Aristotle Onassis* (New York: Summit Books, 1986); "The Happy Jackie, The Sad Jackie, The Bad Jackie, The Good Jackie," *New York Times Magazine,* May 31, 1970; C. David Heymann, *A Woman Named Jackie* (New York: Lyle Stuart/Carol Communications, 1989); "From Camelot to Elysium (Via Olympic Airways)," *Time,* October 25, 1968; Frank Brady, *Onassis: An Extravagant Life* (New York: Prentice-Hall, 1977); Greg Lawrence, "Jackie O, Working Girl," *Vanity Fair,* January 2011; Joyce Maynard, "Jacqueline Onassis Makes a New Debut," *New York Times,* January 14, 1977; "JFK Jr.'s Bash A Socko Show," New York *Daily News,* November 28, 1978; Stephen Birmingham, "The Public Event Named Jackie," *New York Times Magazine,* June 20, 1976; Sally Quinn, "A New Image or Not, Jacqueline Onassis Is an Event," *Washington Post,* November 14, 1975; Helen Lawrenson, "Jackie at 50," *Boston Herald,* July 30, 1979; "Jackie Onassis Builds a $3 Million Hideaway," Associated Press, October 25, 1981; Michael Ryan, "Barry Clifford's Zany Crew—Including JFK Jr.—Prove That Way Down Deep, They're Golddiggers," *People,* August 22, 1983; Marie Brenner, "Jackie Tops at Shunning Limelight," *Los Angeles Times,* October 23, 1983; William Sylvester Noonan with Robert Huber, *Forever Young: My Friendship with John F. Kennedy, Jr.* (New York: Plume/Penguin Books, 2006); Kitty Kelley, *Jackie Oh!* (Secaucus, NJ: Lyle Stuart, 1979); Peter Beard, "John F. Kennedy Jr.—Images of Summer," *Talk,* September 1999; Robert T. Littell, *The Men We Became: My Friendship with John F. Kennedy, Jr.* (New York: St. Martin's Press, 2004).

CHAPTERS 9 AND 10

For these chapters, the author drew on conversations with David Halberstam, James Young, Jack Anderson, Bia Ayiotis, Richard Schaffer, Bobby Zarem, Malcolm Forbes, Alex Gotfryd, John Perry Barlow, Frank Ratcliff, Rick Guy, Daniel Patrick Moynihan, Michael Cherkasky, Ed Koch, Judith Hope, Erika Belle, Carolina Herrera, John Sargent, Arthur Marx, Steve Baranello, Letitia Baldrige, Rick Lazio, Michael Gross, David McGough, Angie Coqueran, Wickham Boyle, Cranston Jones, Paul Adao, Barry Schenck, John Marion, Howie Montaug, Anne Vanderhoop.

Among the published sources consulted: Christina Haag, *Come to the Edge* (New York: Spiegel & Grau, 2011); Marylou Tousignant and Malcolm Gladwell, "In Somber Ceremony Jacqueline Kennedy Onassis Is Laid to Rest," *Washington Post*, May 24, 1994; Frank Rich, "The Jackie Mystery," *New York Times*, May 26, 1994; Martha Sherrill, "Private People, Public Lives," *Harper's Bazaar*, November 1995; Elizabeth Gleick, "The Prying Eyes," *Time*, November 6, 1995; Carole Radziwill, *What Remains* (New York: Scribner, 2005); "The Sexiest Man Alive" (1988), *People*, September 12, 1988; Taki Theodoracopulos, "Jackie O: A Perfect Mom," *New York Post*, May 23, 1994; Annette Tapert, "Jackie's Dearest Wish," *Good Housekeeping*, July 1994; *Oprah* transcript, September 3, 1996; Tina Brown, "A Woman in Earnest," *New Yorker*, September 15, 1997; David Michaelis, "Great Expectations," *Vanity Fair*, September 1999; Martha Brant and Evan Thomas, "Coming of Age," *Newsweek*, August 14, 1995; Michael Gross, "Citizen Kennedy," *Esquire*, September 1995; Rosemarie Terenzio, *Fairy Tale Interrupted* (New York: Gallery Books, 2012); Rebecca Mead, "Does John Kennedy Sell Magazines?," *New York*, August 7, 1995; "Princess Carolyn," *W*, August 1996; Rebecca Mead, "Meet the Mrs.," *New York*, October 7, 1996; Michael Bergin, *The Other Man* (New York: ReganBooks/HarperCollins, 2004); John F. Kennedy Jr., "Don't Sit Under the Apple Tree," *George*, September 1997; "In J.F.K. File, Hidden Illness, Pain and Pills," *New York Times*, November 17, 2002; Tom Squitieri, "Could a Kennedy Be Loosening Family Ties?," *USA*

Today, August 12, 1997; Karen Duffy, "The Spell They Cast," *Glamour*, October 1999; "Prince of the City," *New York*, August 2, 1999; "A Sad Goodbye," *Newsweek*, August 2, 1999; "John Kennedy, New Yorker," *New York Observer*, July 26, 1999; "Kennedy Family Wanted Dignified Burial at Sea to Avoid Spectacle," *Cape Cod Times*, July 26, 1999; Cindy Adams, "Report: John and Carolyn Spent Last Nights Apart," *New York Post*, August 6, 1999; Jesse Kornbluth, "Daryl's Winning Sheen," *Vanity Fair*, January 1990; Anthony Wilson-Smith, "The Curse of the Kennedys," *Maclean's*, July 26, 1999; Jane Farrell, "An Unbreakable Bond," *McCall's*, October 1999; "John Kennedy: A Tribute," *George*, October 1999; "Goodbye," *Newsday*, July 23, 1999; "Talk of the Town," *New Yorker*, August 2, 1999; Terry Pristin, "Families, Employees and Charities Named in Kennedy Will," *New York Times*, September 25, 1999; Ed Klein, "Secrets and Lies," *Vanity Fair*, April 2003; "Farewell, John," *Time*, August 2, 1999; Charles Gandee, "Goodbye to All That," *Vogue*, September 1999; Isabel Vincent and Melissa Klein, "Kennedys Feuded Before Bodies Were Recovered," *New York Post*, November 3, 2013; Jocelyn McClurg, "Memories of JFK JR. and the Heady Days at *George*," *USA Today*, May 22, 2014; "Goodbye, America's Little Prince," *Paris Match*, August 1999.

Bibliography

Acheson, Dean. *Power and Diplomacy*. Cambridge, MA: Harvard University Press, 1958.

Adams, Cindy, and Susan Crimp. *Iron Rose: The Story of Rose Fitzgerald Kennedy and Her Dynasty*. Beverly Hills, CA: Dove Books, 1995.

Alford, Mimi. *Once Upon a Secret*. New York: Random House, 2012.

Amory, Cleveland. *The Proper Bostonians*. New York: E. P. Dutton, 1947.

Andersen, Christopher. *The Day John Died*. New York: William Morrow, 2000.

———. *Jack and Jackie: Portrait of an American Marriage*. New York: William Morrow, 1996.

———. *Madonna Unauthorized*. New York: Simon & Schuster, 1991.

———. *Sweet Caroline*. New York: William Morrow, 2003.

———. *These Few Precious Days*. New York: Gallery Books, 2013.

Anson, Robert Sam. *"They've Killed the President!" The Search for the Murderers of John F. Kennedy*. New York: Bantam, 1975.

Anthony, Carl Sferrazza. *As We Remember Her*. New York: HarperCollins, 1997.

Baldwin, Billy. *Billy Baldwin Remembers*. New York: Harcourt Brace Jovanovich, 1974.

Baldrige, Letitia. *Of Diamonds and Diplomats*. Boston: Houghton Mifflin, 1968.

———. *A Lady First: My Life in the Kennedy White House and the American Embassies of Paris and Rome*. New York: Viking Penguin, 2001.

Beard, Peter. *Longing for Darkness: Kamante's Tales from "Out of Africa."* San Francisco: Chronicle Books, 1990.

Bergin, Michael. *The Other Man: A Love Story*. New York: ReganBooks/ HarperCollins, 2004.

Beschloss, Michael R. *Kennedy and Roosevelt: The Uneasy Alliance.* New York: Norton, 1980.

———. *Taking Charge: The Johnson White House Tapes, 1963–1964.* New York: Simon & Schuster, 1997.

Birmingham, Stephen. *Jacqueline Bouvier Kennedy Onassis.* New York: Grosset & Dunlap, 1978.

———. *Real Lace: America's Irish Rich.* New York: Harper & Row, 1973.

Bishop, Jim. *The Day Kennedy Was Shot.* New York: Funk & Wagnalls, 1968.

Blair, Joan, and Clay Blair Jr. *The Search for JFK.* New York: Berkley, 1976.

Bouvier, Jacqueline, and Lee Bouvier. *One Special Summer.* New York: Delacorte Press, 1974.

Bouvier, Kathleen. *To Jack with Love, Black Jack Bouvier: A Remembrance.* New York: Kensington, 1979.

Braden, Joan. *Just Enough Rope.* New York: Villard, 1989.

Bradlee, Ben. *Conversations with Kennedy.* New York: Norton, 1975.

———. *A Good Life.* New York: Simon & Schuster, 1995.

Brady, Frank. *Onassis.* Englewood Cliffs, NJ: Prentice-Hall, 1977.

Brando, Marlon, with Robert Lindsey. *Songs My Mother Taught Me.* New York: Random House, 1995.

Bryant, Traphes, and Frances Spatz Leighton. *Dog Days at the White House.* New York: Macmillan, 1975.

Buck, Pearl S. *The Kennedy Women: A Personal Appraisal.* New York: Harcourt, 1969.

Burke, Richard E. *My Ten Years with Ted Kennedy.* New York: St. Martin's Press, 1992.

Burns, James MacGregor. *Edward Kennedy and the Camelot Legacy.* New York: Norton, 1976.

———. *John Kennedy: A Political Profile.* New York: Harcourt, 1960.

Cameron, Gail. *Rose: A Biography of Rose Fitzgerald Kennedy.* New York: G. P. Putnam's Sons, 1971.

Cassini, Oleg. *In My Own Fashion: An Autobiography.* New York: Simon & Schuster, 1987.

———. *A Thousand Days of Magic.* New York: Rizzoli, 1995.

Cheshire, Maxine. *Maxine Cheshire, Reporter.* Boston: Houghton Mifflin, 1978.

Clarke, Gerald. *Capote.* New York: Simon & Schuster, 1988.

Cohn, Roy. *McCarthy.* New York: New American Library, 1968.

Collier, Peter, and David Horowitz. *The Kennedys: An American Drama.* New York: Summit Books, 1984.

Damore, Leo. *The Cape Cod Years of John Fitzgerald Kennedy.* Englewood Cliffs, NJ: Prentice-Hall, 1967.

Davis, John. *The Bouviers: Portrait of an American Family.* New York: Farrar, Straus, 1969.

———. *The Kennedys: Dynasty and Disaster*. New York: McGraw-Hill, 1984.

Dempster, Nigel. *Heiress: The Story of Christina Onassis*. London: Weidenfeld & Nicolson, 1989.

DuBois, Diana. *In Her Sister's Shadow: An Intimate Biography of Lee Radziwill*. Boston: Little, Brown, 1995.

Duchin, Peter. *Ghost of a Chance*. New York: Random House, 1996.

Evans, Peter. *Ari: The Life and Times of Aristotle Socrates Onassis*. New York: Summit Books, 1986.

———. *Nemesis*. New York: HarperCollins, 2004.

Exner, Judith, as told to Ovid Demaris. *My Story*. New York: Grove Press, 1977.

Fay, Paul B., Jr. *The Pleasure of His Company*. New York: Harper & Row, 1966.

Fisher, Eddie. *Eddie: My Life, My Loves*. New York: Harper & Row, 1981.

Fontaine, Joan. *No Bed of Roses: An Autobiography*. New York: William Morrow, 1978.

Frank, Gerold. *Zsa Zsa Gabor, My Story*. New York: World, 1960.

Fraser, Nicolas, Phillip Jacobson, Mark Ottaway, and Lewis Chester. *Aristotle Onassis*. Philadelphia: Lippincott, 1977.

Frischauer, Willi. *Jackie*. London: Michael Joseph, 1967.

———. *Onassis*. New York: Meredith Press, 1968.

Galbraith, John Kenneth. *Ambassador's Journal: A Personal Account of the Kennedy Years*. Boston: Houghton Mifflin, 1969.

Gallagher, Mary Barelli. *My Life with Jacqueline Kennedy*. New York: David McKay, 1969.

Giancana, Antoinette, and Thomas C. Renner. *Mafia Princess: Growing Up in Sam Giancana's Family*. New York: William Morrow, 1984.

Goodwin, Doris Kearns. *The Fitzgeralds and the Kennedys: An American Saga*. New York: Simon & Schuster, 1987.

Granger, Stewart. *Sparks Fly Upward*. New York: G. P. Putnam's Sons, 1981.

Haag, Christina. *Come to the Edge*. New York: Spiegel & Grau, 2011.

Halberstam, David. *The Best and the Brightest*. New York: Random House, 1969.

Hall, Gordon Langley, and Ann Pinchot. *Jacqueline Kennedy*. New York: Frederick Fell, 1964.

Hamilton, Nigel. *JFK: Reckless Youth*. New York: Random House, 1992.

Heymann, C. David. *Bobby and Jackie: A Love Story*. New York: Atria, 2009.

———. *A Woman Named Jackie: An Intimate Biography of Jacqueline Bouvier Kennedy Onassis*. New York: A Lyle Stuart Book/Carol Communications, 1989.

Hill, Clint, with Lisa McCubbin. *Mrs. Kennedy and Me*. New York: Gallery Books, 2012.

Kelley, Kitty. *His Way: The Unauthorized Biography of Frank Sinatra*. New York: Bantam, 1986.

———. *Jackie Oh!* Secaucus, NJ: Lyle Stuart, 1979.

———. *Nancy Reagan: The Unauthorized Biography.* New York: Simon & Schuster, 1991.

Kennedy, Caroline. *The Best-Loved Poems of Jacqueline Kennedy Onassis.* New York: Hyperion, 2001.

———. *Jacqueline Kennedy: Historic Conversations on Life with John F. Kennedy: Interviews with Arthur Schlesinger, Jr., 1964.* New York: Hyperion, 2011.

Kennedy, Caroline, and Ellen Alderman. *In Our Defense: The Bill of Rights in Action.* New York: William Morrow, 1991.

———. *The Right to Privacy.* New York: Knopf, 1995.

Kennedy, John F. *Profiles in Courage.* New York: Harper & Row, 1965.

———. *Why England Slept.* New York: Wilfred Funk, 1940.

Kennedy, Rose Fitzgerald. *Times to Remember.* New York: Doubleday, 1974.

Kessler, Ronald. *Inside the White House.* New York: Pocket Books, 1995.

Klein, Edward. *Just Jackie: Her Private Years.* New York: Ballantine Books, 1998.

———. *The Kennedy Curse.* New York: St. Martin's Press, 2003.

Koskoff, David E. *Joseph P. Kennedy: A Life and Times.* Englewood Cliffs, NJ: Prentice-Hall, 1974.

Krock, Arthur. *Memoirs: Sixty Years on the Firing Line.* New York: Funk & Wagnalls, 1968.

Kunhardt, Philip B., Jr., ed. *Life in Camelot.* Boston: Little, Brown, 1988.

Lash, Joseph P. *Eleanor and Franklin.* New York: Norton, 1971.

Latham, Caroline, with Jeannie Sakol. *The Kennedy Encyclopedia.* New York: New American Library, 1989.

Lawford, Patricia Seaton, with Ted Schwarz. *The Peter Lawford Story.* New York: Carroll & Graf, 1988.

Lawliss, Charles. *Jacqueline Kennedy Onassis.* New York: JG Press, 1994.

Leamer, Laurence. *The Kennedy Women: The Saga of an American Family.* New York: Villard, 1994.

———. *Sons of Camelot.* New York: William Morrow, 2004.

Leigh, Wendy. *Prince Charming: The John F. Kennedy Jr. Story.* New York: Signet, 1994.

Lilly, Doris. *Those Fabulous Greeks: Onassis, Niarchos, and Livanos.* New York: Cowles, 1970.

Littell, Robert T. *The Men We Became: My Friendship with John F. Kennedy, Jr.* New York: St. Martin's Press, 2004.

Lowe, Jacques. *Jacqueline Kennedy Onassis: A Tribute.* New York: A Jacques Lowe Visual Arts Project, 1995.

Lowe, Jacques. *JFK Remembered.* New York: Random House, 1993.

Mailer, Norman. *Of Women and Their Elegance.* New York: Simon & Schuster, 1980.

————. *Marilyn*. New York: Grosset & Dunlap, 1973.

Manchester, William. *The Death of a President*. New York: Harper & Row, 1967.

————. *Portrait of President: John F. Kennedy in Profile*. Boston: Little, Brown, 1962.

Martin, Ralph. *A Hero for Our Time*. New York: Ballantine, 1984.

Moutsatsos, Kiki Feroudi. *The Onassis Women*. New York: G. P. Putnam's Sons, 1998.

McCarthy, Joe. *The Remarkable Kennedys*. New York: Dial Press, 1960.

Montgomery, Ruth. *Hail to the Chiefs: My Life and Times with Six Presidents*. New York: Coward-McCann, 1970.

Noonan, William Sylvester, with Robert Huber. *Forever Young: My Friendship with John F. Kennedy, Jr.* New York: Plume, 2006.

O'Connor, Edwin. *The Last Hurrah*. New York: Bantam Books, 1970.

O'Donnell, Kenneth P., and David F. Powers, with Joe McCarthy. *"Johnny We Hardly Knew Ye."* Boston: Little, Brown, 1970.

O'Neill, Tip, with William Novak. *Man of the House: The Life and Political Memoirs of Speaker Tip O'Neill*. New York: Random House, 1987.

Ogden, Christopher. *Life of the Party: The Biography of Pamela Digby Churchill Hayward Harriman*. New York: Warner Books, 1994.

Oppenheimer, Jerry. *The Other Mrs. Kennedy*. New York: St. Martin's Press, 1994.

Parmet, Herbert S. *Jack: The Struggles of John F. Kennedy*. New York: Dial Press, 1980.

————. *J.F.K.: The Presidency of John F. Kennedy*. New York: Dial Press, 1983.

Parker, Robert. *Capitol Hill in Black and White*. New York: Dodd, Mead, 1987.

Pepitone, Lena, and William Stadiem. *Marilyn Monroe Confidential*. New York: Pocket Books, 1979.

Radziwill, Carole. *What Remains*. New York: Scribner, 2005.

Reed, J. D., Kyle Smith, and Jill Smolowe. *John F. Kennedy Jr.: A Biography*. New York: People Profiles/Time, 1998.

Reeves, Richard. *President Kennedy: Profile of Power*. New York: Simon & Schuster, 1993.

————. *A Question of Character: A Life of John F. Kennedy*. Rocklin, CA: Prima, 1992.

Salinger, Pierre. *P.S.: A Memoir*. New York: St. Martin's Press, 1995.

————. *With Kennedy*. Garden City, NY: Doubleday, 1966.

Schlesinger, Arthur M., Jr. *A Thousand Days*. Boston: Houghton Mifflin, 1965.

Sgubin, Marta. *Cooking for Madam: Recipes and Reminiscences from the Home of Jacqueline Kennedy Onassis*. New York: A Lisa Drew Book/Scribner, 1998.

Shaw, Maud. *White House Nannie: My Years with Caroline and John Kennedy, Jr.* New York: New American Library, 1965.

Shulman, Irving. *"Jackie"! The Exploitation of a First Lady*. New York: Trident Press, 1970.

Sidey, Hugh. *John F. Kennedy, President*. New York: Atheneum, 1964.

Smith, Sally Bedell. *Grace and Power*. New York: Random House, 2004.

Sorensen, Theodore C. *Kennedy*. New York: Harper & Row, 1965.

Spada, James. *John and Caroline: Their Lives in Pictures*. New York: St. Martin's Press, 2001.

———. *Peter Lawford: The Man Who Kept the Secrets*. New York: Bantam, 1991.

Spignesi, Stephen. *The J.F.K. Jr. Scrapbook*. Secaucus, NJ: Carol, 1997.

Stack, Robert, with Mark Evans. *Straight Shooting*. New York: Macmillan, 1980.

Storm, Tempest, with Bill Boyd. *Tempest Storm: The Lady Is a Vamp*. Atlanta: Peachtree, 1987.

Summers, Anthony. *Goddess: The Secret Lives of Marilyn Monroe*. New York: Macmillan, 1985.

Swanson, Gloria. *Swanson on Swanson*. New York: Random House, 1980.

Taraborrelli, J. Randy. *Jackie, Ethel, Joan*. New York: Grand Central, 2012.

ter Horst, J. F., and Ralph Albertazzie. *The Flying White House*. New York: Coward, McCann & Geoghegan, 1979.

Terenzio, RoseMarie. *Fairy Tale Interrupted*. New York: Gallery Books, 2012.

Thayer, Mary Van Rensselaer. *Jacqueline Bouvier Kennedy*. Garden City, NJ: Doubleday, 1961.

Thomas, Bob. *Golden Boy: The Untold Story of William Holden*. New York: St. Martin's Press, 1983.

Thomas, Helen. *Dateline: White House*. New York: Macmillan, 1975.

Tierney, Gene, with Mickey Herskowitz. *Self-Portrait*. New York: Simon & Schuster, 1979.

Travell, Janet. *Office Hours: Day and Night*. New York: World, 1968.

Vidal, Gore. *Palimpsest: A Memoir*. New York: Random House, 1995.

Warhol, Andy. *The Andy Warhol Diaries*. New York: Warner Books, 1989.

The Warren Report. New York: Associated Press, 1964.

Watney, Hedda Lyons. *Jackie*. New York: Leisure Books, 1971.

West, J. B., with Mary Lynn Kotz. *Upstairs at the White House*. New York: Coward, McCann & Geoghegan, 1973.

White, Theodore H. *In Search of History*. New York: Warner Books, 1978.

———. *The Making of the President 1960*. New York: Atheneum, 1961.

Widmer, Ted. *Listening In: The Secret White House Recordings of John F. Kennedy*. New York: Hyperion, 2012.

Wills, Garry. *The Kennedy Imprisonment*. Boston: Atlantic–Little, Brown, 1981.

Index